AAT

NVQ FOUNDATION

REVISION **COMPANION** Units 1–4

Unit 1: Income and Receipts

Unit 2: Payments

Unit 3: Ledger Balances and
an Initial Trial Balance

Unit 4: Information for
Management Control

BPP
PROFESSIONAL EDUCATION®

Sixth edition May 2006
First edition 2001

ISBN 07517 2606 0 (previous ISBN 07517 2238 3)

British Library Cataloguing-in-Publication Data
A catalogue record for this book is available from the British Library

Published by

BPP Professional Education
Aldine House,
Aldine Place,
London W12 8AW

Printed in Great Britain

We are grateful to the AAT for permission to reproduce the specimen simulations, assessments and answers, of which the AAT holds the copyright. All other activities and answers have been produced by BPP Professional Education.

CONTENTS

INTRODUCTION

This is BPP's innovative Revision Companion for AAT NVQ Foundation Units 1-4. It is part of an integrated package of AAT materials.

It has been written in conjunction with the BPP Course Companion, and has been carefully designed to enable students to practise all aspects of the requirements of the Standards of Competence and performance criteria. It is fully up to date as at April 2006.

This Revision Companion contains these key features:

- graded activities corresponding to each chapter of the Course Companion

- the AAT's sample simulations and answers for each Unit

- the AAT's specimen exam for Unit 3

- the AAT's exams for Unit 3 set in June 2005 and December 2005

The emphasis in all activities and questions is on the practical application of the skills acquired.

All activities, practice assessments and simulations have full answers prepared by BPP Professional Education.

A further bank of activities relating to each chapter of the Course Companion and practice assessments, with answers prepared by BPP Professional Education, is available in the Tutor Companion, available only to colleges which adopt the BPP Companion material for this unit.

chapter 1:
INTRODUCTION TO BUSINESS

1 What are the main differences between a sole trader, a partnership and a limited company in terms of:

- ownership and management

- liability for debts

- methods of taking out profit?

2 For each of the following transactions state whether they are cash or credit transactions:

		Cash or credit?
i)	purchase of goods for £200 payable by cash in one weeks time	....
ii)	writing a cheque for the purchase of a new computer	....
iii)	sale of goods to a customer where the invoice accompanies the goods	....
iv)	receipt of a cheque from a customer for goods purchased today	....
v)	purchase of goods where payment is due in three week's time	....

3 For each of the following transactions state whether they are capital or revenue transactions:

Capital or revenue?

i) purchase of a new computer paid for by cheque ....

ii) purchase of computer discs by cheque ....

iii) purchase of a new business car on credit ....

iv) payment of road tax on a new business car ....

v) payment of rent for the business premises ....

4 Explain briefly the difference between a profit and loss account and a balance sheet.

chapter 2:
BUSINESS DOCUMENTS – SALES

1 On your desk is a pile of sales invoices that have already had the list price of the goods entered onto them and been totalled. You now have to calculate and deduct the 15% trade discount that is allowed on each of these invoices.

	List price total	Trade discount	Net total
i)	£416.70	....	....
ii)	£105.82	....	....
iii)	£ 96.45	....	....
iv)	£263.46	....	....
v)	£350.90	....	....

2 There is a further pile of invoices which have the net total entered for which you are required to calculate the VAT charge.

	Net total	VAT	Invoice total
i)	£258.94	....	....
ii)	£316.78	....	....
iii)	£82.60	....	....
iv)	£152.99	....	....
v)	£451.28	....	....

3 You now discover that for each of the invoices from the previous activity a 3% settlement discount has been offered. Recalculate the VAT charge to correctly reflect the settlement discount.

	Net total	VAT	Invoice total
i)	£258.94	....	....
ii)	£316.78	....	....
iii)	£82.60	....	....
iv)	£152.99	....	....
v)	£451.28	....	....

4 You work in the accounts department for Southfield Electrical and on your desk are three purchase orders received from customers today. The purchase orders have already been checked to the purchase quotations and the prices are correct on each purchase order.

You also have on your desk the customer details file which gives you the following information about the three customers:

Customer name	Sales ledger code	Trade discount	Settlement discount
Whitehill Superstores	SL 44	10%	4% – 10 days
Quinn Ltd	SL 04	15%	–
Harper & Sons	SL 26	10%	3% – 14 days

You are now required to complete the three blank sales invoices given for each of these purchase orders. The last sales invoice sent out was 57103. Today's date is 8 January 2006. If no settlement discount is offered or taken then payment is due within 30 days.

PURCHASE ORDER

WHITEHILL SUPERSTORES
28 Whitehill Park
Benham DR6 5LM
Tel 0303446 Fax 0303447

To: Southfield Electrical
Industrial Estate
Benham DR6 2FF

Number: 32431

Date: 4 Jan 2006

Delivery address: Whitehill Superstores
28, Whitehill Park
Benham DR6 5LM

Product code	Quantity	Description	Unit list price £
6060	8	Hosch Tumble Dryer	300.00
4425	2	Zanpoint Dishwasher	200.00

Authorised by: P. Williams **Date:** 04/01/06

PURCHASE ORDER

QUINN LTD
High Rocks Estate
Drenchley
DR22 6PQ
Tel 0310442 Fax 0310443

To: Southfield Electrical
Industrial Estate
Benham DR6 2FF

Number: 24316

Date: 5 Jan 2006

Delivery address: As above

Product code	Quantity	Description	Unit list price £
3170	14	Temax Mixer	35.00
3174	6	Temax Mixer	46.00

Authorised by: J. P. Walters

Date: 05/01/06

PURCHASE ORDER

HARPER & SONS
30/34 High Street
Benham DR6 4ST
Tel 0303419 Fax 0303464

To: Southfield Electrical
    Industrial Estate
    Benham DR6 2FF

Number: 04367

Date: 4 Jan 2006

Delivery address: 30/34 High Street
                  Benham DR6 4ST

Product code	Quantity	Description	Unit list price £
6150	3	Hosch Washing Machine	260.00

Authorised by: *S. Stevens* .... **Date:** .... *05/01/06* ....

INVOICE

Southfield Electrical
Industrial Estate
Benham DR6 2FF
Tel 0303379 Fax 0303152
VAT Reg 0264 2274 49

To:

Invoice number:

Date/tax point:

Order number:

Account number:

Quantity	Description	Stock code	Unit amount £	Total £

	Net total	
	VAT	
	Invoice total	

Terms

INVOICE

Southfield Electrical
Industrial Estate
Benham DR6 2FF
Tel 0303379 Fax 0303152
VAT Reg 0264 2274 49

To:

Invoice number:

Date/tax point:

Order number:

Account number:

Quantity	Description	Stock code	Unit amount £	Total £
			Net total	
			VAT	
			Invoice total	

Terms

INVOICE

Southfield Electrical
Industrial Estate
Benham DR6 2FF
Tel 0303379 Fax 0303152
VAT Reg 0264 2274 49

To:

Invoice number:

Date/tax point:

Order number:

Account number:

Quantity	Description	Stock code	Unit amount £	Total £
			Net total	
			VAT	
			Invoice total	

Terms

5 You have on your desk two further sales invoices that have been prepared by your assistant. You are required to check these invoices prior to them being sent out and note any errors that you find in the space given.

You are also given extracts from Southfield's price list and customer details listing.

PRICE LIST EXTRACT

CODE	DESCRIPTION	UNIT PRICE £
HOSCH		
6040	Tumble dryer	250.00
6050	Tumble dryer	280.00
6060	Tumble dryer	300.00
6140	Washing machine	220.00
6150	Washing machine	260.00
6160	Washing machine	300.00
6170	Washing machine	340.00
TEMAX		
3160	Food processor	100.00
3162	Food processor	120.00
3164	Food processor	140.00
3170	Mixer	35.00
3172	Mixer	40.00
3174	Mixer	46.00

CUSTOMER DETAILS EXTRACT

Customer name	Sales ledger code	Trade discount	Settlement discount
Weller Enterprises	SL 18	10%	4% - 14 days
QQ Stores	SL 37	12%	-

Weller Enterprises –

QQ Stores –

INVOICE

Southfield Electrical
Industrial Estate
Benham DR6 2FF
Tel 0303379 Fax 0303152
VAT Reg 0264 2274 49

To: Q Q Stores

Invoice number: 57107

Date/tax point: 9 Jan 2006

Order number: 03611

Account number: SL 27

Quantity	Description	Stock code	Unit amount £	Total £
7	Temax Processor	3162	140.00	890.00
10	Temax Mixer	3170	35.00	350.00
				1,240.00
	Trade Discount			186.00

Net total	1,054.00
VAT	184.45
Invoice total	1,238.45

Terms
Net 30 days
E & OE

INVOICE

Southfield Electrical
Industrial Estate
Benham DR6 2FF
Tel 0303379 Fax 0303152
VAT Reg 0264 2274 49

To: Weller Enterprises

Invoice number:

Date/tax point:

Order number:

Account number:

Quantity	Description	Stock code	Unit amount £	Total £
3	Hosch Tumble Dryer	6060	300.00	900.00
7	Hosch Washing Machine	6160	300.00	2,100.00
				3,000.00
	Trade discount			300.00

Net total		2,700.00
VAT		472.50
Invoice total		3,172.50

Terms
Net 30 days
E & OE

14

chapter 3:
DOUBLE ENTRY BOOKKEEPING

1 James has just started up in business and in his first month had the following transactions:

i)   James paid £20,000 into a business bank account in order to start the business;

ii)   He paid an initial rental of £2,500 by cheque for the shop that he is to trade from;

iii) He purchased a van by cheque for £7,400;

iv)   He purchased £6,000 of goods for resale on credit;

v)   He sold goods for £1,000 - the customer paid by cheque;

vi)   He sold goods on credit for £4,800;

vii) He paid shop assistant's wages by cheque totalling £2,100;

viii) He made further sales on credit for £3,900;

ix)   He purchased a further £1,400 of goods for resale by cheque;

x)   £3,700 was received from credit customers;

xi)   He paid £3,300 to credit suppliers;

xii) He withdrew £800 from the business for living expenses.

State the two effects of each of these transactions in the space given below.

i)   James paid £20,000 into a business bank account in order to start the business;

Effect 1   **Effect 2**

ii)   He paid an initial rental of £2,500 by cheque for the shop that he is to trade from;

Effect 1   **Effect 2**

iii)   He purchased a van by cheque for £7,400;

Effect 1   **Effect 2**

iv)   He purchased £6,000 of goods for resale on credit;

Effect 1   **Effect 2**

v)   He sold goods for £1,000 - the customer paid by cheque;

Effect 1   **Effect 2**

vi)   He sold goods on credit for £4,800;

Effect 1   **Effect 2**

vii)   He paid shop assistant's wages by cheque totalling £2,100;

Effect 1   **Effect 2**

viii)   He made further sales on credit for £3,900;

Effect 1   **Effect 2**

ix)   He purchased a further £1,400 of goods for resale by cheque;

Effect 1   **Effect 2**

x)   £3,700 was received from credit customers;

Effect 1   **Effect 2**

xi)   He paid £3,300 to credit suppliers;

Effect 1   **Effect 2**

xii)   He withdrew £800 from the business for living expenses.

Effect 1   **Effect 2**

2   Using the information above about James's early transactions enter them into the given ledger accounts.

Bank account

£	£

Capital account

£	£

Rent account

£		£

Van account

£		£

Purchases account

£		£

Creditors account

£		£

Sales account

£		£

Debtors account

£		£

Wages account

£		£

Drawings account

£		£

3 Balance each of the ledger accounts from above that have more than one entry. Then prepare a trial balance.

4 During this first month of trading James decides that he must keep more detailed records of his sales and purchases on credit. Explain to James how he could do this by keeping a subsidiary ledger for sales and purchases as well as the main ledger accounts.

5 James decides to put your recommendations into practice and informs you of the details of his sales on credit and receipts from debtors during the first month.

	£
Sales:	
To H Simms	1,800
To P Good	3,000
To K Mitchell	910
To C Brown	2,990
Receipts:	
From H Simms	900
From P Good	1,400
From K Mitchell	910
From C Brown	490

You are now required to record these transactions in the main ledger accounts and in the subsidiary ledger, the sales ledger.

Main ledger

Sales ledger control account

£	£

Sales account

£	£

Subsidiary ledger

H Simms account

£	£

P Good account

£	£

K Mitchell account

£	£

C Brown account

£	£

chapter 4:
ACCOUNTING FOR CREDIT SALES

1 Natural Productions is a small business that manufactures a variety of soaps and bath products which it sells directly to shops. During January 2006 the following credit sales took place:

2 Jan	Invoice No. 6237 to Hoppers Ltd £547 plus VAT
5 Jan	Invoice No. 6238 to Body Perfect £620 plus VAT
6 Jan	Invoice No. 6239 to Esporta Leisure £346 plus VAT
9 Jan	Invoice No. 6240 to Langans Beauty £228 plus VAT
12 Jan	Invoice No. 6241 to Body Perfect £548 plus VAT
16 Jan	Invoice No. 6242 to Superior Products £221 plus VAT
18 Jan	Invoice No. 6243 to Esporta Leisure £416 plus VAT
23 Jan	Invoice No. 6244 to Hoppers Ltd £238 plus VAT
26 Jan	Invoice No. 6245 to Langans Beauty £274 plus VAT

You are required to:

a) enter these transactions into the sales day book given below

b) cast the columns of the sales day book and check that they cross cast

c) post the totals of the sales day book to the main ledger accounts given

d) post the individual entries to the subsidiary ledger, the sales ledger

Sales Day Book

Date	Customer	Invoice number	SL Ref	Gross £	VAT £	Net £

Main ledger

Sales ledger control account

£		£

VAT account

£		£

Sales account

£		£

Subsidiary ledger

Hoppers Ltd account

£		£

Body Perfect account

£		£

Esporta Leisure account

£		£

Langans Beauty account

£		£

Superior Products account

£		£

2   Given below are four sales invoices sent out by Short Furniture, a business that manufactures wooden garden furniture for sale to retail outlets. These are the only invoices that have been issued this week.

You are required to:

a)   enter the invoices into the sales day book given

b)   total and check the sales day book

c)   post the sales day book to the main ledger and the subsidiary ledger, the sales ledger, given.

INVOICE

Short Furniture
Eridge Estate
Benham DR6 4QQ
Tel 0303312 Fax 0303300
VAT Reg 0361 3282 60

To: Rocks Garden Suppliers
14 Windmill Lane
Benham

Invoice number: 08663

Date/tax point: 5 Jan 2006

Order number: 4513

Account number: SL 22

Quantity	Description	Stock code	Unit amount £	Total £
2	6 Seat Dining Table	DT613	344.00	688.00
	Trade Discount			103.20
			Net total	584.80
			VAT	102.34
			Invoice total	687.14

Terms
Net 30 days
E & OE

INVOICE

Short Furniture
Eridge Estate
Benham DR6 4QQ
Tel 0303312 Fax 0303300
VAT Reg 0361 3282 60

To: Eridge Nurseries
Eridge Estate
Benham

Invoice number: 08664

Date/tax point: 7 Jan 2006

Order number: 61735F

Account number: SL 07

Quantity	Description	Stock code	Unit amount £	Total £
15	Plant Stands	PL006	23.85	357.75

Net total	357.75
VAT	62.60
Invoice total	420.35

Terms
Net 30 days
E & OE

INVOICE

Short Furniture
Eridge Estate
Benham DR6 4QQ
Tel 0303312 Fax 0303300
VAT Reg 0361 3282 60

To: Abergaven Garden Centre
Drenchley

Invoice number: 08665

Date/tax point: 7 Jan 2006

Order number: S129

Account number: SL 16

Quantity	Description	Stock code	Unit amount £	Total £
3	Lounger Chairs	LC400	285.00	855.00
	Trade discount			85.50
			Net total	769.50
			VAT	134.66
			Invoice total	904.16

Terms
Net 30 days
E & OE

INVOICE

Short Furniture
Eridge Estate
Benham DR6 4QQ
Tel 0303312 Fax 0303300
VAT Reg 0361 3282 60

To: Rother Nurseries
Rother Road
Benham

Invoice number: 08666

Date/tax point: 9 Jan 2006

Order number: 06112

Account number: SL 13

Quantity	Description	Stock code	Unit amount £	Total £
2	Coffee Table	CT002	96.00	192.00
6	Dining Chairs	DC416	73.00	438.00
		Net total		630.00
		VAT		110.25
		Invoice total		740.25

Terms
Net 30 days
E & OE

a) and b)

Sales day book

Date	Customer	Invoice number	SL Ref	Gross £	VAT £	Net £

c)

Main ledger

Sales ledger control account

£	£

VAT account

£	£

Sales account

£	£

Subsidiary ledger

	Eridge Nurseries		SL 07
£			£

	Rother Nurseries		SL 13
£			£

	Abergaven Garden Centre		SL 16
£			£

	Rocks Garden Supplies		SL 22
£			£

3   Returning to Natural Productions, during January the following credit notes were issued:

17 Jan   Credit note No. 1476 to Hoppers Ltd £68.70 plus VAT
23 Jan   Credit note No. 1477 to Esporta Leisure £89.23 plus VAT
30 Jan   Credit note No. 1478 to Superior Products £11.75 plus VAT

You are required to:

a)   enter these transactions into the sales returns day book given below

b)   cast the columns of the sales returns day book and check that they cross cast

c)   post the totals of the sales returns day book to the main ledger accounts given

d)   post the individual entries to the subsidiary ledger accounts used in the earlier activity

Sales returns day book

Date	Customer	Invoice number	SL Ref	Gross £	VAT £	Net £

Main ledger

Sales ledger control account

	£		£
31 Jan SDB	4,039.64		

VAT account

	£		£
		31 Jan SDB	601.64

Sales returns account

	£		£

4   Short Furniture also sent out a credit note on 9 January 2006 which is given below. Credit notes are not recorded in a separate returns day book but instead are recorded in the sales day book.

You are required to:

a)   record the credit note in the partially completed sales day book given below

b)   total and check the casting of the sales day book

c)   post the totals to the main ledger accounts given below

d)   post the individual entries to the subsidiary ledger accounts given below.

CREDIT NOTE

SHORT FURNITURE
Eridge Estate
Benham DR6 4QQ
Tel 0303312 Fax 0303300
VAT Reg 0361 3282 60

Credit note to:

Rocks Garden Supplies
14 Windmill Lane
Benham

Credit note number:	1468
Date/tax point:	9 Jan 2006
Order number	4513
Account number:	SL 22

Quantity	Description	Stock code	Unit amount	Total
			£	£
1	6 Seat Dining Table	DT613	344.00	344.00
	Trade Discount			51.60

	Net total	292.40
	VAT	51.17
	Gross total	343.57

Reason for credit note:

Damaged - two legs scratched

Sales day book

Date	Customer	Invoice number	SL Ref	Gross £	VAT £	Net £
5 Jan	Rocks Garden Supp	08663	22	687.14	102.34	584.80
7 Jan	Eridge Nurseries	08664	07	420.35	62.60	357.75
7 Jan	Abergaven G C	08665	16	904.16	134.66	769.50
9 Jan	Rother Nurseries	08666	13	740.25	110.25	630.00

Main ledger

Sales ledger control account

£	£

VAT account

£	£

Sales account

£	£

Subsidiary ledger

	Eridge Nurseries		SL 07
£			£

	Rother Nurseries		SL 13
£			£

	Abergaven Garden Centre		SL 16
£			£

	Rocks Garden Supplies		SL 22
£			£

chapter 5:
RECEIVING MONEY

1 Given below is a completed cheque.

Who is the drawee?   -

Who is the payee?   -

Who is the drawer?   -

first national   20 - 26 - 33
                                                  003014   40268134
        26 Pinehurst Place, London EC1 2AA   Date *9 January 2006*

Pay *J Peterson*

     Twenty pounds only   Account payee   £   *20.00*

140600
Cheque No.   Sort Code   Account No.   *F. Ronald*

  003014   20 - 26 - 33   40 268134   F. Ronald

2 Given below are four cheques received by Southfield Electrical today 9 January 2006. Check each one thoroughly and make a note in the table provided of any errors or problems that you encounter.

	Comments
Cheque from B B Berry Ltd	
Cheque from Q Q Stores	
Cheque from Dagwell Enterprises	
Cheque from Weller Enterprises	

Central Bank

18 - 26 - 44
010629 32791641

44, Main Road, Walkingham

Date *5 January 2006*

Pay *Southfield Electrical*

Six hundred and seventy nine

pounds and 83 pence

£ *697.83*

140600
Cheque No.   Sort Code   Account No.

J. L. Smith

010629   18-26-44   32791641

B. B. Berry Ltd

Northern Bank

22 - 44 - 16
10128 12976844

High Street, Drenchley

Date *7 January 2006*

Pay *Southfield Electrical*

Two hundred and twenty eight

pounds and 60 pence

£ *228.60*

140600
Cheque No.   Sort Code   Account No.

10128   22-44-16   12976844

Q Q Stores

First Western

30 - 11 - 46
001276 43216900

High Street, Benham

Date *2 January 2006*

Pay *Southfield Electronics*

Two hundred and forty three

Pounds only

£ *243.00*

140600
Cheque No.   Sort Code   Account No.

001276   30-11-46   43216900

J. Dagwell

Dagwell Ent.

Great National Bank

14 - 23 - 18
006411 32714986

25/27 Main Road, Benham

Date *6 January 2005*

Pay *Southfield Electrical*

Nine hundred and eighty five

pounds and 73 pence only

£ *985.73*

140600
Cheque No.   Sort Code   Account No.

006411   14-23-18   32714986

T. Johnson

Weller Enterprises

3 Southfield Electrical have also received the following cheque - is it valid and is there anything about it that you should note?

First Western	30 - 11 - 46

First Western

High Street, Benham

Date *2 Jan 2006*

Pay *Southfield Electrical*

One hundred pounds only

Northern Bank
Drichley

£ *100.00*

L P Townsend

140600
Cheque No.   Sort Code   Account No.

O46121   30−11−46   36994361

Polygon Stores

4 You work in Newmans, a music shop, and today, 7 January 2006, you were offered the following cheques and cheque guarantee cards for payment for goods.

In the table supplied explain any problems encountered with these payments and the action that you took.

	Comment and action
Cheque from T M Spence	
Cheque from B Withers	
Cheques from C J Long	

first national

20 - 26 - 33
004177 26194382

26 Pinehurst Place, London EC1 2AA

Date *7 January 2006*

Pay *Newmans*

Twenty eight pounds and 30 pence

Account payee

£ **28.30**

140600
Cheque No.   Sort Code   Account No.

T. M. Spence

004177   20-26-33   26194382   T. M. Spence

This is given to you together with a cheque guarantee card – limit £200, sort code 20-26-33, account number 26194382, expiry date December 2005.

Northern Bank

22 - 44 - 30
004166 22193870

144 West Street, Tunfield

Date

Pay *Newmans*

Sixteen pounds only

Account payee

£ **16.00**

140600
Cheque No.   Sort Code   Account No.

B. Withers

004166   22-44-30   22193870   B. Withers

This is given to you together with a cheque guarantee card - limit £100, sort code 22-44-30, account number 22193621, expiry date May 2006.

Central Bank

18 - 26 - 44
006277 63416002

44, Main Road, Walkingham

Date *7 January 2006*

Pay *Newmans*

One hundred pounds only

Account payee

£ **100.00**

140600
Cheque No.   Sort Code   Account No.

C. J. Long

006277   18-26-44   63416002   C. J. Long

```
Central Bank                                    18 - 26 - 44
                                                006278 63416002
        44, Main Road, Walkingham        Date  7 January 2006

Pay   Newmans
                                            £        75.63
      Seventy five pounds and

      63 pence
140600                                      C. J. Long
Cheque No.       Sort Code      Account No.

  006278      18-26-44    63416002          C. J. Long
```

These two cheques were given to you together with a cheque guarantee card - limit £100, sort code 18-26-44, account number 63416002, expiry date June 2006.

5   Short Furniture has received the following cheques and remittance advices through the post in the week ending 7 February 2006. The remittance advices from Rocks Garden Centre and Eridge Nurseries were the ones sent out by Short Furniture with the monthly statement. However the remittance advices from Abergaven Garden Centre and Rother Nurseries were prepared by their accounts department and must therefore be checked to their accounts in the subsidiary ledger, the sales ledger, which are given below.

Check each payment thoroughly and record any problems or comments in the table provided.

Subsidiary ledger

Rother Nurseries			SL 16
	£		£
9 Jan SDB – 08666	740.25	20 Jan SDB – 1470	96.50
16 Jan SDB – 08674	214.78		
24 Jan SDB – 08681	337.89		
5 Feb SDB – 08695	265.98		

	Abergaven Garden Centre	SL 17
	£	£
7 Jan SDB – 08665	904.16	
13 Jan SDB – 08672	623.56	
26 Jan SDB – 08685	316.58	
3 Feb SDB – 08692	415.76	

	Comments
Payment from Rocks Garden Supplies	
Payment from Eridge Nurseries	
Payment from Abergaven Garden Centre	
Payment from Rother Nurseries	

First Western

30 - 11 - 46
001234 36142910

High Street, Benham

Date *4 February 2006*

Pay *Short Furniture*

Account payee

Seven hundred and seventy

£ **773.75**

three pounds and 75 pence

P. S. Hammond

140600
Cheque No.   Sort Code   Account No.

001234   30-11-46   36142910

Rocks Garden Supplies

REMITTANCE ADVICE

To: Short Furniture
Eridge Estate
Benham DR6 4QQ
Tel 0303312 Fax 0303300

From: Rocks Garden Supplies

Date: 4 February 2006

Reference	Amount	Paid (✓)
08663	687.14	✓
1468	(343.57)	✓
08675	521.18	✓
08686	732.40	

CHEQUE ENCLOSED	£773.75

Northern Bank

22 - 44 - 16
04061 17694398

High Street, Drenchley

Date *3 February 2006*

Pay *Short Furniture*

Five hundred and ninety nine

pounds and 30 pence

Account payee

£ *595.30*

S. Stephenson

140600
Cheque No.

Sort Code

Account No.

04061   22-44-16   17694398

Eridge Nurseries

REMITTANCE ADVICE

To: Short Furniture
Eridge Estate
Benham DR6 4QQ
Tel 0303312 Fax 0303300

From: Eridge Nurseries

Date: 3 February 2006

Reference	Amount £	Paid (✓)
08664	420.35	✓
08676	381.18	✓
1471	(206.23)	✓
08687	640.20	
08690	381.62	

CHEQUE ENCLOSED	£595.30

Central Bank

18 - 26 - 44
004621 31640390

44, Main Road, Walkingham

Date *4 February 2006*

Pay *Short Furniture*

One thousand eight hundred and

forty four pounds and 30 pence

Account payee

£ *1,844.30*

P. Oliver

140600
Cheque No.   Sort Code   Account No.

004621   18-26-44   31640390

Abergaven Garden Centre

REMITTANCE ADVICE

To: Short Furniture
Eridge Estate
Benham DR6 4QQ
Tel 0303312 Fax 0303300

From: Abergaven Garden
Centre

Date: 4 February 2006

Reference	Amount £	Paid (✓)
08665	904.16	✓
08672	623.56	✓
08685	316.58	✓

CHEQUE ENCLOSED	£1,844.30

Great National Bank

14 - 23 - 18
001642 32660987

25/27 Main Road, Benham

Date *3 February 2006*

Pay *Rother Nurseries*

One thousand and ninety six

pounds and 42 pence only

£ *1,096.42*

140600
Cheque No.   Sort Code   Account No.

T. Johnson

001642   14—23—18   32660987

Rother Nurseries

REMITTANCE ADVICE

To: Short Furniture
Eridge Estate
Benham DR6 4QQ
Tel 0303312 Fax 0303300

From: Rother Nurseries

Date: 5 February 2006

Reference	Amount £	Paid (✓)
08666	740.25	✓
08674	114.78	✓
1470	(96.50)	✓
08681	337.89	✓

CHEQUE ENCLOSED	£1,096.42

chapter 6:
RECORDING RECEIPTS

1   The following sales have been made inclusive of VAT. Calculate the amount of VAT on each sale and the net amount of the sale:

		VAT	Net amount
i)	£145.28	....	....
ii)	£68.90	....	....
iii)	£258.73	....	....
iv)	£35.82	....	....
v)	£125.60	....	....

2   You work for Natural Productions. One of your duties is to write up the cash receipts book. Natural Productions makes sales on credit to a number of credit customers and also has some cash sales from a small retail outlet attached to the factory.

The remittance list for the last week in January 2006 is given below.

REMITTANCE LIST
23 Jan   £545.14 from Hoppers Ltd - cash discount £16.86
23 Jan   £116.70 from Superior Products
24 Jan   £128.46 from cash sales including VAT
24 Jan   £367.20 from Esporta Leisure - cash discount £11.36
25 Jan   £86.75 from cash sales including VAT
27 Jan   £706.64 from Body Perfect - cash discount £21.86
27 Jan   £58.90 from cash sales including VAT
27 Jan   £267.90 from Langans Beauty

You are required to:

i) record these receipts in the analysed cash receipts book given below;

ii) total the cash receipts book and check that it cross-casts.

Cash receipts book

Date	Details	Total	VAT	Cash sales	Sales ledger	Sundry	Discounts allowed
		£	£	£	£	£	£

3 What is the double entry required for discounts allowed to customers?

4   Returning to Natural Productions you are required to:

i)   post the totals of the cash receipts book to the main ledger accounts given below;

ii) post each individual receipt from sales ledger customers to their account in the subsidiary ledger given below.

Main ledger

Sales ledger control account

	£		£
20 Jan SDB	3,438.04	20 Jan SRDB	80.72

VAT account

	£		£
20 Jan SRDB	12.02	20 Jan SDB	512.04

Sales account

	£		£
		20 Jan SDB	2,926.00

Discount allowed account

	£		£

Subsidiary ledger

Hoppers Ltd account

	£		£
2 Jan SDB – 6237	642.72	17 Jan SRDB – 1476	80.72

Body Perfect account

	£		£
5 Jan SDB - 6238	728.50		
12 Jan SDB – 6241	643.90		

Esporta Leisure account

	£		£
6 Jan SDB - 6239	406.55		
18 Jan SDB – 6243	488.80		

Langans Beauty account

	£		£
9 Jan SDB - 6240	267.90		

Superior Products account

	£		£
16 Jan SDB - 6242	259.67		

chapter 7:
THE BANKING SYSTEM

1   On 23 January 2006 Natural Productions received a cheque from Hoppers Ltd who bank with Central Bank, Drenchley. Natural Productions pays this cheque into its bank, the Benham branch of the First National Bank.

What happens to this cheque before it appears as cleared funds in Natural Production's bank account?

2   Given below is a summary of the contents of the cash till for a shop at the end of the day.

Notes/coins	Number
£50	3
£20	17
£10	26
£5	35
£2	7
£1	18
50p	15
20p	36
10p	47
5p	23
2p	41
1p	63

What is the total amount of cash in the cash till?

3   Given below is the remittance list for Natural Productions for the last week in January 2006.

REMITTANCE LIST

23 Jan	£545.14 from Hoppers Ltd - cash discount £16.86
23 Jan	£116.70 from Superior Products
24 Jan	£128.46 from cash sales including VAT
24 Jan	£367.20 from Esporta Leisure - cash discount £11.36
25 Jan	£86.75 from cash sales including VAT
27 Jan	£706.64 from Body Perfect - cash discount £21.86
27 Jan	£58.90 from cash sales including VAT
27 Jan	£267.90 from Langans Beauty

All of the cheques are to be paid into the bank today, 27 January 2006.

The cash in the till from the cash sales is made up of the following notes and coins:

Notes/coins	Number
£20	5
£10	12
£5	13
£2	1
£1	17
50p	9
20p	4
10p	15
5p	12
2p	16
1p	19

This is all to be paid into the bank other than the cash float which is always made up as follows:

Notes/coins	Number
£10	2
£5	2
£1	5
50p	2
10p	10
5p	10
2p	10
1p	10

You are required to fill in the paying-in slip given below for payment of the cheques and cash into the bank.

Date			Date	Bank Giro Credit	first national

Cashier's stamp and initials

First National High Street, Benham

Account

Paid in by

	£	p
Cash		
Cheques		
Total		

No. of cheques

DE LA RUE 0514

Sorting code number	Account number	Transcode
20-26-33	40268134	66

Please do not write or mark below this line or fold this voucher

	£	p
Cash		

Cheques +

£

Please detail cash and cheques overleaf

000123   20−26−33   40268134   66

Cash	£	p	Cheques	£	p
£50 notes					
£20 notes					
£10 notes					
£5 notes					
£2 coins					
£1 coins					
Other coins					
Total			Total		

chapter 8:
COMMUNICATION WITH CUSTOMERS

1 Given below are two debtors accounts. You are required to find the closing balance on each account:

Harold & partners

	£		£
1 May Opening balance	1,367.83	7 May CRB	635.78
5 May SDB – 27465	998.20	7 May CRB – discount	33.46
12 May SDB – 27499	478.92	15 May SRDB – CN0364	106.34
20 May SDB – 27524	258.29	30 May CRB	663.66
		30 May CRB – discount	34.93

T N Designs

	£		£
1 May Opening balance	2,643.56	8 May CRB	1,473.28
11 May SDB – 27491	828.40	24 May SRDB CN0381	253.89
18 May SDB – 27513	1,083.65		

2   You work in the accounts department for Short Furniture. On your desk this morning, 5 February 2006, is the debtor listing as at 31 January 2006, showing amounts outstanding and how long they have been outstanding for. Short Furniture's credit terms are that payment should be made within 30 days of the invoice date. Given below is an extract from that debtor listing:

AGED DEBTOR ANALYSIS

Date: 31 January 2006

Account number	Account name	Credit limit £	Balance £	Current £	> 30 days £	> 60 days £	> 90 days £
SL08	Sunshine Sales	2,000.00	1,979.40	558.38	1,421.02	–	–
SL09	Groom Nurseries	1,000.00	368.90	368.90	–	–	–
SL10	Bridge DIY	1,500.00	1,760.47	1,760.47	–	–	–
SL11	Erfield Gardens	500.00	435.77	–	–	435.77	–
SL12	Lye Nursery	2,500.00	2,100.45	1,743.67	267.46	–	89.32

You are required to comment on the credit position of each of the debtors in the table given below:

Debtor	Comment
Sunshine Sales	
Groom Nurseries	
Bridge DIY	
Erfield Gardens	
Lye Nursery	

3   Using the data from the aged debtor analysis above for Short Furniture draft a suitable letter to Erfield Gardens regarding their credit position on behalf of the Sales Ledger manager, Jane Trump. Today's date is 5 February 2006 and your reference code for the letter is EG11/01/01. The letterhead for Short Furniture is given below to use;

SHORT FURNITURE
ERIDGE ESTATE
BENHAM DR6 4QQ
Tel 0303312 Fax 0303300
VAT Reg 0361 3282 60

chapter 9:
BUSINESS DOCUMENTS – PURCHASES

1 Your name is Charlie Rubble and you work in the warehouse at Whitehill Superstores. You have just taken delivery of some goods supplied by Southfield Electrical, delivery note number 34976. You have checked and counted the goods with the following results:

3	Zanpoint fridge freezers	Stock code	4075
2	Zanpoint tumble dryers	Stock code	4120 (one of these is scratched and is returned to Southfield on the van)
1	Hosch washing machine	Stock code	6140

Your assistant Jim Davids has checked that this is correct. Today's date is 14 January 2006 and the last GRN number was 04883. The purchase order that this delivery relates to is 32581.

You are required to complete the goods received note given below.

GOODS RECEIVED NOTE

Whitehill Superstores

Supplier:

GRN number:

Date:

Order number:

Quantity	Description	Stock code

Received by: ....

Checked by: ....

Comments: ....

2   You work in the accounts department of Whitehill Superstores and one of your duties is to request credit notes from suppliers by sending debit notes. Regarding the delivery from Southfield Electrical above you are required to complete the debit note given below relating to this delivery. The purchase order that relates to this delivery is given below. Today's date is 15 January 2006 and the last debit note number used was 0612.

PURCHASE ORDER

WHITEHILL SUPERSTORES
28 Whitehill Park
Benham DR6 5LM
Tel 0303446 Fax 0303447

To: Southfield Electrical
Industrial Estate
Benham DR6 2FF

Number: 32581

Date: 10 Jan 2006

Delivery address: Whitehill Superstores
28, Whitehill Park
Benham DR6 5LM

Product code	Quantity	Description	Unit list price £
6140	1	Hosch Washing Machine	220.00
4075	3	Zanpoint Fridge Freezer	310.00
4120	2	Zanpoint Tumble Dryer	190.00

Authorised by: *J. Hampton*   **Date:** *10 Jan 2006*

DEBIT NOTE

WHITEHILL SUPERSTORES
28 Whitehill Park
Benham DR6 5LM
Tel 0303446 Fax 0303447

To:

Debit note number:

Date/tax point:

Order number

Delivery note number:

Quantity	Description	Stock code	Unit amount	Total
			£	£

Reason: ....

Authorised by: ....   **Date:** ....

3   Your name is Anita Paul and you work in the accounts department of Short Furniture and one of your duties is to check invoices received from suppliers to purchase orders, delivery notes and GRNs.

Given below are three invoices from suppliers and the related supporting documentation. You are required to check each invoice carefully to the supporting documentation and note any discrepancies and the action required to be taken in the table given.

Supplier	Comment
A1 Wood Supplies	
Polish People	
Woodwards Woods	

INVOICE

A1 Wood Supplies
Heath Park
Drenchley DR22 6KL
VAT Reg 4621 3117 04

To:
Short Furniture
Eridge Estate
Benham DR6 4QQ

Invoice number: 764910

Date/tax point: 5 Jan 2006

Order number: 04672

Account number: 504

Quantity	Description	Stock code	Unit amount £	Total £
20m	Stripped Pine	P4612	12.38	247.60
50m	Oak	02611	15.87	793.50
				1,041.10
	Trade Discount			156.17

Net total		884.93
VAT		150.21
Invoice total		1,035.14

Terms
3% settlement discount for payment within 14 days, otherwise 30 days net
E & OE

64

PURCHASE ORDER

SHORT FURNITURE
Eridge Estate
Benham DR6 4QQ
Tel 0303312 Fax 0303300

To: A1 Wood Supplies
Heath Park
Drenchley

Number: 04672

Date: 2 Jan 2006

Delivery address: As above

Product code	Quantity	Description	Unit list price £
04612	20m	Stripped Pine	12.38 per m + VAT
02611	50m	Oak	15.87 per m + VAT

Authorised by: _K. Palmer_   **Date:** _2 Jan 2006_

DELIVERY NOTE

A1 Wood Supplies
Heath Park
Drenchley DR22 6KL
VAT Reg 4621 3117 04

Delivery address:

Short Furniture
Eridge Estate
Benham DR6 4QQ

Number: DN41268
Date: 5 Jan 2006
Order number: 04672

Product code	Quantity	Description
P4612	20m	Stripped Pine
02611	45m	Oak

Received by: [Signature] *A. Hall*   **Print name:** *A. HALL*

Date: *5 Jan 2006*

GOODS RECEIVED NOTE

Short Furniture

Supplier: A1 Wood Supplies

GRN number: 07904

Date: 5 Jan 2006

Order number: 04672

Quantity	Description	Stock code
45m	Oak	02611
20m	Stripped Pine	P4612

Received by: *A. Hall*

Checked by: *J. Finch*

Comments: —

INVOICE

Polish People
23/25 Main Street
Wakeham DR17 4ZF
VAT Reg 692 9417 63

To: Short Furniture
Eridge Estate
Benham DR6 4QQ

Invoice number: 06694

Date/tax point: 4 Jan 2006

Order number: 04668

Account number: SL 13

Quantity	Description	Stock code	Unit amount £	Total £
48 litres	Exterior Wood Polish - cherry	88631	3.16	151.68
24 litres	Exterior Wood Polish - teak	88413	2.83	67.92
		Net total		219.60
		VAT		38.43
		Invoice total		258.03

Terms
Net 30 days
E & OE

PURCHASE ORDER

SHORT FURNITURE
Eridge Estate
Benham DR6 4QQ
Tel 0303312 Fax 0303300

To: Polish People
23/25 Main Street
Wakeham DR17 4ZF

Number: 04668

Date: 23 Dec 2005

Delivery address: As above

Product code	Quantity	Description	Unit list price £
88413	24 litres	Exterior Wood Polish – teak	2.83 per litre + VAT
88631	48 litres	Exterior Wood Polish – cherry	2.99 per litre + VAT

Authorised by: *K. Palmer*

Date: *23 Dec 2005*

DELIVERY NOTE

Polish People
23/25 Main Street
Wakeham DR17 4ZF
VAT Reg 692 9417 63

Delivery address:

Short Furniture
Eridge Estate
Benham DR6 4QQ

Number: 17792

Date: 3 Jan 2006

Order number: 04668

Product code	Quantity	Description
88631	48 litres	Exterior Wood Polish - cherry
88413	24 litres	Exterior Wood Polish - teak

Received by: [Signature]   *A. Hall*   **Print name:**   *A. HALL*

Date: *3 Jan 2006*

GOODS RECEIVED NOTE

Short Furniture

Supplier: ⌐ Polish People   ¬

GRN number: 07903

Date: 4 Jan 2006

Order number: 04668

Quantity	Description	Stock code
24 litres	Exterior Wood Polish – teak	88413
48 litres	Exterior Wood Polish – cherry	88631

Received by: A. Hall

Checked by: J. Finch

Comments: -

INVOICE

Woodwards Woods
Inchpark House
Westfield Road
Benham DR6 4PL
VAT Reg 6671 4289 83

To: Short Furniture
Eridge Estate
Benham DR6 4QQ

Invoice number: 46692

Date/tax point: 5 Jan 2006

Order number: 04671

Account number: SL 56

Quantity	Description	Stock code	Unit amount £	Total £
110m	Teak 10cm planks	T10P	7.23	795.90
	Trade Discount			159.06

Net total		636.24
VAT		108.55
Invoice total		744.79

Terms
2.5% settlement discount for payment within 20 days, otherwise 30 days net
E & OE

PURCHASE ORDER

SHORT FURNITURE
Eridge Estate
Benham DR6 4QQ
Tel 0303312 Fax 0303300

To: Woodwards Woods
Inchpark House
Westfield Road
Benham DR6 4PL

Number: 04671

Date: 2 Jan 2006

Delivery address: As above

Product code	Quantity	Description	Unit list price £
T10P	110m	Teak 10cm planks	7.23 per metre + VAT

Authorised by: *K. Palmer* **Date:** *2 Jan 2006*

DELIVERY NOTE

Woodwards Woods
Inchpark House
Westfield Road
Benham DR6 4PL

Delivery address:

Short Furniture
Eridge Estate
Benham DR6 4QQ

Number: 646921

Date: 5 Jan 2006

Order number: 04671

Product code	Quantity	Description
T10P	~~110m~~ 95m	Teak 10cm plank

Received by: [Signature] *A. Hall*　　**Print name:** *A. HALL*

Date: *5 Jan 2006*

GOODS RECEIVED NOTE

Short Furniture

Supplier: Woodwards Woods

GRN number: 07905

Date: 5 Jan 2006

Order number: 04671

Quantity	Description	Stock code
95m	Teak 10cm plank	T10P

Received by: A. Hall

Checked by: J. Finch

Comments: -

chapter 10:
ACCOUNTING FOR CREDIT PURCHASES

1 Natural Productions is a small business that manufactures a variety of soaps and bath products. It buys materials for the manufacturing process from a number of suppliers on credit. It also buys other items such as stationery and packaging on credit. During January 2006 Natural Productions received the following invoices from credit suppliers:

4 Jan	Invoice No. 03576 from P J Phillips £357 plus VAT for materials
6 Jan	Invoice No. 18435 from Trenter Ltd £428 plus VAT for materials
9 Jan	Invoice No. 43654 from W J Jones £210 plus VAT for stationery
12 Jan	Invoice No. 03598 from P J Phillips £413 plus VAT for materials
16 Jan	Invoice No. 28423 from Packing Supplies £268 plus VAT for packaging
19 Jan	Invoice No. 18478 from Trenter Ltd £521 plus VAT for materials
20 Jan	Invoice No. 84335 from O & P Ltd £624 plus VAT for materials
24 Jan	Invoice No. 28444 from Packing Supplies £164 plus VAT for packaging
28 Jan	Invoice No. 18491 from Trenter Ltd £368 plus VAT for materials
31 Jan	Invoice No. 43681 from W J Jones £104 plus VAT for stationery

You are required to:

a) enter these transactions in the purchases day book given below

b) cast the columns of the purchases day book and check that they cross cast

c) post the totals of the purchases day book to the main ledger accounts given

d) post the individual entries to the subsidiary ledger, the purchases ledger, accounts given

Purchases day book

Date	Supplier	Invoice number	Gross £	VAT £	Purchases £	Stationery £	Packaging £

Main ledger

Purchases ledger control account

£		£

VAT account

£		£

Purchases account

	£		£

Stationery account

	£		£

Packaging account

	£		£

Subsidiary ledger

P J Phillips account

	£		£

Trenter Ltd account

	£		£

W J Jones account

	£		£

Packing Supplies account

	£		£

O & P Ltd account

	£		£

2 Given below are four purchase invoices received by Short Furniture, the only invoices received this week, the week ending 27 January 2006. You are also given an extract from the purchase ledger coding listing.

Purchase ledger coding listing

Calverley Bros	PL03
Cavendish Woods	PL14
Culverden & Co	PL23
Ephraim Supplies	PL39

You are required to:

a) enter the invoices in the purchases day book given - note that purchases are analysed into wood, polish and varnish and other

b) total and check the purchases day book

c) post the purchases day book totals to the main ledger accounts given

d) post the individual entries in the purchases day book to the supplier's accounts in the subsidiary ledger, the purchases ledger, given below

Purchases day book

Date	Supplier	Invoice number	Ref	Gross £	VAT £	Wood Purchases £	Polish/ varnish purchases £	Other purchases £	Sundry £

INVOICE

Ephraim Supplies
24 Mount Street
Benham DR6 8PN

To: Short Furniture
Eridge Estate
Benham DR6 4QQ

Invoice number: 09642

Date/tax point: 24 Jan 2006

Order number: 04697

Account number: SL 02

Quantity	Description	Stock code	Unit amount £	Total £
75m	10cm Teak Pole	461127	4.85	363.75
	Trade Discount			72.75

Net total	291.00
VAT	49.39
Invoice total	340.39

Terms
3% settlement discount for payment within 20 days, otherwise 30 days net
E & OE

INVOICE

Cavendish Woods
Earley House
Wakeham DR17 6TQ
VAT Reg 6291 3714 06

To: Short Furniture
Eridge Estate
Benham DR6 4QQ

Invoice number: 06932

Date/tax point: 23 Jan 2006

Order number: 04696

Account number: SL 14

Quantity	Description	Stock code	Unit amount £	Total £
70m	Teak	46117	11.85	829.50
	Trade Discount			124.43

Net total	705.07
VAT	123.38
Invoice total	828.45

Terms
Net 30 days
E & OE

83

INVOICE

Calverley Bros
Charter House
Main Street
Drenchley DR22 4XJ
VAT Reg 3929 4960 07

To: Short Furniture
Eridge Estate
Benham DR6 4QQ

Invoice number: 67671

Date/tax point: 23 Jan 2006

Order number: 04689

Account number: S03

Quantity	Description	Stock code	Unit amount £	Total £
40 litres	Exterior Wood Varnish – Colour 007	WV407	3.64	145.60

Net total		145.60
VAT		25.48
Invoice total		171.08

Terms
Net 30 days
E & OE

INVOICE

Culverden & Co
Channing Park Estate
Wakeham DR17 4LF
VAT Reg 1273 4522 16

To:
Short Furniture
Eridge Estate
Benham DR6 4QQ

Invoice number: 36004

Date/tax point: 24 Jan 2006

Order number: 04691

Account number: SL 10

Quantity	Description	Stock code	Unit amount £	Total £
20 dozen	3/4″ nails	664327	2.87	57.40

Net total	57.40
VAT	9.84
Invoice total	67.24

Terms
2% settlement discount for payment within 20 days, otherwise net 30 days
E & OE

Main ledger

Purchases ledger control account

£		£

VAT account

£		£

Wood purchases account

£		£

Polish/varnish purchases account

£		£

Other purchases account

£		£

Subsidiary ledger

Calverley Bros account	PL 03
£	£

Cavendish Woods account	PL 14
£	£

Culverden & Co account	PL 23
£	£

Ephraim Supplies account	PL 39
£	£

3 Returning to Natural Productions, during January the following credit notes were received:

10 Jan Credit note No. 04216 from P J Phillips £98 plus VAT
16 Jan Credit note No. CN 0643 from W J Jones £56 plus VAT
30 Jan Credit note No. CN 1102 from O & P Ltd £124 plus VAT

You are required to:

a) enter these transactions in the purchases returns day book given below

b) cast the columns of the purchases returns day book and check that they cross cast

c) post the totals of the purchases returns day book to the main ledger accounts given

d) post the individual entries to the subsidiary ledger accounts also given below

Purchases returns day book

Date	Supplier	Invoice number	Gross £	VAT £	Purchases £	Stationery £	Packaging £

Main ledger

Purchases ledger control account

	£		£
		31 Jan PDB	4,061.96

VAT account

	£		£
31 Jan PDB	604.96		

Purchases account

	£		£
31 Jan PDB	2,711.00		

Stationery account

	£		£
31 Jan PDB	314.00		

Packaging account

	£		£
31 Jan PDB	432.00		

Subsidiary ledger

P J Phillips account

	£		£
		4 Jan PDB 03576	419.47
		12 Jan PDB 03598	485.27

W J Jones account

	£		£
		9 Jan PDB 43654	246.75
		31 Jan PDB 43681	122.20

O & P Ltd account

	£		£
		20 Jan PDB 84335	733.20

chapter 11:
MAKING PAYMENTS TO CREDIT SUPPLIERS

1 Given below is a list of suppliers' invoices that require paying and their payment terms. When a cheque is written to a supplier it generally takes two days to reach the supplier. It is your organisation's policy to take advantage of any settlement discounts wherever possible but, if a discount cannot be taken, to pay the invoice after 30 days. Where settlement discounts are not offered it is your organisation's policy to take the longest period of credit allowed by the supplier. Today's date is 17 January 2006.

	Invoice date	Payment terms	Invoice amount £
i)	9 Jan	30 days	£372.48 plus VAT
ii)	9 Jan	2.5% settlement discount for receipt within 10 days	£275.68 plus VAT
iii)	10 Jan	5% settlement discount for receipt within 7 days	£624.59 plus VAT
iv)	10 Jan	30 days	£168.90 plus VAT
v)	11 Jan	3% settlement discount for receipt within 10 days	£527.00 plus VAT
vi)	11 Jan	3% settlement discount for receipt within 14 days	£473.80 plus VAT

You are required to complete the schedule given below showing the date that the cheque must be sent to the supplier according to your organisation's policies and the amount of the cheque to be sent. There is space after the schedule for any workings that may be required.

Invoice No	Payment date	Amount £
i)		
ii)		
iii)		
iv)		
v)		
vi)		

2 You work for Newmans, the music shop, in the accounts department and one of your responsibilities is to organise the payments to suppliers. You have been off sick for the last week and a half and therefore it is urgent that you consider the invoices that are on your desk requiring payment.

Newman's policy is to pay any invoices that are due each Friday. If a settlement discount is offered by a supplier then this should be taken if it can validly be taken each Friday. Otherwise the policy is to take the maximum amount of credit available. When a cheque is written on a Friday it does not then reach the supplier until Monday, ie three days later.

Today's date is Friday 27 January 2006. Thereafter, the following payment dates are 3 February, 10 February and 17 February. Remember that, as payments take three days to reach the supplier, then any invoice dated earlier than 7 January with a 30 day credit limit must be paid today as if they are delayed until 3 February then the payment will not be received until 6 February, more than 30 days.

The invoices that are on your desk are scheduled below:

Invoice date	Supplier	Terms	Gross £	VAT £	Net £
5 Jan	Henson Press	30 days	329.00	49.00	280.00
8 Jan	GH Publications	30 days	133.95	19.95	114.00
12 Jan	Ely Instruments	20 days 2% discount otherwise 30 days	749.76	109.76	640.00
15 Jan	Hams Instruments	14 days 2.5% discount otherwise 30 days	362.89	52.89	310.00
19 Jan	CD Supplies	10 days 3% discount otherwise 30 days	135.22	19.62	115.60
22 Jan	Jester Press	10 days 3.5% discount otherwise 30 days	149.14	21.54	127.60
22 Jan	Henson Press	30 days	299.62	44.62	255.00
23 Jan	CD Supplies	10 days 3% discount otherwise 30 days	76.50	11.10	65.40
25 Jan	Jester Press	10 days 3.5% discount otherwise 30 days	46.17	6.67	39.50
25 Jan	Buser Ltd	7 days 5% discount otherwise 30 days	285.73	40.73	245.00

In the schedule given below show the date that each invoice should be paid and the amount that the cheque should be written out for.

Invoice		Payment date	Amount of cheque
5 Jan	Henson Press		
8 Jan	GH Publications		
12 Jan	Ely Instruments		
15 Jan	Hams Instruments		
19 Jan	CD Supplies		
22 Jan	Jester Press		
22 Jan	Henson Press		
23 Jan	CD Supplies		
25 Jan	Jester Press		
25 Jan	Buser Ltd		

3 Given below are 6 blank cheques. Using the information for Newmans set out above, for each of the payments to be made today write out the cheque and cheque stub recording any discount taken on the cheque stub. You do not need to sign the cheque as this will be done by the authorised signatories.

first national

20 - 26 - 33
003015 40268134

26 Pinehurst Place, London EC1 2AA

Date

Date
Payee

Pay

Old balance

Account Payee

Deposits

£

£

140600
Cheque No.   Sort Code   Account No.

003015   003015   20−26−33   40268134

first national

20 - 26 - 33
003016 40268134

26 Pinehurst Place, London EC1 2AA

Date

Date
Payee

Pay

Old balance

Account Payee

Deposits

£

£

140600
Cheque No.   Sort Code   Account No.

003016   003016   20−26−33   40268134

first national

20 - 26 - 33
003017 40268134

26 Pinehurst Place, London EC1 2AA

Date

Date
Payee

Pay

Old balance

Account Payee

Deposits

£

£

140600
Cheque No.   Sort Code   Account No.

003017   003017   20−26−33   40268134

first national

20 - 26 - 33
003018 40268134

26 Pinehurst Place, London EC1 2AA

Date

Date
Payee

Pay

Old balance

Account Payee

Deposits

£

140600
Cheque No.   Sort Code   Account No.

£

003018   003018   20−26−33   40268134

first national

20 - 26 - 33
003019 40268134

26 Pinehurst Place, London EC1 2AA

Date

Date
Payee

Pay

Old balance

Account Payee

Deposits

£

140600
Cheque No.   Sort Code   Account No.

£

003019   003019   20−26−33   40268134

4 Given below is a statement received by your organisation, Edgehill Designs, from one of its credit suppliers, P T Supplies, as at 31 January 2006. You are instructed to pay all of the invoices less credit notes up to 10 January. Today's date is 7 February.

You are required to complete the remittance advice attached to the statement and to write out the cheque required for the payment on the blank cheque given. Note that this supplier does not offer a settlement discount to your organisation.

STATEMENT

P. T. Supplies
28 Farm Court Road
Drenchley DR22 4XT

To: Edgehill Designs

Account number: SL 53

Date: 31 January 2006

Date	Details	Debit	Credit	Balance
2006				
1 Jan	Balance b/f	227.63		227.63
6 Jan	Inv 20671	107.22		334.85
8 Jan	Inv 20692	157.63		492.48
9 Jan	Payment – Thank you		227.63	264.85
10 Jan	CN 04722		28.41	236.44
17 Jan	Inv 20718	120.48		356.92
25 Jan	Inv 20734	106.18		463.10
30 Jan	CN 04786		16.15	446.95

Amount now due £446.95

REMITTANCE ADVICE

To: P.T. Supplies
28 Farm Court Road
Drenchley DR22 4XT

From: Edgehill Designs

Date: 7 February 2006

Reference	Amount £	Paid (✓)
20671	107.22	
20692	157.63	
CN 04722	(28.41)	
20718	120.48	
20734	106.18	
CN 04786	(16.15)	

CHEQUE ENCLOSED	£

Central Bank

18 - 26 - 44
004167   23341892

44, Main Road, Walkinghan.

Date

Date
Payee

Pay

Old balance

Account Payee

£

Deposits

£

140600
Cheque No.   Sort Code   Account No.

004167   004167   18−26−44   23341892

Edgehill Designs

chapter 12:
RECORDING PAYMENTS

1 The following purchases have been made for cash inclusive of VAT. Calculate the amount of VAT on each purchase and the net amount of the purchase:

		VAT	Net amount
i)	£254.68	....	....
ii)	£159.28	....	....
iii)	£ 49.69	....	....
iv)	£104.28	....	....
v)	£ 62.48	....	....
vi)	£823.55	....	....

2 A payment is made to a supplier for £367.48 after a settlement discount of £12.50 has been taken. What is the double entry for this transaction?

3   You work for Natural Productions and one of your duties is to write up the cash payments book. Most of the payments are to credit suppliers but there are some cash purchases of materials from small suppliers which include VAT.

The cheque payment listing for the week ending 27 January 2006 is given below:

Cheque Payment Listing

Date	Cheque number	Supplier	Amount £	Discount £
23 Jan	002144	Trenter Ltd	1,110.09	28.47
23 Jan	002145	Cash purchase	105.79	
24 Jan	002146	W J Jones	246.75	
24 Jan	002147	P J Phillips	789.60	
24 Jan	002148	Cash purchase	125.68	
25 Jan	002149	Packing Supplies	305.45	8.04
26 Jan	002150	O & P Ltd	703.87	18.72
27 Jan	002151	Cash purchase	95.00	

You are required to:

a)   record these receipts in the analysed cash payments book given below

b)   total the cash payments book and check that it cross-casts

c)   post the totals of the cash payments book to the main ledger accounts given below;

d)   post each of the individual payments to the suppliers' accounts in the subsidiary ledger given below.

Date	Details	Cheque No	Total £	VAT £	Cash purchases £	Purchases ledger £	Sundry £	Discounts received £

Main ledger

Purchases ledger control account

	£		£
31 Jan PRDB	326.65	31 Jan PDB	4,061.96

VAT account

	£		£
31 Jan PDB	604.96	31 Jan PRDB	48.65

Purchases account

	£		£
31 Jan PDB	2,711.00	31 Jan PRDB	222.00

Discounts received account

	£		£

Subsidiary ledger

P J Phillips account

	£		£
10 Jan PRDB 04216	115.15	4 Jan PDB 03576	419.47
		12 Jan PDB 03598	485.27

W J Jones account

	£		£
16 Jan PRDB CN0643	65.80	9 Jan PDB 43654	246.75
		31 Jan PDB 43681	122.20

O & P Ltd account

	£		£
30 Jan PRDB CN1102	145.70	20 Jan PDB 84335	733.20

Trenter Ltd account

	£		£
		6 Jan PDB 18435	502.90
		28 Jan PDB 18491	432.40

Packing Supplies account

	£		£
		16 Jan PDB 28423	314.90
		24 Jan PDB 28444	192.70

4 Given below are the cheque stubs for the six payments made by Newmans on 27 January.

You have also looked at the standing order and direct debit instruction file and noted that there is a standing order due to be paid to the local council for business rates of £255.00 on the 27th of each month and a direct debit for rent of £500.00 also due on 27th of the month.

You are required to write up the cash payments book given below, total it and post it to the main ledger accounts given and the subsidiary ledger accounts given.

Date _27 Jan 2006_	Date _27 Jan 2006_	Date _27 Jan 2006_
Henson Press	_Ely Instruments_	_Jester Press_
	Discount 12.80	_Discount 4.47_
£ 329.00	£ 736.96	£ 144.67
003014	003015	003016

Date _27 Jan 2006_

CD Supplies

Discount 1.96

£ 74.54

003017

Date _27 Jan 2006_

Jester Press

Discount 1.38

£ 44.79

003018

Date _27 Jan 2006_

Buser Ltd

Discount 12.25

£ 273.48

003019

Cash payments book

Date	Details	Cheque No	Total £	VAT £	Purchases ledger £	Rent & rates £	Sundry £	Discounts received £

Main ledger

Purchases ledger control account

£		£

Rent and rates account

£		£

Discounts received

£		£

Subsidiary ledger

Buser Ltd

£		£

CD Supplies

£		£

Ely Instruments

£ | £

Henson Press

£ | £

Jester Press

£ | £

5 You have received an invoice from a regular supplier for £1,000 plus VAT. However, upon checking the supplier master file, you note that normally this supplier gives your company a 20% trade discount. Draft the wording of a letter to the supplier explaining the problem and requesting a credit note for a suitable amount.

chapter 13:
PETTY CASH PROCEDURES

1 Natural Productions has a petty cash system based on an imprest amount of £100 which is replenished weekly. On Friday 20 January 2006 the total of the vouchers in the petty cash box was £68.34. How much cash is required to replenish the petty cash box?

2 Newmans, the music shop, has an imprest petty cash system based upon an imprest amount of £120.00. During the week ending 27 January 2006 the petty cash vouchers given below were presented, authorised and paid.

PETTY CASH VOUCHER

Number: *0726*   Date: *27 Jan 2006*

Details		Amount
Computer disks		*9 - 35*
	Net	*9 - 35*
	VAT	*1 - 63*
	Gross	*10 - 98*

Claimed by: *D. Player*

Authorised by: *J. Clarke*

PETTY CASH VOUCHER

Number: *0721*   Date: *23 Jan 2006*

Details		Amount
Coffee		*3 - 99*
	Net	*3 - 99*
	VAT	*-*
	Gross	*3 - 99*

Claimed by: *T. Richards*

Authorised by: *J. Clarke*

PETTY CASH VOUCHER

Number: 0722   Date: 23 Jan 2006

Details		Amount
10 Books Postage Stamps		24 - 00
	Net	24 - 00
	VAT	-
	Gross	24 - 00

Claimed by: D. Player

Authorised by: J. Clarke

PETTY CASH VOUCHER

Number: 0723   Date: 24 Jan 2006

Details		Amount
Taxi fare		8 - 94
	Net	8 - 94
	VAT	1 - 56
	Gross	10 - 50

Claimed by: P. L. Newman

Authorised by: J. Clarke

PETTY CASH VOUCHER

Number: 0724   Date: 24 Jan 2006

Details		Amount
Printer paper		2 - 99
Envelopes		2 - 95
	Net	5 - 94
	VAT	1 - 03
	Gross	6 - 97

Claimed by: T. Richards

Authorised by: J. Clarke

```
PETTY CASH VOUCHER

Number: 0725                    Date: 26 Jan 2006

Details                         Amount

Train fare                          13 - 60
                    Net             13 - 60
                    VAT               -
                    Gross           13 - 60

Claimed by:      P. L. Newman
Authorised by:    J. Clarke
```

You are required to:

a)   write up the petty cash vouchers in the petty cash book

b)   total the petty cash payments side and check that it cross casts

c)   post the totals of the payments side to the main ledger accounts given.

RECEIPTS			PAYMENTS								
Date	Details	Amount £	Date	Details	Voucher number	Total £	VAT £	Travel £	Post £	Stationery £	Office supplies £
16 Jan	Bal b/f	120.00									

Main ledger

VAT account

£		£

Travel expenses account

£		£

Postage account

£		£

Stationery account

£		£

Office supplies account

£		£

chapter 14:
PAYROLL ACCOUNTING PROCEDURES

1 Peter Knight is one of the employees at Short Furniture and has a gross weekly wage of £440.00. For this week his income tax payable through the PAYE system is £77.76. The employee's National Insurance Contribution for the week is £43.18 and 5% of his gross wage is deducted each week as a pension contribution. The employer's National Insurance Contribution for the week is £49.35.

a) Calculate Peter's net wage for the week.

b) What payments and to whom will Short Furniture be making in regard to Peter's wages this week?

c) Show how all of the elements of this wage payment would be entered into the accounting records by writing up the ledger accounts given.

Wages expense account

£	£

Gross wages control account

£		£

PAYE/NIC creditor account

£		£

Pension contribution account

£		£

2 Short Furniture has five employees who are paid on a monthly basis. For each one you are required to calculate their net monthly salary.

Each employee has a personal allowance of £4,300 and they pay income tax at a rate of 10% on the first £1,500 per annum and 22% on the remainder.

National Insurance contributions are calculated at 10% of the gross salary but the first £300 of monthly income is exempt from this.

In the table given below show the calculation of the net annual pay for each employee.

Employee	Gross annual salary £	Taxable annual salary £	Income tax @ 10% £	Income tax @ 22% £	NIC £	Net annual salary £
J Short	30,000					
P Nielson	24,000					
J Taylor	17,400					
M Harris	15,500					
J Philpott	14,600					

chapter 15:
BANK RECONCILIATION STATEMENT

1 Would each of the following transactions appear as a debit or a credit on the bank statement?

Transaction	Debit or credit?

i)   £470.47 paid into the bank ....

ii) Standing order of £26.79 ....

iii) Cheque payment of £157.48 ....

iv) Interest earned on the bank balance ....

v)   BACS payment for wages ....

2 Given below is the cash payments book for Newmans for the week ending 27 January 2006.

Cash Payments Book

You are given information about the receipts during the same week:

Date	Cheque No	Details	Total £	VAT £	Purchases ledger £	Rent and rates £	Sundry £	Discounts received £
27 Jan	003014	Henson Press	329.00		329.00			
27 Jan	003015	Ely Instr	736.96		736.96			12.80
27 Jan	003016	Jester Press	144.67		144.67			4.47
27 Jan	003017	CD Supplies	74.54		74.54			1.96
27 Jan	003018	Jester Press	44.79		44.79			1.38
27 Jan	003019	Buser Ltd	273.48		273.48			12.25
27 Jan	SO	Rates	255.00			255.00		
27 Jan	DD	Rent	500.00			500.00		

From Tunfield District Council £594.69
From Tunshire County Orchestra £468.29 – discount taken of £14.48
Cash sales for music (no VAT) £478.90
From Tunfield Brass Band £1,059.72 – discount taken of £33.03
Cash sales from instruments (including VAT) £736.58
Cash sales from CDs (including VAT) £251.67

You are required to write up and total the cash receipts book given below:

Date	Details	Total £	VAT £	Sales ledger £	Music sales £	Instrument sales £	CD sales £	Discounts allowed £	Sundry £

3 Given below is the bank statement for Newmans for the week ending 27 January 2006. You are required to compare the cash payments book and cash receipts book from earlier in this chapter to the bank statement. Note any unmatched items in the space given below and state what action you would take.

Unmatched item   **Action to be taken**

STATEMENT

first national
26 Pinehurst Plance
London
EC1 2AA

NEWMANS

Account number: 20-26-33 40268134

CHEQUE ACCOUNT

Sheet 023

Date		Paid out	Paid in	Balance
2006				
20 Jan	Balance b/f			379.22 CR
24 Jan	BGC - Tunsfield		594.69	
	BGC - TunshireCo.		468.29	
24 Jan	SO - British Elec	212.00		1230.20 CR
25 Jan	BGC - Tunfield AOS		108.51	1338.71 CR
26 Jan	Cheque No 003014	329.00		
	Credit		478.90	1488.61 CR
27 Jan	Cheque No 003017	74.54		
	Cheque No 003015	736.96		
	Credit		1,059.72	
	Credit		736.58	
	SO - TDC	255.00		
	DD - Halpern Properties	500.00		
	Bank interest		3.68	1722.09 CR

4   Amend the cash receipts and payments books and find the balance on the cash books at 27 January. You can assume that the opening bank statement balance is the same as the opening cash book balance.

5   Prepare the bank reconciliation statement as at 27 January 2006.

chapter 16:
CONTROL ACCOUNT
RECONCILIATIONS

1 The balances on your organisation's sales ledger control account on 1 January 2006 were:

	£
Debit balances	12,589
Credit balances	900

The transactions that take place during January 2006 are summarised below:

	£
Credit sales	12,758
Sales returns	1,582
Cash received from debtors	11,563
Discounts allowed to debtors	738
Bad debt to be written off	389
Returned cheque	722

There were no credit balances on any debtor accounts at the end of January 2006.

You are required to write up the sales ledger control account for the month of January 2006 in the blank account given below.

Sales ledger control account

£	£

2   The opening balance on your organisation's purchases ledger control account at 1 January 2006 was £8,347. The transactions for the month of January have been summarised below:

	£
Credit purchases	9,203
Purchases returns	728
Payments to creditors	8,837
Discounts received	382

You are required to write up the purchases ledger control account for the month of January 2006 in the blank account given below.

Purchases ledger control account

£	£

3   When considering the reconciliation of sales ledger and purchases ledger control accounts to the list of balances from the subsidiary ledger, would the following errors affect the relevant control account, the list of balances or both?

		Control account	List of balances	Both
i)	Invoice entered into the sales day book as £980 instead of £890			
ii)	Purchase day book overcast by £1,000			
iii)	Discounts allowed of £20 not entered into the cash receipts book			
iv)	An invoice taken as £340 instead of £440 when being posted to the subsidiary ledger			
v)	Incorrect balancing of a subsidiary ledger account			
vi)	A purchase return not entered into the purchases returns day book			

4 In an earlier chapter we came across James who had just completed his first month of trading. James makes sales on credit to four customers and the transactions during his second month of trading were as follows:

	£
Sales	
To H Simms	2,000
To P Good	2,700
To K Mitchell	1,100
To C Brown	3,800
Receipts	
From H Simms	2,400
From P Good	3,600
From K Mitchell	1,100
From C Brown	4,800

All the sales are inclusive of VAT.

You are required to:

a) show these transactions in total in the sales ledger control account given and in detail in the individual subsidiary ledger accounts given. Each of the accounts given shows the opening balance at the start of month two.

b) balance the sales ledger control account and the individual subsidiary ledger accounts

c) reconcile the list of subsidiary ledger balances to the balance on the control account in the pro-forma given.

Main ledger

Sales ledger control account

	£		£
Opening balance	5,000		

Subsidiary ledger

H Simms account

	£		£
Opening balance	900		

P Good account

	£		£
Opening balance	1,600		

K Mitchell account

	£		£

C Brown account

	£		£
Opening balance	2,500		

Reconciliation of subsidiary ledger balances with control account balance

£

H Simms
P Good
K Mitchell
C Brown

Sales ledger control account

5   James also buys goods on credit from three suppliers. The transactions with these suppliers in month two are summarised below:

£

Purchases:
From J Peters   1,600
From T Sands   2,500
From L Farmer   3,200

Payments:
To J Peters   1,700
To T Sands   3,200
To L Farmer   3,000

All the purchases are inclusive of VAT.

You are required to:

a) show these transactions in total in the purchases ledger control account given and in detail in the individual subsidiary ledger accounts given. Each of the accounts given shows the opening balance at the start of month two

b) balance the purchases ledger control account and the individual subsidiary ledger accounts

c) reconcile the list of subsidiary ledger balances to the balance on the control account in the pro-forma given.

Main ledger

Purchases ledger control account

	£		£
		Opening balance	2,700

Subsidiary ledger

J Peters account

	£		£
		Opening balance	300

T Sands account

	£		£
		Opening balance	1,700

L Farmer account

	£		£
		Opening balance	700

Reconciliation of subsidiary ledger balances with control account balance

	£
J Peters	
T Sands	
L Farmer	
	———
Purchases ledger control account	———

6   The balance on a business's sales ledger control account at 30 June 2006 was £13,452. However the list of balances in the subsidiary ledger totalled to £12,614. The difference was investigated and the following errors were discovered:

i)   the sales returns day book was undercast by £100

ii)   a payment from one debtor had been correctly entered into the cash receipts book as £350 but had been entered into the subsidiary ledger as £530

iii) a bad debt of £200 had been written off in the subsidiary ledger but had not been entered into the main ledger accounts

iv)   a balance of £358 due from one debtor had been omitted from the list of subsidiary ledger balances.

You are required to write up the corrected sales ledger control account and to reconcile this to the corrected list of subsidiary ledger balances.

7   The balance on an organisation's purchases ledger control account at 30 June 2006 was £26,677 whereas the total of the list of subsidiary ledger balances for creditors was £27,469. The following errors were discovered:

i)   one total in the purchases day book had been undercast by £1,000

ii)   a discount received from a supplier of £64 had not been posted to his account in the subsidiary ledger

iii) a debit balance of £120 had been included in the list of subsidiary ledger balances as a credit balance

iv)   discounts received of £256 were credited to both the discounts received account and to the creditors' control account.

You are required to correct the purchases ledger control account and to reconcile the corrected balance to the corrected list of subsidiary ledger balances.

8   Short Furniture has a petty cash imprest system based upon an imprest amount of £150.00 each month. During the month of January 2006 the following petty cash vouchers were authorised and paid:

Voucher No.	£
0473	12.60
0474	15.00
0475	19.75
0476	9.65
0477	10.00
0478	13.84
0479	4.26
0480	16.40

The cash in the petty cash box at 31 January 2003 was made up as follows:

£10 note	1
£5 note	4
£2 coin	3
£1 coin	7
50p coin	5
20p coin	8
10p coin	9
5p coin	4
2p coin	11
1p coin	8

a)   Reconcile the petty cash in the petty cash box and the vouchers at the end of January 2006 in the space below.

b) The petty cash control account in the main ledger is given below:

Petty cash control

	£			£
1 Jan Balance b/d	150.00	31 Jan	Petty cash book	101.50

You are to balance the petty cash control account and reconcile the balance to the amount of cash in the petty cash box on 31 January 2006.

chapter 17:
PREPARING AN INITIAL TRIAL BALANCE

1   Given below are the sales ledger and purchases ledger control accounts for your organisation. You are required to balance the accounts and show the closing balance carried down and brought down.

Sales ledger control account

	£		£
Opening balance	16,387	Cash receipts	15,388
Sales	17,385	Discounts allowed	734
		Sales returns	1,297
		Bad debt written off	479

Purchases ledger control account

	£		£
Cash payments	10,756	Opening balance	11,529
Discounts received	529	Purchases	10,487
Purchases returns	926		

2   You are given the following account balances from the main ledger of your organisation. Would each balance be a debit or a credit balance in the trial balance?

Ledger account	Balance	Debit or credit?
Sales	625,679	....
Telephone	1,295	....
Debtors	52,375	....
Wages	104,288	....
Purchases returns	8,229	....
Bank overdraft	17,339	....
Purchases	372,589	....
Drawings	38,438	....
Sales returns	32,800	....
Motor car	14,700	....
Creditors	31,570	....

3   Given below is the list of ledger balances for your organisation at 31 January 2006. You are required to prepare a trial balance as at 31 January 2006.

	£
Motor vehicles	76,800
Office equipment	36,440
Sales	285,600
Purchases	196,800
Bank overdraft	2,016
Petty cash	36
Capital	90,000
Sales returns	5,640
Purchases returns	4,320
Sales ledger control	42,960
Purchases ledger control	36,120
VAT (credit balance)	15,540
Stock	12,040
Telephone	1,920
Electricity	3,360
Wages	74,520
Loan	36,000
Discounts allowed	7,680
Discounts received	4,680
Rent	14,400
Bad debts written off	1,680

chapter 18:
ERRORS AND THE TRIAL BALANCE

1   Given below are two ledger accounts. Examine them carefully and then re-write them correcting any errors that have been made.

Sales ledger control account

	£		£
Sales	15,899	Balance b/d	1,683
Discounts allowed	900	Cash received	14,228
Sales returns	1,467	Bad debts written off	245
		Balance c/d	2,110
	18,266		18,266

VAT account

	£		£
VAT on sales	2,368	Balance b/d	2,576
VAT on purchases returns	115	VAT on purchases	1,985
Balance c/d	2,078		
	4,561		4,561

2 Given below is a trial balance that does not balance. Examine it carefully and then re-draft it having corrected any errors that you can find - it should then balance.

	£	£
Motor vehicle	18,720	
Stock	2,520	
Bank (debit balance)	10,956	
Sales ledger control	5,280	
Purchases ledger control		3,840
Capital		48,000
Sales		78,000
Sales returns		6,000
Purchases	50,400	
Purchases returns		3,240
Bank charges	120	
Discounts allowed		1,080
Discounts received	720	
Wages and salaries	26,160	
Rent and rates		7,440
Telephone	1,224	
Electricity	3,060	
Bad debts written off	840	
	120,000	147,600

	£	£
Motor vehicle		
Stock		
Bank (debit balance)		
Sales ledger control		
Purchases ledger control		
Capital		
Sales		
Sales returns		
Purchases		
Purchases returns		
Bank charges		
Discounts allowed		
Discounts received		
Wages and salaries		
Rent and rates		
Telephone		
Electricity		
Bad debts written off		

3   The trial balance of Harry Parker & Co has been prepared by the bookkeeper and the total of the debit balances is £428,365 whilst the total of the credit balances is £431,737. The difference was dealt with by setting up a suspense account and then the ledger accounts were investigated to try to find the causes of the difference. The following errors and omissions were found:

i)   the sales day book was undercast by £1,000

ii) the balance on the electricity account of £1,642 had been completely omitted from the trial balance

iii) discounts allowed of £865 had been entered on the wrong side of the discounts allowed account

iv) receipts from debtors of £480 had been entered into the accounts as £840

v)   a discount received of £120 had been completely omitted from the cash payments book.

You are required to:

a)   draft journal entries to correct each of these errors or omissions.

b)   write up the suspense account showing clearly the opening balance and how the suspense account is cleared after correction of each of the errors.

chapter 19:
BUSINESS TRANSACTIONS AND THE LAW

1   Short Furniture send out a purchase quotation to a customer, Rother Nurseries, for two dining tables at a cost of £340.00 plus VAT. Rother Nurseries respond by sending a purchase order for these tables.

i)   Who is the offeror and who is the offeree?

ii)   Is there a valid contract at this stage?

iii)   If Rother Nurseries state on the purchase order that the tables must be delivered the following day - is there a valid contract? Explain your answer.

2   Short Furniture place an advertisement in the local newspaper for their products. Unfortunately there is a typing error and a sun lounger has been shown at a price of £50 instead of £250. Three customers have telephoned to place orders for the sun lounger.

Is Short Furniture obliged to sell the sun loungers at the advertised price of £50? Explain your answer.

3   Short Furniture have just employed a new salesman, Paul Finch. Paul has just taken a telephone call from a customer showing interest in a garden bench priced at £120 plus VAT. Paul has explained that this price is only available for the rest of this week and finished the conversation by saying to the customer "if I have not heard from you by Friday I will assume that you wish to go ahead with the purchase".

If the customer does not call back by Friday is there a contract of sale between the customer and Short Furniture? Explain your answer.

4   Paul Finch is also dealing with a further customer who is interested in the garden benches priced at £120 plus VAT. Paul has again explained that the price is only available this week and the customer agrees to send a purchase order for the benches.

The purchase order is not received until Tuesday of the following week although the post mark clearly shows that it was posted on the Friday of this week.

Does Short Furniture have to sell the garden benches to the customer at the price of £120 plus VAT? Explain your answer.

5   a)   What type of information is covered by by the Data Protection Act 1998?

b)   What are the eight principles of good information handling?

chapter 20:
INTRODUCTION TO MANAGEMENT INFORMATION

1   Given below are a number of different typical management tasks. For each one decide whether this is an example of management's role of decision-making, planning or control.

Management task	Management role
i) estimating advertising costs for the following year	....
ii) comparing this month' sales income to that for last month	....
iii) considering the opening of an additional factory	....
iv) determining how many production employees are required for the following quarter's production	....
v) comparing the actual costs for the month to the budgeted costs	....
vi) considering taking out a loan to help fund expansion	....

2   If the management of a business need to decide how many production employees are required for the next quarter what information might they need?

3   If the management of a business need to know the total cost of materials for the following quarter what budgets would be required?

chapter 21:
ELEMENTS OF COST

1   Given below are a variety of costs that are incurred by Short Furniture, makers of wooden garden furniture. You are required to classify each one as materials, labour or expense.

Cost		Classification
i)	advertising costs in local paper	A C ✓
ii)	cost of imported wood	DM ✓
iii)	store keeper's wages	IDL ✓
iv)	new blades for saws	IDM/E ✓
v)	cost of wood polish	DM ✓
vi)	accountant's salary	AC ✓
vii)	repair cost of delivery van	AC ✓
viii)	insurance of the cutting machinery	IDE ✓
ix)	telephone bill	AC ✓

2 Short Furniture has just received a delivery of wood which has been recorded on the following goods received note.

GOODS RECEIVED NOTE

Short Furniture

Supplier: A1 Wood Supplies

GRN number: 07904

Date: 5 Jan 2006

Order number: 04672

Quantity	Description	Stock code
45m	Oak	02611
20m	Stripped Pine	P4612

Received by: *A. Hall*

Checked by: *J. Finch*

Comments: -

You are required to write up the stock record cards given to reflect this delivery.

STOCK RECORD CARD

Stock code 02611

Date	In	Out	Balance
2006 1 Jan 2 Jan		25 metres	35 metres 10 metres

STOCK RECORD CARD

Stock code P4612

Date	In	Out	Balance
2006 1 Jan 4 Jan		10 metres	15 metres 5 metres

3 Short Furniture employs 15 weekly paid employees. There is one production supervisor, ten production workers and four administrative staff. There are three grades of production workers but the administrative staff are all paid at the same rate per hour.

The hourly rates of pay are:

Production supervisor		£10.20
Production workers	– Grade I	£8.50
	Grade II	£7.20
	Grade III	£6.50
Administrative staff		£7.10

All employees work a 35 hour week with any overtime being paid at time and a half.

The hours worked by each employee for the week ending 27 January 2006 are as follows:

Employee	Hours
Supervisor:	
P Knight	38
Production workers:	
P Anil (Grade II)	35
K Chappatte (Grade I)	39
H Dennis (Grade II)	37
K Fisher (Grade III)	38
J Hunt (Grade I)	40
D Jones (Grade III)	38
L Minns (Grade II)	41
S Percy (Grade II)	35
I Roberts (Grade I)	39
G Tracy (Grade III)	35
Administrative staff:	
F Albert	37
L Gill	35
J Norman	41
T Stevens	38

The employer's National Insurance Contribution is calculated at 12.8% of the weekly gross pay for each employee other than the first £97 each week which is exempt.

In the table below you are required to calculate the total gross pay and employer's NIC for each of the employees for the week ending 27 January 2006.

Employee	Total hours	Basic hours	Overtime hours	Basic pay £	Overtime pay £	Total gross pay £	Employers' NIC £
P Knight P Anil K Chappatte H Dennis K Fisher J Hunt D Jones L Minns S Percy I Roberts G Tracy F Albert L Gill J Norman T Stevens							

4 Short Furniture has the following cost centres for management accounting purposes:

Production cost centres:

■ cutting
■ assembly
■ finishing

Service cost centres:

■ marketing
■ administration

Summarised below are the total wage costs for the month to 27 January 2006 for the weekly paid employees together with the cost centre in which each employee works:

Employee	Cost centre	Gross wage £	Employer's NIC £
P Knight	(see note below)	1,612.70	159.59
P Anil	Assembly	1,008.00	84.00
K Chappatte	Cutting	1,327.55	123.94
H Dennis	Finishing	1,026.85	86.36
K Fisher	Assembly	1,026.40	86.30
J Hunt	Assembly	1,445.00	138.63
D Jones	Finishing	1,004.35	83.54
L Minns	Finishing	1,267.20	116.40
S Percy	Cutting	1,008.00	84.00
I Roberts	Assembly	1,284.60	118.58
G Tracy	Finishing	945.60	76.20
F Albert	Administration	1,079.20	92.90
L Gill	Marketing	994.00	82.25
J Norman	Marketing	1,234.70	112.34
T Stevens	Marketing	1,121.80	98.22
		17,385.95	1,543.25

P Knight is the production supervisor and as such works in all three production departments. His labour cost is to be split equally between all three production cost centres.

Short Furniture's policy is to allocate the employer's NIC as a labour cost to each cost centre as well as the total gross wage.

You are required to show the weekly labour cost for each cost centre in the table below:

	Cutting cost centre £	Assembly cost centre £	Finishing cost centre £	Marketing cost centre £	Admin cost centre £	Total £
Gross wages						
Employer's NIC						

chapter 22:
CODING

1 Short Furniture makes sales to two types of organisation, garden centres/nurseries and high street stores. Each of these sales functions is a profit centre. It also has five cost centres, cutting, assembly, finishing, marketing and administration.

An extract from the coding manual is given below:

Profit centre codes:

110	Garden centres/nurseries
120	High street stores

The third digit of the sales code denotes the type of sale:

001	Dining furniture
002	Benches
003	Sun loungers
004	Coffee tables
005	Other

Cost centre codes:

210	Cutting
220	Assembly
230	Finishing
240	Marketing
250	Administration

The third digit of the cost codes denotes the type of expense:

001	Wood
002	Screws/nails
003	Glue
004	Polish
005	Labour
006	Expenses

You are given below some sales invoices and purchase invoices from the end of the month of January 2006.

You are also given the coding listing which shows the total income or expense for each code to date.

INVOICE

Short Furniture
Eridge Estate
Benham DR6 4QQ
Tel 0303312 Fax 0303300
VAT Reg 0361 3282 60

To: Rother Nurseries
Rother Road
Benham

Invoice number: 08721

Date/tax point: 27 Jan 2006

Order number: 06148

Account number: SL 13

Quantity	Description	Stock code	Unit amount £	Total £
2	Coffee Table	CT002	96.00	192.00
6	Dining Chair	DC416	73.00	438.00

Net total	630.00
VAT	110.25
Invoice total	740.25

Terms
Net 30 days
E & OE

INVOICE

Short Furniture
Eridge Estate
Benham DR6 4QQ
Tel 0303312 Fax 0303300
VAT Reg 0361 3282 60

To: Fenband Stores
Victory Shopping Centre
Benham

Invoice number: 08722

Date/tax point: 27 Jan 2006

Order number: 43217

Account number: SL 61

Quantity	Description	Stock code	Unit amount £	Total £
7	Sunlounger	SL642	210.00	1,470.00
1	Bench	B443	110.00	110.00
				1,580.00
	Trade Discount			158.00

Net total	1,422.00
VAT	248.85
Invoice total	1,670.85

Terms
Net 30 days
E & OE

INVOICE

A1 Wood Supplies
Heath Park
Drenchley DR22 6KL
VAT Reg 4621 3117 04

To: Short Furniture
Eridge Estate
Benham DR6 4QQ

Invoice number: 764989

Date/tax point: 27 Jan 2006

Order number: 46794

Account number: S04

Quantity	Description	Stock code	Unit amount £	Total £
30m	Stripped Pine	P4612	12.38	371.40
40m	Oak	02611	15.87	638.80
				1,010.20
	Trade Discount			151.53
		Net total		858.67
		VAT		145.75
		Invoice total		1,004.42

Terms
3% settlement discount for payment within 14 days, otherwise net 30 days
E & OE

INVOICE

Polish People
23/25 Main Street
Wakeham DR17 4ZF
Tel 0421666 Fax 0421667
VAT Reg 3692 9417 63

To:
Short Furniture
Eridge Estate
Benham DR6 4QQ

Invoice number: 06715

Date/tax point: 27 Jan 2006

Order number: 04701

Account number: SL 13

Quantity	Description	Stock code	Unit amount £	Total £
40 litres	Exterior Wood Polish – cherry	88631	3.16	126.40
20 litres	Exterior Wood Polish – teak	88413	2.83	56.60
		Net total		183.00
		VAT		32.02
		Invoice total		215.02

Terms
Net 30 days
E & OE

INVOICE

J. T. Turner
Black Horse House
Budlett DR4 6TM
VAT Reg 3667 1294 61

To: Short Furniture
Eridge Estate
Benham DR6 4QQ

Invoice number: 06302

Date/tax point: 27 Jan 2006

Order number: 04699

Account number: SL 43

Quantity	Description	Stock code	Unit amount £	Total £
12 dozen	4″ cross head 2/8 screws	S428	3.83	45.96
30 dozen	3″ cross head 1/8 screws	S318	1.94	58.20
				104.16
	Trade Discount			15.62

Net total	88.54
VAT	14.87
Invoice total	103.41

Terms
4% settlement discount for payment within 10 days, otherwise 30 days net
E & OE

Coding listing – Income and expenditure – January 2006

Code	Balance £	Amendment £	Updated balance £
111	16,387.50		
112	13,265.95		
113	9,326.20		
114	3,587.90		
115	1,037.00		
121	10,385.30		
122	7,256.30		
123	3,646.70		
124	3,027.60		
125	926.40		
211	35,287.74		
215	–		
216	–		
222	1,285.47		
223	1,036.80		
225	–		
226	–		
234	8,385.40		
235	–		
236	–		
245	–		
246	–		
255	–		
256	–		

You are required to code each of the invoices given and to enter the net amounts onto the coding listing for each code (ignore VAT as the management accounting records are only concerned with the net of VAT costs).

2 Given below is the summary of the wages costs for the month to 27 January 2006 prepared earlier.

	Cutting cost centre £	Assembly cost centre £	Finishing cost centre £	Marketing cost centre £	Admin cost centre £	Total £
Gross wages	2,873.12	5,301.57	4,781.56	3,350.50	1,079.20	17,385.95
Employer's NIC	261.14	480.70	415.70	292.81	92.90	1,543.25
	3,134.26	5,782.27	5,197.26	3,643.31	1,172.10	18,929.20

You are required to code each total and to enter them into the coding listing for the relevant codes. The coding listing from the previous question is to be used.

3 Given below is the expense schedule for January 2006 produced earlier.

Expense	Total £	Cutting £	Assembly £	Finishing £	Marketing £	Admin £
Blades	340	340				
Electricity 60% x 1,560	1,560	936	156	156	156	156
Advertising	550				550	
Rent 2,100 x 1,000/7,000 2,100 x 3,000/7,000 2,100 x 2,000/7,000 2,100 x 500/7,000	2,100	300	900	600	150	150
Telephone 70% x 420 30% x 420	420				294	126
	4,970	1,576	1,056	756	1,150	432

You are required to code the totals and to enter them into the coding listing for the relevant codes. The coding listing from the earlier question is to be used.

4   Finally you are required to complete the coding listing for January 2006 by calculating the updated balance for each code.

5   A business has the following balances on each of its cost codes at 1 June 2006.

Code	Balance £
10101	28,375
10102	13,773
10103	12,356
10201	17,365
10202	21,925
10203	11,482

During the month of June 2006 the following costs were incurred for each cost code.

Code	Cost £
10101	6,234
10102	3,154
10103	1,783
10201	4,254
10202	4,793
10203	2,015

Set up a computer spreadsheet to find the closing balance on each cost code at the end of June 2006.

	A	B	C	D	E
1					
2					
3					
4					
5					
6					
7					

chapter 23:
COMPARISON OF COSTS AND INCOME

1 During the month of December 2006 the production costs of Natural Productions were summarised as:

	£
Raw materials	2,968
Labour	1,635
Expenses	372

You are Jane Mitchell and you have been asked by the owner of the business, Phil McKenna, to compare these costs to those of the previous month. The costs for November 2006 are summarised as:

	£
Raw materials	5,216
Labour	2,667
Expenses	552

You mention to Phil that the November costs are much larger than those for December as production was greater due to Christmas demand. He therefore asks you to compare the December 2006 costs to those for December 2005. The relevant figures for December 2005 are:

	£
Raw materials	2,537
Labour	1,367
Expenses	350

You are required to prepare a memo to the owner showing separate comparisons of the December 2006 costs to those of the previous month and those of the corresponding month last year. Today's date is 5 January 2007.

MEMO

To:

From:

Date:

Subject:

---

2 Phil McKenna has now asked you send him a note comparing the actual costs for December 2006 to the forecast costs for that month and showing any variances. You find the budgeted figures for December 2006 in the filing system and they are:

	£
Raw materials	2,700
Labour	1,650
Expenses	420

Prepare a note to Phil showing the comparison and the variances.

3 Newmans, the music shop, has an accounting year that runs from 1 July through to 30 June. The forecast sales for figures for the year from 1 July 2006 to 30 June 2007 are:

July	Aug	Sept	Oct	Nov	Dec	Jan	Feb	Mar	Apr	May	June
£ 8,700	8,100	9,800	8,600	8,500	9,900	7,400	7,800	8,400	8,500	8,700	8,800

The actual sales for the year to date are:

July	Aug	Sept	Oct	Nov	Dec	Jan	Feb	Mar	Apr	May	June
£ 8,500	8,500	9,900	9,000	8,500	9,600	7,100					

You have been asked to prepare a table that shows a comparison of the actual monthly sales and the cumulative sales to date to the forecast figures. Show the actual figures up to January 2007 but complete the forecast figures until June 2007 in order that the actual figures can be inserted when each month's sales are known.

4 The actual and budgeted costs for material, labour and expenses for a business for the last month are given:

	Actual £	Budget £
Materials	41,705	45,000
Labour	68,376	60,000
Expenses	25,357	22,500

All variances which exceed 5% of the budgeted figure are to be investigated.

Set up a computer spreadsheet to calculate each variance and the percentage that each variance is of the budgeted figure.

	A	B	C	D	E
1					
2					
3					
4					
5					
6					
7					

AAT

SAMPLE SIMULATION
UNIT 1

TUBNEY TECHNOLOGY LTD

> This is the AAT's Sample Simulation for Unit 1. Its purpose is to give you an idea of what an AAT simulation looks like. It is not intended as a definitive guide to the tasks you may be required to perform.
>
> This simulation is in two parts. It is suggested that you spend approximately 90 minutes on each part.
>
> Total time: 3 hours

SIMULATION

Coverage of performance criteria and range statements

All performance criteria are covered in this simulation.

Element	PC Coverage
1.1	**Process documents relating to goods and services supplied**
a)	Accurately prepare **invoices and credit notes** in accordance with organisational requirements and check against **source documents**.
b)	Ensure invoices and credit notes are correctly authorised and coded before being sent to customers.
c)	Ensure invoices and credit notes are correctly **coded**.
d)	Enter invoices and credit notes into **books of prime entry** according to organisational procedures.
e)	Enter invoices and credit notes in the appropriate **ledgers.**
f)	Produce **statements** of account for despatch to debtors.
g)	**Communicate** politely and effectively with customers regarding accounts, using the relevant information from the aged debtors analysis.
1.2	**Process receipts**
a)	Check **receipts** against relevant supporting information.
b)	Enter receipts in appropriate **accounting records.**
c)	Prepare paying-in documents and reconcile to relevant records.
d)	Identify **unusual features** and either resolve or refer to the appropriate person.

All range statements are covered in this simulation.

DATA AND TASKS

INSTRUCTIONS

This simulation is designed to let you show your ability to record income and receipts.

You should read the whole simulation before you start work, so that you are fully aware of what you will have to do.

You are allowed **three hours** to complete your work.

Write your answers in the Answer Booklet provided on pages 189 to 212. If you need more paper for your answers, ask the person in charge.

You should write your answers in blue or black ink, **not** pencil.

You may use correcting fluid, but in moderation. You should cross out your errors neatly and clearly.

You may pull apart and rearrange your booklets if you wish to do so, but you must put them back in their original order before handing them in.

Your work must be accurate, so check your work carefully before handing it in.

You are not allowed to refer to any unauthorised material, such as books or notes, while you are working on the simulation. If you have any such material with you, you must hand it to the person in charge before you start work.

Any instances of misconduct will be reported to the AAT, and disciplinary action may be taken.

Coverage of performance criteria and range statements

It is not always possible to cover all performance criteria and range statements in a single simulation. Any performance criteria and range statements not covered must be assessed by other means by the assessor before a candidate can be considered competent.

Performance criteria and range statement coverage for this simulation is shown on page 156.

THE SITUATION

Tubney Technology Limited is based at a business park in Oxford. It is a small company with a factory where it manufactures standard parts used in the production of computers and mobile phones. It also makes some special parts to the customer's specification.

You are Lynsey Jones, Accounts Assistant. You report directly to Samir Aleffi, who is the Accounts Manager of Tubney Technology Ltd.

All sales are made on credit to customers, which are computer and mobile phone manufacturers. Tubney Technology Ltd is registered for VAT and all its sales are standard rated at 17.5%.

A settlement discount of 3% for payment within 14 days is offered to all customers. Established customers also receive trade discount.

Accounting system

Tubney Technology Ltd operates a partially computerised sales and accounting system.

- Invoices and credit notes are prepared manually and details are input to a computer, which produces a Discount Analysis.

- The Sales Day Book and Sales Returns Day Book are prepared manually. The relevant totals are entered by hand into the manual main ledger containing a sales ledger control account, and into the manual subsidiary (sales) ledger, which is not part of the double entry system.

- Receipts are entered first into the manual cash book, which is part of the main ledger, and this is posted manually to the other main ledger accounts and the subsidiary (sales) ledger. Details of receipts are also entered into the computer, which produces the Aged Debtors Analysis.

Today's date is Thursday 18 September 2006.

THE TASKS TO BE COMPLETED

PART 1 PROCESS DOCUMENTS RELATING TO GOODS AND SERVICES SUPPLIED (90 MINUTES)

Invoice preparation

All sales to customers are made against purchase orders received from the customer, or sales orders prepared by the Sales Manager, Mark Alberts. For sales of special parts there is also a quotation setting out the work to be done and the rates to be charged. Delivery notes accompany all deliveries to the customer. If the order and the delivery note do not agree in any respect, the sale is not invoiced but is referred back to Mark Alberts. The prices charged are calculated with reference to either the quotation or the price list on page 164 of this book. Trade discount details are taken from the Subsidiary (Sales) Ledger Account List, which is on page 164 of this book.

Task 1

Refer to the documents on pages 164-175 of this book.

- Check each order against the relevant delivery note. Make a note of any discrepancy on page 189 of the Answer Booklet.

- Prepare invoices for the sales that you have agreed. Use the invoice forms on pages 190-194 of the Answer Booklet. You do not need to fill in the customer's address. VAT, trade discount and settlement discount should be rounded down to the nearest penny.

Credit Note Preparation

Credit notes for parts returned are raised against return notes. The return notes are completed and signed by Ian Smith, the Factory Manager, to indicate that he has approved the return.

Task 2

Refer to the return notes on pages 176-177 of this book.

- Prepare credit notes using the credit note forms on pages 195-196 of the Answer Booklet. You do not need to fill in the customer's address.

Task 3

Before invoices and credit notes are despatched to customers or recorded, they must be authorised.

- On page 197 of the Answer Booklet, make a note of who should authorise the invoices and credit notes for despatch: Mark Alberts (Sales Manager), Samir Aleffi (Accounts Manager) or Ian Smith (Factory Manager)?

Assume that you have obtained authorisation as required.

- Make appropriate entries in the Sales Day Book and the Sales Return Day Book on pages 197-198 of the Answer Booklet.

- Calculate the total settlement discount that the computer's Discount Analysis will show is available to customers on the day's invoice. Make a note on page 197 of the Answer Booklet.

Task 4

- Total the entries in the Sales Day Book and Sales Returns Day Book.

- Insert the appropriate main ledger and subsidiary (sales) ledger codes in the Day Books.

- Make the necessary entries in the main ledger and subsidiary (sales) ledger accounts on pages 199-203 of the Answer Booklet. (For some ledger accounts there will be no entries at this stage.)

Note: There are transactions already shown on some of the ledger accounts. You do NOT need to balance any accounts after you have made your entries.

PART 2 PROCESS RECEIPTS (90 minutes)

Banking receipts

Cash and cheques received from customers are checked against supporting documentation and then entered into the cash book. Some customers make automated payments, which appear on the bank statement. These are entered into the cash book when they have been checked to the weekly bank statement, and the supporting documentation.

Where the receipt does not agree with supporting documentation, the payment is banked and entered into the cash book, but a communication is sent to the customer outlining the effect of the transaction on the debtor's account. Wrongly completed cheques are returned to the customer with a request for a correctly completed cheque to be issued.

Task 5

Refer to the documents on pages 178-182 of this book relating to amounts received, and the subsidiary (sales) ledger accounts on pages 201-203 of the Answer Booklet.

■　　Refer to the Discount Analysis printout on page 178 of this book and check the receipt and remittance advices on pages 178-182 of this book to ensure that any settlement discount taken by customers is allowable. You should bear in mind that only a 14 day period is offered and that the month of August has 31 days. Make notes on page 204 of the Answer Booklet of any queries, and the action that needs to be taken.

■　　On page 205 of the Answer Booklet, calculate a total for the cash received from Kendrick & Co, and agree this to the receipt that Samir gave to the customer.

■　　Check that the cheques have been correctly completed and agree with supporting documentation. If a cheque cannot be paid into the bank today, or does not agree with supporting documentation, make notes on page 204 of the Answer Booklet as to the reason, and the action that needs to be taken.

■　　Agree the automated receipt on the bank statement on page 183 of this book to the supporting documentation.

Task 6

■　　Write up the cash book (receipts side) on page 206 of the Answer Book for the cash and cheques that will be paid into the bank, and subtotal the amount to be paid in.

■　　Write up the cash book (receipts side) for the automated payment received.

Note: You do NOT need to calculate any totals in the cash book (receipts side) at this stage.

Task 7

Prepare the paying-in slip on page 207 of the Answer Booklet for the cash and cheques that need to be paid into the bank today. Make sure that the total on the paying-in slip agrees with paying-in total in the cash book total (receipts side) that you calculated in Task 6.

Task 8

- Calculate the totals for the cash book (receipts side).

- Enter appropriate main ledger and subsidiary (sales) ledger codes into the cash book (receipts side) in preparation for posting.

- Post the cash book (receipts side) to the relevant main ledger and subsidiary (sales) ledger accounts.

Task 9

For the two customers for whom statements are provided on page 208 of the Answer Booklet:

- calculate a balance on the appropriate subsidiary (sales) ledger account;

- complete the statements as at today's date.

Chasing payments

The company policy for debtors who have debts which are more than 60 days old is to put the whole account on 'stop'. This means that that no more sales are made until settlement has been received as agreed.

Task 10

Refer to the extract from the aged debtor analysis on page 184 of this book, and to the letter from Kendrick & Co to Mark Alberts on page 185 of this book. Samir has made some notes on both documents.

- Draft a letter to Slomax & Partners from Samir Aleffi, in accordance with Samir's notes on the Aged debtor analysis. Use the letterhead on page 209 of the Answer Booklet. Note that the contact name and address for the customer have been completed for you.

- Draft a memo to Mark Alberts concerning the letter from Kendrick & Co and Samir's notes on it. Use page 210 of the Answer Booklet.

Task 11

The Finance Director has asked Samir to find ways in which the computer can be used more fully by the Accounts Department without disrupting matters too much. Samir has asked you for some ideas.

- Using page 211 of the Answer Booklet, draft an email to Samir, with answers to the following points:

    - If we move to a fully computerised system, do we have to change the sequence of our invoice and credit note numbers and the ledger codes?

    - We already input details to the computer so that we have a Discount Analysis and an Aged Debtor Analysis. How will further computerisation help in completing the Day Books and the main and subsidiary ledgers, and in preparing statements?

MAIN LEDGER ACCOUNT CODES (EXTRACT)

Ledger code	Account name
1000	Cash
2000	Sales Ledger Control
3000	Discount Allowed
4000	Sales
5000	Returns
6000	VAT

SUBSIDIARY (SALES) LEDGER ACCOUNT CODES (EXTRACT)

Ledger code	Account name	Trade discount
100	Ardington plc	0
200	Dreadnought PC Ltd	5%
300	Kendrick & Co	0
400	Lineman plc	0
500	PrimeTime Mobiles	5%
600	Rondar plc	0
700	Slomax & Partners	0

TUBNEY TECHNOLOGY LTD: PRICE LIST

Part reference	£ per unit
AD897	0.35
DF014	3.60
GW208	12.80
MM936	0.50
PA220	5.55
RL188	9.75

QUOTATION

From: Tubney Technology Ltd, Oxford Business Park, Oxford OX2 8VN

To: Dreadnought PC Ltd
Saddleworth Laner
Halifax LS6 8WL

Date: 8 September 2006

Further to your enquiry, we have pleasure in providing this firm quotation to carry out the necessary work as per your specification.

Description

Manufacture and testing of 500 HighDensity 10 cm SIM cards as per your specification of 1 September 2006.

Including packing and delivery   £1,950 plus VAT

Signed: M Alberts   Date: 8 September 2006

PURCHASE ORDER

Ardington plc
90/94 Grove Road
Wantage OX16 9AS

To: Tubney Technology Lrd,
Oxford Business Park,
Oxford, OX2 8VN

Date: 15 September 2006

Please supply us with 2,000 AD897 and 1,000 MM936 parts as
soon as possible.

Yours faithfully

C Timms

Ardington plc

DELIVERY NOTE

Tubney Technology
Oxford Business Park
Oxford
OX2 8VN

Delivery address:

Ardington plc
90/94 Grove Road
Wantage OX16 9AS

Date: 16 September 2006

Item	Quantity
MM936	1,000
AD897	2,000

Received by: [Signature]   *C Timms*

Date: *16 September 2006*

PURCHASE ORDER

DREADNOUGHT PC Ltd
Saddleworth Lane
Halifax, LS6 8WL

To: Tubney Technology Lrd,
Oxford Business Park,
Oxford, OX2 8VN

Date: 10 September 2006

Please supply 500 special parts in accordance with your
quotation of 8 September, which we accept.

Yours faithfully

S Parsons

Dreadnought PC Ltd

DELIVERY NOTE

Tubney Technology
Oxford Business Park
Oxford
OX2 8VN

Delivery address:

Dreadnought PC Ltd
Saddleworth Lane
Halifax LS6 8WL

Date: 16 September 2006

Item	Quantity
High Density 10 cm SIM cards as per quotation	500

Received by: [Signature]   *S Parsons*

Date: *16 September 2006*

PURCHASE ORDER

Kendrick & Co
110-120 Banbury Road
Bicester OX6 9QW

To: Tubney Technology Lrd,
    Oxford Business Park,
    Oxford, OX2 8VN

Date: 15 September 2006

Please supply 100 PA220 parts as soon as possible.

Yours faithfully

O Kendrick

Kendrick & Co

DELIVERY NOTE

Tubney Technology
Oxford Business Park
Oxford
OX2 8VN

Delivery address:

Kendrick & Co
110-120 Banbury Road
Bicester OX6 9QW

Date: 17 September 2006

Item	Quantity
RL188	1,000

Received by: [Signature]   *O Kendrick*

Date: *17 September 2006*

SALES ORDER

Tubney Technology
Oxford Business Park
Oxford
OX2 8VN

Customer: Lineman plc

Delivery address:

Hamilton House
Oxford Science Park
Oxford OX3 3PR

Date: 15 September 2006

Item	Quantity
AD897	3,000
DF014	200
GW208	150

Received by: [Signature]   *M Alberts*

Date: *15 September 2006*

DELIVERY NOTE

Tubney Technology
Oxford Business Park
Oxford
OX2 8VN

Delivery address:

Lineman plc
Hamilton House
Oxford Science Park
Oxford OX3 3PR

Date: 17 September 2006

Item	Quantity
GW208	150
DF014	200
AD897	3,000

Received by: [Signature]   *P Patel*

Date: *17 September 2006*

SALES ORDER

Tubney Technology
Oxford Business Park
Oxford
OX2 8VN

Customer: PrimeTime Mobiles

Delivery address:

Penny Hinton Road
Morpath
Cambridge CB13 8DF

Date: 16 September 2006

Item	Quantity
PA220	250
MM936	3,000

Received by: [Signature]   *M Alberts*

Date: *16 September 2006*

DELIVERY NOTE

Tubney Technology
Oxford Business Park
Oxford
OX2 8VN

Delivery address:

PrimeTime Mobiles
Penny Hinton Road
Morpath
Cambridge CB13 8DF

Date: 17 September 2006

Item	Quantity
PA220	250
MM936	3,000

Received by: [Signature]   *A Colley*

Date: *17 September 2006*

RETURN NOTE

Tubney Technology
Oxford Business Park
Oxford
OX2 8VN

Customer: Kendrick & Co

Date: 12 September 2006

Item	Quantity
GW208 see invoice 8900 8-Sept-05	20

Reason for return   Faulty parts

Received by: [Signature]   *Ian Smith*

Date: *12 September 2006*

RETURN NOTE

Tubney Technology
Oxford Business Park
Oxford
OX2 8VN

Customer: Rondar plc

Date: 15 September 2006

Item	Quantity
PA220 see invoice 8905 10-Sept-05	15

Reason for return   Faulty parts

Received by: [Signature]   *Ian Smith*

Date: *15 September 2006*

Discount analysis (extract)

Invoice number	Date 2006	Customer account	SDB folio	Invoice subtotal £	VAT £	Invoice total £	Settlement discount £
8750	19 Sept	Dreadnought PC Ltd	200	8,550.00	1,443.88	9,993.88	299.25
8765	20 Aug	PrimeTime Mobiles	500	4,264.05	616.05	4,264.05	127.68
8790	22 Aug	Ardington plc	100	438.75	74.09	512.84	15.35
8890	5 Sept	Kendrick & Co	300	360.00	60.79	420.79	12.60
8910	8 Sept	Lineman plc	400	487.50	82.32	569.82	17.06

```
                                    Receipt no:51

        18 September 2006

        To: Barry Kendrick, Kendrick & Co

        Receipt for cash received

        Received with thanks £408.19 in full
        settlement of Invoice 8890 (discount taken:
        £12.60)

        S Aleffi

        Accounts Manager

        Tubney Technology Ltd          ✓
```

REMITTANCE ADVICE

To: Tubney Technology Ltd,
Oxford Business Park,
Oxford, OX2 8VN

From: Ardington plc
90/94 Grove Road
Wantage, OX16 9AS

Date	Transaction reference	Amount (£)
28-Aug-06	Invoice 8790	512.84
17-Sept-06	Cheque attached	-512.84

✓

Oxford Bank plc

20 - 26 - 33
003014 40268134

26 Pinehurst Place, London EC1 2AA

Date *17 Sept 2006*

Pay *Tubney Technology*

Five hundred and twelve

pounds and 84 pence

Account Payee

£ *512.84*

C Timms

Cheque No.	Sort Code	Account No.	
455847	25−45−78	03216875	Ardington plc

REMITTANCE ADVICE

To: Tubney Technology Ltd,
Oxford Business Park,
Oxford, OX2 8VN

From: PrimeTime Mobiles,
Morpath, Cambridge,
CB13 8DF

Date	Transaction reference	Amount (£)
21-Aug-06	Invoice 8765	4,264.05
17-Sept-06	Cheque attached	-4,264.05

Cambridge Bank pkc

35 - 45 - 91

Castle Hill, Cambridge CB2 1TA

Date *17 Sept 2006*

Pay *Tubney Technology*

Four thousand, two hundred and

sixty four pounds and 5p

£ *4,264.05*

Cheque No.	Sort Code	Account No.

464647   35—45—91   77575461

PrimeTime Mobiles

REMITTANCE ADVICE

To: Tubney Technology Ltd,
Oxford Business Park,
Oxford, OX2 8VN

From: Dreadnought PC Ltd
Saddleworth Lane,
Halifax LS6 8WL

Date	Transaction reference	Amount (£)
19-Aug-06	Invoice 8750	9,939.88
17-Sept-06	Cheque attached	-9,939.88

MidNorth Bank plc

50 - 46 - 30

Denby Road, Halifax LS9 7FG

Date *17 Sept 2006*

Pay *Tubney Technology*

Nine thousand, nine hundred and thirty nine pounds and 88p

£ *9,939.88*

K Betts

Cheque No.	Sort Code	Account No.
30 2695	50—46—30	97198715

Dreadnought PC Ltd

REMITTANCE ADVICE

To: Tubney Technology Ltd,
Oxford Business Park,
Oxford, OX2 8VN

From: Lineman plc,
Hamilton House,
Oxford Science,
Oxford, OX3 3PR

Date	Transaction reference	Amount (£)
8-Sept 06	Invoice 8910	569.82
17-Sept-06	BACS	-552.76
17-Sept-06	Settlement discount taken	-17.06

✓

STATEMENT

Oxford Bank plc
High Street,
Oxford,
OX2 7DF

Account name: Tubney Technology
Oxford Business Park
Oxford OX2 8VN

Account number: 98746510

Sort code: 25-45-78

Statement no: 109

Details	Date	Debit £	Credit £	Balance £
	2006			
Balance forward	11 Sept			25,946.46
CC	11 Sept		9,457.08	
Cheque 4900	11 Sept	15,789.43		
Cheque 4899	11 Sept	6,913.30		12,700.81
CC	12 Sept		12,879.63	
Cheques 4901	12 Sept	8,673.00		
CC	12 Sept		500.00	17,047.44
BACS payment - salaries	15 Sept	21,067.90		
CC	15 Sept		7,560.49	3,900.03
Cheque 4902	16 Sept	681.34		
BACS receipt	17 Sept		552.76	3,771.45

Key CC: Cash and/or cheques   **BACS:** Banks automated clearing service

Aged Debtor Analysis

Customer	Subsidiary (sales) ledger code	Credit limit	Total	Not yet due 0-30 days £	30-60 days £	60+ days £	Action taken
Slomax & Partners	700	2,000.00	3,972.09	0.00	1,893.44	2,078.65	In error we allowed them to exceed their credit limit, then we received a cheque dated 16 September 2005 for £2,078.65, plus an order goods worth £1,280.00. Draft a letter for my signature - point out why we could not bank this cheque (which we will return with the letter, asking for a corrected one), and confirm our company policy on the state of their account.

Kendrick & Co

111-120 Banbury Road
Bicester OX6 9QW
Phone: 01869 654641 Fax: 01869 567684

Mr M Alberts
Sales Manager
Tubney Technology Ltd
Oxford Business Park
Oxford OX2 8VN

16 September 2006

Dear Mark

As you know, I often pay your invoices in cash, so that we can take advantage of the settlement discount you offer. I have recently acquired a corporate credit card. If you are agreeable, I propose to pay our bills in future by this method. I shall pop in on Friday to settle our account as it stands in full with the card.

Yours sincerely

O Kendrick

Ollie Kendrick
Partner

Lynsey

Mark and his sales team are able to take credit card payments using vouchers, but our floor limit is only £100. And what is the state of Kendrick & Co's account currently? Will he be able to settle it in full on Friday? Please drop a memo to Mark about this, and let me have a copy.

Samir

ANSWER BOOKLET

ANSWERS (Task 1)

Note on sale not invoiced:

Kendrick + Co – purchase order does not match delivery note – PO is for 100 PA220 parts, DN is for 1000 RL188 ✓

Action to be taken:

Refer back to M Alberts, do not write invoice ✓

Note on sale not invoiced:

Action to be taken:

ANSWERS (Task 1, continued)

INVOICE

Tubney Technology Ltd
Oxford Business Park
Oxford OX2 8VN
Phone: 01865 444555
Fax 01865 444666

To: Ardington PLC

Invoice number: 8950

VAT Registration: 305 034 97 63

Date/tax point: 18 Sept 06

Subsidiary (sales) ledger code: 100

Item	Quantity	Price £	Total £
MM936	1,000	0.50	500.00
AD897	2,000	0.35	700.00

Goods total	1200.00
Trade discount @ %	0.00
Sub-total	1200.00
VAT @ 17.5%	202.65
Invoice total	1402.65

Settlement discount: 3.5% for payment in 14 days
(to be deducted when computing VAT)

£42. ✓

ANSWERS (Task 1, continued)

INVOICE

Tubney Technology Ltd
Oxford Business Park
Oxford OX2 8VN
Phone: 01865 444555
Fax 01865 444666

To: Dreadnaght RCLtd

Invoice number: 8951

VAT Registration: 305 034 97 63

Date/tax point: 18 Sept 06

Subsidiary (sales) ledger code: 200

Item	Quantity	Price £	Total £
High Density 10cm SIM cards as per quotation.	500	1950.00	1950.00

Goods total	1950.00
Trade discount @ 5 %	97.50
Sub-total	1852.50
VAT @ 17.5%	312.84
Invoice total	2165.34

Settlement discount: 3.5% for payment in 14 days
(to be deducted when computing VAT)

£64.83

ANSWERS (Task 1, continued)

INVOICE

Tubney Technology Ltd
Oxford Business Park
Oxford OX2 8VN
Phone: 01865 444555
Fax 01865 444666

To: Lineman PLC

Invoice number: 8952

VAT Registration: 305 034 97 63

Date/tax point: 18 Sept 06

Subsidiary (sales) ledger code: 400

Item	Quantity	Price £	Total £
GW208	150	12.80	1920.00
DF014	200	3.60	720.00
AD897	3000	0.35	1050.00

Goods total	3690.00
Trade discount @ %	0.00
Sub-total	3690.00
VAT @ 17.5%	623.14
Invoice total	4313.14

Settlement discount: 3.5% for payment in 14 days
(to be deducted when computing VAT)

129.15 ✓

ANSWERS (Task 1, continued)

INVOICE

Tubney Technology Ltd
Oxford Business Park
Oxford OX2 8VN
Phone: 01865 444555
Fax 01865 444666

To: Prime Time Mobiles

Invoice number: 8953

VAT Registration: 305 034 97 63

Date/tax point: 18 Sept 06

Subsidiary (sales) ledger code: 500

Item	Quantity	Price £	Total £
PA 220	250	5.55	1387.50
MM936	3000	0.50	1500.00

Goods total	2887.50
Trade discount @ 5 %	144.37
Sub-total	2743.13
VAT @ 17.5%	463.28 ✗ 463.24
Invoice total	3206.41 ✗ 3206.37.
	96.00
	106.11

Settlement discount: 3.5% for payment in 14 days
(to be deducted when computing VAT)

ANSWERS (Task 1, continued)

INVOICE

Tubney Technology Ltd
Oxford Business Park
Oxford OX2 8VN
Phone: 01865 444555
Fax 01865 444666

To:

Invoice number: 8954

VAT Registration: 305 034 97 63

Date/tax point:

Subsidiary (sales) ledger code:

Item	Quantity	Price £	Total £

Goods total	
Trade discount @ %	
Sub-total	
VAT @ 17.5%	
Invoice total	

Settlement discount: 3.5% for payment in 14 days
(to be deducted when computing VAT)

ANSWERS (Task 2)

CREDIT NOTE

Tubney Technology Ltd
Oxford Business Park
Oxford OX2 8VN
Phone: 01865 444555
Fax 01865 444666

To: Kendrick + Co.

Credit note number: 650

VAT Registration: 305 034 97 63

Date/tax point: 18 Sept 06.

Subsidiary (sales) ledger code: 300

Item	Quantity	Price £	Total £
6W208	20	12.80	256.00

Goods total	256.00
Trade discount @ %	0.00
Sub-total	256.00
VAT @ 17.5%	43.23
Credit note total	299.23 ✓
	£8.96

ANSWERS (Task 2, continued)

CREDIT NOTE

Tubney Technology Ltd
Oxford Business Park
Oxford OX2 8VN
Phone: 01865 444555
Fax 01865 444666

To: Rondar PLC

Credit note number: 651

VAT Registration: 305 034 97 63

Date/tax point: 18 Sept 06.

Subsidiary (sales) ledger code: 600

Item	Quantity	Price £	Total £
PA220	15	5.55	83.25

Goods total	83.25
Trade discount @ 0 %	0.00
Sub-total	83.25
VAT @ 17.5%	14.05
Credit note total	97.30
	£2.91

ANSWERS (Tasks 3 and 4)

Invoices and credit notes should be authorised before despatch by: _Sams Alam_

Day's total settlement discount on invoices (to be agreed to discount analysis): £331.98

SALES DAY BOOK

Folio: SDB 38

Date 2006	Customer	Subsidiary (sales) ledger code: DR	Invoice number	Total £	VAT £	Net £
18/09/06	Ardington PLC	100	8950	1402.65	202.65	1200.00
18/09/06	Deadnought PLC Ltd	200	8951	2165.34	312.84	1852.50
18/09/06	Lureman PLC	400	8952	4313.14	623.14	3690.00
16/09/06	Primetime Mobiles	500	8953	3206.41	463.28	2743.13
Totals				11087.54	1601.91	9485.63
Main ledger codes				3000 DR	6000 CR	4000 CR

ANSWERS (Tasks 3 and 4, continued)

SALES RETURNS DAY BOOK Folio: SRDB 9

Date 2006	Customer	Subsidiary (sales) ledger code: DR	Credit note number	Total £	VAT £	Net £
18/9/06	Kendrick + Co	300	650	299.23	43.23	256.00
18/9/06	Ponder PLC	600	651	97.30	14.05	83.25
Totals				396.53	57.28	339.25
Main ledger codes				2000 CR	6000 DR	5000 DR

ANSWERS (Tasks 4 and 7)

MAIN LEDGER

2000 SALES LEDGER CONTROL ACCOUNT

Date 2006	Details	Folio	Amount £	Date 2006	Details	Folio	Amount £
18/09	Invoices	SDB 38	11087.54	18/09	Returns	SRDB 9	376.53
				18/09	Payments	CB 38	1443.67
				18/09	discounts	CB 38	2229.66 ✓

3000 DISCOUNT ALLOWED

Date 2006	Details	Folio	Amount £	Date 2006	Details	Folio	Amount £
18/09	discounts	CB 38	29.66 ✓				

4000 Sales

Date 2006	Details	Folio	Amount £	Date 2006	Details	Folio	Amount £
				18/09	Invoices	SDB 38	9485.63 ✓

ANSWERS (Tasks 4 and 7, continued)

MAIN LEDGER

5000 SALES RETURNS

Date 2006	Details	Folio	Amount £	Date 2006	Details	Folio	Amount £
18/09	Returns	SRDB 9	339.25				

6000 VAT

Date 2006	Details	Folio	Amount £	Date 2006	Details	Folio	Amount £
18/09	Returns	SRDB 9	57.28	18/09	Invoices	SDB 38	1601.54

ANSWERS (Tasks 4 and 7, continued)

SUBSIDIARY (SALES) LEDGER

100 ARDINGTON PLC

Date 2006	Details	Folio	Amount £	Date 2006	Details	Folio	Amount £
22-Aug	Inv 8790	SDB 34	512.84	18/09	Payment	CB 38	512.84 ✓
18-Sept	Inv 8950	SDB 38	402.65				

200 DREADNOUGHT PC LTD

Date 2006	Details	Folio	Amount £	Date 2006	Details	Folio	Amount £
19-Aug	Inv 8750	SDB 34	9,993.88	18/09	Payment	CB 38	9939.88
18-Sept	Inv 8951	SDB 38	2165.34	18/09	Bal c/d		2219.34
			12159.22				12159.22
18/09	Bal b/d		2219.34				✓

300 KENDRICK & CO

Date 2006	Details	Folio	Amount £	Date 2006	Details	Folio	Amount £
5-Sept	Inv 8890	SDB 36	420.79	18-Sept	CN 660	SRDB 9	299.23
8-Sept	Inv 8900	SDB 37	1,496.16	18/09	Payment	CB 38	408.19
				18/09	Discount	CB 38	12.60
				18/09	Bal b/d		1196.93
			1916.95				1916.95
18/09	Bal c/d		1196.93				✓

ANSWERS (Tasks 4 and 7, continued)

SUBSIDIARY (SALES) LEDGER

400 LINEMAN PLC

Date 2006	Details	Folio	Amount £	Date 2006	Details	Folio	Amount £
8-Sep	Inv 8910	SDB 37	569.82	18/09	Payment	CB 38	552·76
18-Sept	Inv 8952	SDB38	438.14	18/09	discount	CB 38	17·06

500 PRIMETIME MOBILES

Date 2006	Details	Folio	Amount £	Date 2006	Details	Folio	Amount £
20-Aug	Inv 8765	SDB 34	4,264.05				
18-Sept	Inv 8953	SDB 38	3206.41				

600 RONDAR PLC

Date 2006	Details	Folio	Amount £	Date 2006	Details	Folio	Amount £
13-May	Inv 6535	SDB 7	169.86	18-Sept	CN 651	SRDB 9	97.30
2-Jun	Inv 6590	SDB 10	210.87				

ANSWERS (Tasks 4 and 7, continued)

SUBSIDIARY (SALES) LEDGER

700 SLOMAX & PARTNERS

Date 2006	Details	Folio	Amount £	Date 2006	Details	Folio	Amount £
18-Sep	Balance		3,972.09				

ANSWERS (Task 5)

Notes

Dreadnought PLC – amount should be for
9993.88, cheque + remittance advice show
value of £993.88. ~~Cheque + remittance should~~
~~be sent back with request for the right~~
~~amount~~ Cheque can be banked but letter should
be written to customer to let them know money
still owed.
Prime Time Mobiles – cheque not signed,
send back to customer to sign.

ANSWERS (Task 5, continued)

Contents of envelope handed in by Mark Albert with Kendrick & Co receipt

		£
£50	4	200.00
£20	8	160.00
£10	4	40.00
£5	1	5.00
£2	0	0.00
£1	2	2.00
50p	1	0.50
20p	2	0.40
10p	1	0.10
5p	3	0.15
2p	1	0.02
1p	2	0.02
		408.19 ✓

ANSWERS (Tasks 6 and 8)

MAIN LEDGER

1000 CASH BOOK CB 38

RECEIPTS

Date 2006	Details	Ref	Receipt £	Discount allowed £	Customer account £	Subsidiary (sales) ledger code
18/09	Arlington PLC	Chq	512.84		512.84	100
18/09	Dreadnought PLC	Chq	9139.88		9139.88	200
18/09	Kendrick + Co	Cash	408.19	12.60	408.19	300
	Paying in amount		10360.91			
18/09	Tynman PLC	BACS	552.76	17.06	552.76	400
			11413.67	29.66	11413.67	
Main ledger codes				3000-DR.	2000-CR	
				2000-CR		

ANSWERS (Task 7)

bank giro credit	Please detail cheques and cash overleaf		
Date 15/09/06	£50 Notes	200	—
Cashier's stamp	£20 Notes	160	—
Oxford Bank plc High Street, Oxford OX2 7DF	£10 Notes	40	—
	£5 Notes	5	—
	£2		
Account	£1	2	—
Tubney Technology Ltd	50p	0	50
	20p	0	40
	10p, 5p	0	25
Paid in by/Ref.	2p, 1p	0	04
	Total cash	408	19
NO. OF CHEQUES **2** 25-45-78 98746510	Cheques, PO's	10452	72
	£	16860	91

Please do not write or mark below this line or fold this voucher

Details of cheques	Amount	
	£	P
Ardington PLC	512	84
Dreadnought PLC	9939	88
Total cheques carried over	10452	72

ANSWERS (Task 9)

STATEMENT OF ACCOUNT
Tubney Technology Ltd, Oxford Business Park, Oxford OX2 8VN

Customer: Dreadnought PC Ltd
Date: 18 Sept 06
Subsidiary (sales) ledger code: 200

Date 2006	Transaction reference	Debit £	Credit £	Balance outstanding £
19/08	Inv 8750	9993.88		9993.88
18/09	Inv 8951	2165.34		12159.22
18/09	Chq received		9939.88	2219.34
Balance outstanding				2219.34

Our terms are strictly 30 days, with 3.5% cash settlement discount available for payment within 14 days.

STATEMENT OF ACCOUNT
Tubney Technology Ltd, Oxford Business Park, Oxford OX2 8VN

Customer: Kendrick & Co
Date: 18 Sept 06
Subsidiary (sales) ledger code: 300

Date 2006	Transaction reference	Debit £	Credit £	Balance outstanding £
05/09	Inv 8890	420.79		420.79
08/09	Inv 8900	1496.16		1916.95
18/09	CN 650		299.23	1617.72
18/09	Cash received		408.19	1209.53
18/09	Discount taken		12.60	1196.93
Balance outstanding				1196.93

Our terms are strictly 30 days, with 3.5% cash settlement discount available for payment within 14 days.

ANSWERS (Task 10)

Tubney Technology Ltd
Oxford Business Park, Oxford OX2 8VN
Phone: 01865 444555 Fax 01865 444666

Ms U Ogangwe
Slomax & Partners
Success House
200 Old Kent Road
London SE2 9CV

18 Sept 06

Dear Ms Ogangwe,

We received your payment, however the cheque which you sent was dated 16 September 2005 this means the cheque is out of date, therefore can you arrange a new cheque to written and sent to us as soon as possible? of £2078.65

Please note that this payment is more than 60 days overdue and it is company policy that no further sales be made to you until this payment has been received.

You should also note that you have a total of £1893.44 which is also due This total is very close to your credit limit of £2000 so we would appreciate it if this balance was also paid as soon as possible.

We look forward to hearing from you.

Yours sincerely.

S Aleffi
Accounts Manager.

ANSWERS (Task 10, continued)

MEMO

To: M Alberts
From: L Jones
CC: S Aleffi
Subject: Kendrick + Co
Date: 18 Sept 06.

Kendrick + Co have requested to pay all further bills via credit card and O Kendrick has suggested coming in on Friday to pay off the remainder of their balance. Currently they owe a total of £1196.93, as our floor limit is £100 they will obviously not be able to pay their full balance via credit card, without us first receiving authorisation from the credit card company.

As most of their invoices total more than £100 we may need to think about having our floor limit increased. If this is not possible I would suggest that it is inconvinient for Kendrick + Co to pay their invoices on credit card.

ANSWERS (Task 11)

EMAIL

From: lynsey.jones@tubneytech.co.uk

To: samir.aleffi@tubneytech.co.uk

CC:

Subject: Computerisation

Date: 18 September 2006

Message

Samir,

If we were to move to fully computerised system we should be able to keep our system of coding of invoices, we may need to change our ledger codes however.

If we continue to input all information to the computer it can prepare our day books for us + prepare statements for customers this will obviously save a great deal of time.

lsh

If using this page, please state clearly which task you are answering.

AAT

SAMPLE SIMULATION
UNIT 2

AMICA PRINTING CO.

This is the AAT's Sample Simulation for Unit 2. Its purpose is to give you an idea of what an AAT simulation looks like. It is not intended as a definitive guide to the tasks you may be required to perform.

This simulation is in two parts. It is suggested that you spend approximately 90 minutes on each part.

Total time: 3 hours

SIMULATION

COVERAGE OF PERFORMANCE CRITERIA AND RANGE STATEMENTS

All performance criteria are covered in this simulation.

Element	PC Coverage
2.1	**Process documents relating to goods and services received**
a)	Check suppliers' invoices and credit notes against relevant **documents** for validity.
b)	Checked **calculations** on suppliers' invoices and credit notes for accuracy.
c)	Identify and deduct available **discounts**.
d)	Correctly **code** invoices and credit notes.
e)	Correctly enter invoices and credit notes into **books of prime entry** according to organisational procedures.
f)	Enter invoices and credit notes in the appropriate **ledgers**.
g)	Identify **discrepancies** and either resolve or refer to the appropriate person if outside own authority.
h)	**Communicate** appropriately with suppliers regarding accounts.
2.2	**Process payments**
a)	Calculate **payments** from relevant **documentation**.
b)	Schedule payments and obtain authorisation.
c)	Use the appropriate **payment method** and timescale, in accordance with organisational procedures.
d)	Enter payments into **accounting records**.
e)	Identify **queries** and resolve or refer to the appropriate person.
f)	Ensure security and confidentiality is maintained according to organisational requirements.

The following range statements are **not** covered in this simulation and should be assessed separately.

Element	Range Statement
2.1	**Code:** computerised systems **Books of prime entry:** relevant computerised records **Ledgers:** computerised ledgers **Discrepancies:** duplicated invoices
2.2	**Accounting records:** computerised records

DATA AND TASKS

INSTRUCTIONS

This simulation is designed to let you show your ability to make and record payments.

You should read the whole simulation before you start work, so that you are fully aware of what you will have to do.

You are allowed three hours to complete your work.

Write your answers in the Answer Booklet provided on pages 239-288. If you need more paper for your answers, ask the person in charge.

You should write your answers in blue or black ink, **not** pencil.

You may use correcting fluid, but in moderation. You should cross out your errors neatly and clearly.

You may pull apart and rearrange your booklets if you wish to do so, but you must put them back in their original order before handing them in.

Your work must be accurate, so check your work carefully before handing it in.

You are not allowed to refer to any unauthorised material, such as books or notes, while you are working on the simulation. If you have any such material with you, you must hand it to the person in charge before you start work.

Any instances of misconduct will be reported to the AAT, and disciplinary action may be taken.

Coverage of performance criteria and range statements

It is not always possible to cover all performance criteria and range statements in a single simulation. Any performance criteria and range statements not covered must be assessed by other means by the assessor before a candidate can be considered competent.

Performance criteria and range statement coverage for this simulation is shown on page 214.

THE SITUATION

You are Hei Lam Cheng, Accounts Assistant at Amica Printing Company, a business situated in the town of Wantage. Your duties include accounting for purchases on credit, making payments and controlling petty cash. You report to Alex Cook, the Accountant. The business is owned by Sam Fisher.

Amica Printing Company prints brochures and leaflets for businesses and public sector organisations in the UK.

The company employs 20 people, most of whom work in the printing factory. The Factory Supervisor is Henry Lynch, who reports to Edward Hunt, the Factory Manager. Nearly all the factory staff are employed on a permanent basis, but there are three temporary factory staff to whom special payroll procedures apply. All staff are paid monthly by bankers automated clearing system (BACS), unless they do not have a bank account, in which case they are paid in cash.

Accounting system

Amica Printing Company operates a main ledger, which contains the Cash Book, the Petty Cash Book and the Purchase Ledger Control Account. Each supplier has a separate account in the subsidiary (purchases) ledger, which is not part of the double entry system.

The company is registered for VAT.

Today's date is Tuesday 23 September 2006.

THE TASKS TO BE COMPLETED

PART 1 PROCESSING DOCUMENTS RELATING TO GOODS AND SERVICES RECEIVED (90 MINUTES)

Handling Purchase Invoices

You are responsible for processing documents relating to goods and services received.

- Most of Amica Printing Company's purchases are made via the internet. You match invoices received to the following supporting documentation: the supplier master file, printouts of Amica Printing Company purchase orders, delivery notes from the supplier, and Amica Printing Company goods received notes (for factory purchases only).

- If an invoice does not agree with the supporting documentation, the discrepancy is discussed initially with either Edward Hunt, the factory manager, or Alex Cook, the accountant. If appropriate, the invoice is recorded once it has been signed by one of them to show that the discrepancy has been resolved.

- For any other type of error, the invoice is not recorded but is returned to the supplier with a letter from you on headed notepaper, requesting a corrected invoice.

Task 1

Refer to the invoices on pages 239-249 of the Answer Booklet and the supporting documentation on pages 224-230 of this book. The last invoice recorded in the purchase day book was numbered 6069.

- Check each invoice against the supporting documentation, and check all the calculations, including settlement discount and VAT (which should always be rounded down to the nearest penny). Where appropriate, mark any errors or discrepancies beneath each invoice, and state the action to be taken.

- Allocate an invoice number to each invoice that can be recorded, and write the relevant number in the space beneath each document.

- If it is appropriate, prepare notes for conversations with either Edward Hunt or Alex Cook. Use page 251 of the Answer Booklet.

- If it is appropriate, prepare letters to suppliers. Use the letterheads on pages 252 and 253 of the Answer Booklet.

Handling Credit Notes

- Credit notes must be agreed to goods returned notes, which are prepared by Edward Hunt.

- A credit note which does not agree to the goods returned note is discussed with either Edward Hunt or Alex Cook, as appropriate. If the discrepancy is resolved by this method, the credit note is recorded once one of them has signed it.

- For any other type of error, the credit note is not recorded, but is returned to the supplier with a letter from you on headed notepaper, requesting a corrected credit note.

Task 2

Refer to the credit notes on pages 254-257 of the Answer Booklet and the supporting documentation on page 230 of this book. The last credit note recorded in the purchase returns day book was numbered 276.

- Check each credit note against the supporting documentation, and check all the calculations, including discount and VAT (which should always be rounded down to the nearest penny). Where appropriate, mark any errors or discrepancies beneath each credit note, and state the action to be taken.

- Allocate a credit note number to each credit note to be recorded, and write the relevant number in the space provided beneath each document.

- If you have found any errors relating to the supporting documentation, prepare notes for conversations with either Edward Hunt or Alex Cook. Use page 251 of the Answer Booklet.

- If you have found any other errors, prepare a letter to the relevant supplier. Use the letterhead on page 258 of the Answer Booklet.

Task 3

For all invoices and credit notes in Tasks 1 and 2 that have not been queried with Edward Hunt or Alex Cook, and so can be recorded, enter and analyse the details of invoices in the purchase day book, and of credit notes in the Purchase Returns Day Book on pages 259-260 of the Answer Booklet.

Task 4

- Total the columns in the purchase day book and the purchase returns day book.

- Enter the relevant main ledger and subsidiary (purchase) ledger account codes in the Day Books in preparation for posting. Show which sides of the accounts will be posted by writing either 'DR' or 'CR' as appropriate.

- Make the required entries in the main ledger and subsidiary (purchase) ledger accounts on pages 261-266 of the Answer Booklet.

Note: There are transactions already shown on some of the ledger accounts. You do NOT need to balance any ledger accounts after you have made your entries.

PART 2 PROCESS PAYMENTS (90 MINUTES)

Payments to suppliers and others

Twice a month you prepare cheque runs and BACS payments to be received by the payee on the second Friday and the last Friday of each month (the payment date). If settlement discount is available on any invoices at the payment date in question, you always take it. Otherwise, you take the maximum credit available according to the supplier's terms at the payment date. When assessing whether settlement discount is still available, you should treat the payment date for suppliers this week as 26 September 2006, as this is the date that cheques and BACS payments will be received by suppliers. The next payment date after the present one will be Friday 10 October 2006.

Task 5

Refer to the suppliers' statements on pages 267-271 of the Answer Booklet. Alex Cook has made a note on each statement of which invoices should be paid and how much settlement discount should be taken.

- Check the statements against the relevant ledger accounts on pages 265-266 of the Answer Booklet. On the ledger accounts, tick each item that is due for payment. Beneath each statement, write any settlement discount that is available. Also make a note of any discrepancies, and the action to be taken about them.

- Complete the remittance advices on pages 272-274 of the Answer Booklet for all payments to suppliers that will be made. You do not need to fill in the supplier's address.

- Refer to the cheque requisitions on page 231 of this book and check them against the supporting documentation on page 232 of this book. Make notes on page 275 of the Answer Booklet as to what further action is required, if any.

- Write up the Cash Book (Payments side) on page 276 of the Answer Booklet with the amounts to be paid to suppliers and others today. In the Folio column, write the documentation that supports each payment.

Note: The BACS and cheque payments will be prepared later. You do not need to fill in relevant cheque numbers, and main and subsidiary (purchases) account numbers, nor total the Cash Book (Payments side), at this stage.

Payroll payments

All staff are paid monthly in arrears on the last Friday of the month for the four (sometimes five) weeks ending the previous Friday. All factory staff are paid for a basic working week of 37.5 hours, plus overtime pay at time-and-a-half for hours over 37.5 hours per week. They can also receive occasional bonuses.

A payroll bureau, PrintPay Ltd, calculates gross pay and deductions and prepares payslips for all staff, and makes BACS payments by autopay to all permanent staff. You are sent a Factory Payroll with all amounts for permanent factory staff already inserted, plus payslips for temporary factory staff. Overtime and bonuses for temporary factory staff are listed on your Factory Pay List, which is signed by Edward Hunt and Alex Cook. You check this against the payslips, and then make the payments to any temporary factory staff from the payslips by cheque.

You raise queries about gross pay for temporary factory staff with Edward Hunt in person, and about the calculation and preparation of payslips with Robert Kane at PrintPay Ltd by phone.

You complete the Factory Payroll from the temporary factory staff payslips. Except where there is an error in the calculation of net pay you always include payslips for temporary staff in the Factory Payroll.

Task 6

- Check the payslips of the temporary factory staff shown on pages 277 and 278 of the Answer Booklet against the factory pay list and employee master file on page 233 of this book. Make notes beneath any payslip which contains an error or discrepancy, and state the action to be taken.

- Check the calculation of net pay on the payslips of each of the temporary staff.

Note: You do not need to check how the PAYE and NIC figures, and the year to date figures, are calculated, so you do not need tax tables to perform this task.

- Write up the factory payroll on page 279 of the Answer Booklet for the temporary factory staff payslips, indicating the amounts to be paid by cheque.

- Write up the cash book (payments side) on page 276s of the Answer Booklet with the amounts to be paid to individual temporary factory staff by cheque.

- Write up the cash book (payments side) for the total BACS payments by autopay that have been made by PrintPay Ltd to permanent factory staff.

Note: You need not fill in the references, nor total the cash book (payments side), at this stage.

Task 7

Refer to the email from Henry Lynch, the Factory Supervisor, on page 234 of this book.

■ Draft an email to Henry in response to his memo, outlining the course of action you need to take. Use page 280 of the Answer Booklet.

Petty cash payments

Each day you are responsible for writing up petty cash vouchers from valid receipts for the expenditure paid out. Receipts are only valid if signed by the recipient and authorised by Alex Cook. Employees can only make petty cash claims up to £40. If they wish to claim for more than this amount, they are required to fill out an expenses claim form. You top up the petty cash to £300 each time the amount of cash in the petty cash box falls below £60.

Task 8

Refer to the list of ledger accounts on page 223 of this booklet and the authorised receipts on page 235 of this book.

■ Complete vouchers on page 281 of the Answer Booklet, calculating VAT as appropriate (round VAT down to the nearest penny), for all receipts that you are able to pay from petty cash.

■ Make notes on page 282 of the Answer Booklet on why you have not prepared a voucher for all the receipts.

■ Refer to the list of notes and coin in the petty cash box on page 283 of the Answer Booklet. On this list, write in what notes and coin are being paid out in respect of the valid receipts. You should use the highest denominations of notes and coin that are available. Then calculate a revised total for notes and coin in the petty cash box.

Note: You can assume that the cash has now been paid to the recipients.

■ Write up the petty cash book on page 284 of the Answer Booklet for the vouchers you have prepared and paid, analysing the expenditure.

■ Total the petty cash book and calculate the balance. Ensure that the petty cash book balance agrees with the amount of cash in the petty cash box which you have just calculated.

■ Calculate any necessary top-up for petty cash and include the payment for this in the cash book (payments side) on page 276 of the Answer Booklet. You do not need to fill in the cheque number at this stage.

■ Enter the relevant main ledger codes in the petty cash book in preparation for posting to the main ledger.

- Write up the petty cash book for the top-up and calculate the balance at the end of the day.

Note: You may assume that all the payments you have listed out in the Cash Book (payments side) have been authorised by Alex Cook on behalf of Sam Fisher.

Task 9

- Complete the cheques on pages 285-287 of the answer booklet for all the items that you have written up in the cash book (payments side). These will be signed by Sam Fisher.

- Enter the cheque numbers in the cash book (payments side).

- Total the cash book (payments side) and insert the relevant main and subsidiary (purchase) ledger codes in preparation for posting to the ledgers.

Task 10

- From the cash book (payments side), the payroll and the petty cash book, make the appropriate entries in the ledger accounts on pages 261-266 of the Answer Booklet.

- Calculate the balance on the purchase ledger control account in the main ledger, and on all the subsidiary ledger accounts. Show also the balance brought down on 24 September for each of these accounts.

The following are extracts from the lists of ledger codes.

MAIN LEDGER

Ledger account	Ledger code
Administration	090
Cash book	100
Purchase ledger control account	110
Discount received	120
Factory wages control	130
Factory wages expense	140
PAYE/NIC creditor	150
Petty cash book	160
Postage	170
Production expense	180
Purchases	190
Purchases returns	200
Stationery	210
VAT	220

SUBSIDIARY (PURCHASES) LEDGER

Ledger account	Ledger code
Abingdon Paper Ltd	1101
Feltham Bindery Ltd	1102
Hamburg Print Plates Ltd	1103
Ilsley Inks Ltd	1104
Sidney Stationers	1105
Wantage Engineering	1106

SUPPLIER MASTER FILE

Subsidiary (purchases) ledger account code	Name of supplier	Trade disount %	Settlement terms	Agreed payment methods	Bank account number	Sort code
1101	Abingdon Paper Ltd	5	30 days net	Cheque	N/a	N/a
1102	Feltham Bindery Ltd	0	30 days net	Cheque	N/a	N/a
1103	Hamburg Print Plates Ltd	0	3%/7 days, 30 days net	BACS	67461313	80-16-74
1104	Ilsley Inks Ltd	5	30 days net	Cheque	N/a	N/a
1105	Sidney Stationers	0	30 days net	Cheque	N/a	N/a
1106	Wantage Engineering Ltd	10	1%/21 days, 30 days net	Cheque	N/a	N/a

Hamburg Print Plates Ltd

Price list

Plate for:	£ (each)
Hamburg 250 print press	25.00
Hamburg 500 print press	30.00
Hamburg 1000 print press	35.00
Myobi 400 press	20.00
Myobi 600 press	37.50
Myobi 800 press	50.00

Amica Printing Company
McLaren Trading Estate, Wantage OX12 8SD Tel: 01235 687465

INTERNET PURCHASE ORDER

To: Abingdon Paper Ltd, Milton Park, Abingdon, Oxon OX13 9AS

Description of item(s) ordered	Quantity	Price from website (£)
100gsm Nordic White A1 (500 kg pack)	5	200.00
260 gsm Polar Ice A1 (500 kg pack)	4	350.00

Ordered: Edward Hunt   **Date:** 15 September 2006   **Expense classified as:** Purchases

---

Abingdon Paper Ltd
Milton Park, Abingdon, Oxon OX13 9AS   Tel: 01235 412 233

DELIVERY NOTE

To: Amica Printing Company, Mclaren Trading Estate, Wantage OX12 8SD

Description of item(s) ordered	Quantity
100gsm Nordic White A1 (500 kg pack)	5
260 gsm Polar Ice A1 (500 kg pack)	4

Signed for by: Edward Hunt   **Date:**   22 September 2006

Amica Printing Company
GOODS RECEIVED NOTE

From: Abingdon Paper Ltd

Description of item(s) ordered	Quantity	Received in good condition?
100gsm Nordic White A1 (500 kg pack)	5	Yes
260 gsm Polar Ice A1 (500 kg pack)	4	Yes

Signed: Edward Hunt   **Date:**   22 September 2006

Amica Printing Company
McLaren Trading Estate, Wantage OX12 8SD Tel: 01235 687465

PURCHASE ORDER

To: Feltham Bindery Ltd, Chertsey Road Trading Estate, Feltham, Mddx TW12 5AB

Description of item(s) ordered	Quantity	Fixed price agreed (£)
Consultancy report on installation of a fully automated binding line at the Wantage factory	1	3,250.00 plus VAT

Signed: Sam Fisher   **Date:** 2 September 2006   **Expense classified as:** Production expenses

Lam,
I've received this report now so you can pay the bill when it comes in.
Sam 19 September 2006

Amica Printing Company
McLaren Trading Estate, Wantage OX12 8SD Tel: 01235 687465

INTERNET PURCHASE ORDER

To: Hamburg Print Plates Ltd, Highgrove Road, Newbury, Berks, NY9 4BW

Description of item(s) ordered	Quantity
Hamburg 250 print press plates	100
Hamburg 1000 print press plates	50
Myobi 600 press plates	70

Ordered: Edward Hunt   **Date:** 18 September 2006   **Expense classified as:** Purchases

---

Hamburg Print Plates
Highgrove Road, Newbury, Berks NY9 4BW

DELIVERY NOTE

To: Amica Printing Company, Mclaren Trading Estate, Wantage OX12 8SD

Description of item(s) ordered	Quantity
Myobi 600 press plates	70
Hamburg 1000 print press plates	50
Hamburg 250 print press plates	100

Signed for by: Edward Hunt   **Date:** 22 September 2006

Amica Printing Company
GOODS RECEIVED NOTE
From: Hamburg Print Plates Ltd

Description of item(s) ordered	Quantity	Received in good condition?
Myobi 600 press plates	70	Yes
Hamburg 1000 print press plates	50	Yes
Hamburg 250 print press plates	100	Yes

Signed: Edward Hunt   **Date:** 22 September 2006

Amica Printing Company
McLAren Trading Estate, Wantage OX12 8SD TEl: 01235 687465

PURCHASE ORDER

To: Sidney Stationers, 40 Market Square, Wantage OX12 5KK

Description of item(s) ordered	Quantity	Rate agreed (£)
Red A4 lever arch files	200	1.49

Ordered: Alex Cook   **Date:** *16 September 2006*   **Expense classified as:** *Stationery*

Sidney Stationers Ltd
40 Market Square, Wantage OX12 5KK

DELIVERY ORDER

To: Amica Printing Company, McLaren Trading Estate, Wantage OX12 8SD

Description of item(s) ordered	Quantity
Red A4 lever arch files	200

Ordered: Alex Cook   **Date:** 22 September 2006

Amica Printing Company
McLaren Trading Estate, Wantage OX12 8SD Tel: 01235 687465

INTERNET PURCHASE ORDER

To: Wantage Engineering Ltd, Grove Road, Wantage OX12 7SM

Description of item(s) ordered	Quantity	Price from website (£)
Machine Oil	10 litres	5.00/litre
Print press cleaning fluid	50 litres	6.50/litre
Press tester units	25	15.00 each

Ordered: Edward Hunt   **Date:** 15 September 2006   **Expense classified as:** Purchases

---

Wantage Engineering Ltd
Grove Road, Wantage OX12 7SM

DELIVERY NOTE

To: Amica Printing Company, Mclaren Trading Estate, Wantage OX12 8SD

Description of item(s) ordered	Quantity
Print press cleaning fluid	50 litres
Machine oil	10 litres
Press tester units	25

Agreed by: Edward Hunt   **Date:** 22 September 2006

Amica Printing Company
GOODS RECEIVED NOTE

From: Wantage Engineering Ltd

Description of item(s) ordered	Quantity	Received in good condition?
Print press cleaning fluid	50 litres	Yes
Machine oil	10 litres	Yes
Press tester units	25	Yes

Signed: Edward Hunt   **Date:** 22 September 2006

Amica Printing Company
GOODS RETURNED NOTE

To: Hamburg Print Plates

Description	Quantity	Rate agreed (£)
Hamburg 500 print press plates	5	On inspection, these plates are damaged and cannot be used in the printing machines

Signed: Edward Hunt   **Date:** *15 September 2006*   **Return classified as:** *Purchase returns*

Amica Printing Company
GOODS RETURNED NOTE

To: Ilsley Inks Ltd

Description	Quantity	Rate agreed (£)
Special order pigment 291 - ordered at £25.00 per kilo	10 kilos	On examination, the ink is not of the correct pigment and cannot be used

Signed: Edward Hunt   **Date:**   *15 September 2006*   **Return classified as:** *Purchase returns*

Amica Printing Company

CHEQUE REQUISITION

Payee: _Yarnton Estates Ltd_ **Date:** _22 September 2006_

Amount: _£150.00 + VAT_

Supporting documentation: _To follow_

Expense classified as:

Signed: _Henry Lynch, Factory Supervisor_

Amica Printing Company

CHEQUE REQUISITION

Payee: _Children in Need_ **Date:** _22 September 2006_

Amount: _£300_

Supporting documentation: _This is the amount that our Pudsy Bear campaign raised. Please see the memo attached_

Expense classified as: _Administration_

Signed: _Henry Lynch, Factory Supervisor_

MEMO

To: All staff members
From: Sam Fisher
Subject: Children in Need – Pudsey Bear campaign
Date: 19 September 2006

As you know, we spent a very productive and enjoyable day this week doing silly things to help the Pudsey Bear campaign raise funds for Children in Need. I said to you that I would donate £300 to Children in Need if the day proved a success. I'm delighted that it exceeded even my expectations, so i'm happy to donate the £300.

I'd like to thank all those who took part.

Sam Fisher

Alex

Please issue a cheque for £300, and analyse it to Administration

Sam   9-Sept-06

TO BE DISPLAYED ON ALL NOTICE BOARDS UNTIL
30 SEPTEMBER

Amica Printing Company

Factory Pay List - Temporary Factory Workers only

Date: 23 September 2006
Four weeks ending: 19 September 2006

Name	Basic hours	Overtime hours worked	Bonus
Pippa Allen	150.00	12	£15.00
Usha Gupta	37.50	4	£5.00

Signed Edward Hunt   **Authorised:** Alex Cook

Amica Printing Company

Employee Master File - Temporary Factory Workers

Name	Employee number	NI Number	Tax code	Basic hourly rate (£)	Pay by
Pippa Allen	FT683	KS 82 01 92 M	475L	5.50	Cheque
Ushta Gupta	FT685	WL 29 30 48 P	475L	5.50	Cheque

EMAIL

To: heilamcheng@amica.co.uk
From: henrylynch@amica.co.uk
CC:
Subject: Larry Haynes
Date: 22 September 2006

Message

Hi Lam

Larry approached me yesterday to say that he has recently applied for a mortgage and the lender needs confirmation of his pay and benefits, plus copies of his last three payslips. He hasn't kept any of the documentation we have given him in the past on these matters, so I said I would get hold of copies and go through any queries he may have about him in person. Please leave these on my desk in the factory first thing tomorrow.

Henry

POST OFFICE LTD

Mon 22 September 2006

Special Delivery

2 @ £18.95	37.90
2 @ £6.50	13.00
Total due to Post Office	50.90
Cash from customer	50.90
Balance	0.00

Dispatch of leaflets to customers
Martha Collins   23-Sep-06

Approved: Alex Cook

Larkhill Stationers

VAT 0576761338

Stapler (inc VAT)	6.99
Total	6.00
Cash tendered	10.00
Change amount	3.01

Date: 22 Sept 2006   Time 09.17

Office stapler to replace missing
stapler in factory.
Edward Hunt

Approved: Alex Cook

Sparkbrook Tools

Mon 22 September 2006

5" spanner	15.99
Total due (inc VAT)	15.99
Cash from customer	20.00
Change	4.01

Urgent purchase for factory
Larry Haynes

Approved: Alex Cook

VAT 9870257119

ANSWER BOOKLET

ANSWERS (Tasks 1 and 3)

INVOICE

Abingdon Paper Ltd
Milton Park
Abingdon
Oxon OX13 9AS
T: 01235 412233
F: 01235 412866

To: Amica Printing Company
McLaren Trading Estate
Wantage OX2 8SD

VAT Registration: 9175698745

Date/tax point: 22 September 2006

Quantity	Description	Unit amount £	Total £
5	100gsm Nordic White A1	200.00	1,000.00
4	260gsm Polar Ice A1	350.00	1,400.00

Good total		2,400.00
Trade discount @ 5%		120.00
Sub-total		2,280.00
VAT @ 17.5%		399.00
Invoice total		2,679.00

Terms
30 days net
E & OE

Errors or discrepancies:

None ✓

Action to be taken:

Process as normal. ✓

Invoice number:

6070 ✓

ANSWERS (Tasks 1 and 3, continued)

INVOICE

Feltham Bindery Ltd
Chertsey Road Trading Estate
Feltham
Middlesex TW12 5AB
T/F: 020 8371 5987

To: Amica Printing Company
McLaren Trading Estate
Wantage OX12 8SD

VAT Registration: 6873687344

Date/tax point: 22 September 2006

Description	Rate £	Total £
Consultancy report on installation of fully automated binding line, as per Sam Fisher's purchase order of 2 September 2006, and conversation with Alex Cook	4,250.00	4,250.00
Sub-total		4,250.00
VAT @ 17.5%		743.75
Invoice total		4,993.75

Terms: strictly 30 days net

Terms
30 days net
E & OE

Errors or discrepancies:

Purchase order states price as £3250 +
VAT, invoice has price of £4250 + VAT.

Action to be taken:

Discuss with Alex Cook and get his
approval of invoice.

Invoice number:

N/A

ANSWERS (Tasks 1 and 3, continued)

INVOICE

HAMBURG PRINT PLATES LTD
Highgrove Road
Newbury
Berks NY9 4BW
T: 01461 476431
F: 01461 547643

To: Amica Printing Company
McLaren Trading Estate
Wantage OX12 8SD

VAT Registration: 0547351034

Date/tax point: 22 September 2006

Description	Quantity	Rate £	Total £
Myobi 600 press plates	70	37.50	2,625.00
Hamburg 1000 print press plates	50	35.00	1,750.00
Hamburg 250 print press plates	100	25.00	2,500.00

Goods total	6,875.00
Trade discount @ 0%	0.00
Sub-total	6,875.00
VAT @ 17.5%	1,167.03
Invoice total	8,042.03

Cash (settlement) discount: 3% for payment in 7 days (to be deducted when computing VAT), otherwise 30 days net	£206.25

Errors or discrepancies:

None ✓

Action to be taken:

Process as normal ✓

Invoice number:

6071 ✓

ANSWERS (Tasks 1 and 3, continued)

INVOICE

Ilsley Inks Ltd
Ridgeway House
East Ilsley
Berks NY7 1LS
T: 01461 7576764
F: 01461 343463

To: Amica Printing Company
McLaren Trading Estate
Wantage OX12 8SD

VAT Registration: 0917757537

Date/tax point: 22 September 2006

Description	Quantity	Rate £	Total £
Cyan ink for Hamburg colour presses	15	20.00	300.00
Yellow ink for Myobi presses	20	12.50	250.00

Goods total	550.00
Trade discount @ 5%	27.50
Sub-total	522.50
VAT @ 17.5%	91.43
Invoice total	613.93

Terms: strictly 30 days net

Errors or discrepancies:

No Purchase order or goods received note.✓

Action to be taken:

Talk to Edward Hunt, check goods received & documentation held.✓

Invoice number:

N/A ✓

ANSWERS (Tasks 1 and 3, continued)

INVOICE

Sidney Stationers Ltd
40 Market Square
Wantage OX12 5KK
T: 01235 497611
F: 01235 576643

To: Amica Printing Company
McLaren Trading Estate
Wantage OX12 8SD

VAT Registration: 1473658734

Date/tax point: 22 September 2006

Description	Quantity	Price £	Total £
A4 lever arch files - red	200	1.49	298.00

Goods total		298.00
Trade discount	0%	0.00
Sub-total		298.00
VAT	17.5%	52.15
Invoice total		350.15

Terms: strictly 30 days net

Errors or discrepancies:

None.

Action to be taken:

Process as normal. ✓

Invoice number:

6072 ✓

ANSWERS (Tasks 1 and 3, continued)

INVOICE

Wantage Engineering Ltd
Grove Road
Wantage OX12 7SM
T: 01235 232155
F: 01235 235698

To: Amica Printing Company
McLaren Trading Estate
Wantage OX12 8SD

VAT Registration: 4654646446

Date/tax point: 22 September 2006

Description	Quantity	Price £	Total £
Print press cleaning fluid	50 litres	6.50	250.00
Machine oil	10 litres	5.00	60.00
Press tester units	25	15.00	475.00

Goods total			785.00
Trade discount	10%		78.00
Sub-total			707.00
VAT	17.5%		123.72
Invoice total			830.72

Cash (settlement) discount: 1% for payment in 21 days
(to be deducted when computing VAT), otherwise 30 days net   £7.07

Handwritten annotations (right margin): 325. / -50. / 3 375 / 750 / 75 / 675 / 116.94 / 791.94 / 6.75

Errors or discrepancies:

Calculations of net prices are wrong for all products - write all probs with inv.

Action to be taken:

Write to company asking them to reissue invoice with correct figures ✓

Invoice number:

N/A ✓

ANSWERS (Tasks 1 and 2)

Notes for conversation with Alex Cook

Invoice from Feltham Bindery Ltd does not match Original purchase order, purchase order was for £3,250+VAT, invoice is for £4,250+VAT, ~~was~~ this as per your conversation?

Notes for conversation with Edward Hunt

Ilsley Inks Ltd - doesn't seem to be a purchase order or goods received note for products, do you have this documentation? And were goods received?

ANSWERS (Task 1)

AMICA PRINTING COMPANY

McLaren Trading Estate, Wantage OX12 8SD

Tel: 01235 687465 Fax: 01235 687412

Wantage Engineering Ltd
Gore Road
Wantage
Ox 12 7SM

22nd September 2000

Dear Sir,

Re: Your invoice ~~no~~ dated 22/09/06.

we received your invoice, unfortunately
there is a problem with the total
amounts calculated.

~~The print price~~ ~~Print pr~~ ~~fluid~~ fluid of which we
ordered 50 litres at 6.50 per litre is
totaled on your invoice as £250.00, this

ANSWERS (Task 1, continued)

AMICA PRINTING COMPANY

McLaren Trading Estate, Wantage OX12 8SD

Tel: 01235 687465 Fax: 01235 687412

should be £375.00. Similarly Machine Oil which we ordered 10 litres of at 5.00 per litre is priced at £60.00, this should be £50.00. Finally we ordered 25 press tester units at 15.00 each, this is stated as 475.00 on your invoice, it should be £375.00. With these corrections and trade discount and VAT I believe the total for the invoice should be £791.94 not £830.72 as stated. Please can a new invoice be issued with the correct figures and this previous one be deleted.

I look forward to hearing from you.

Yours faithfully,

~~E Bloomer~~ M Lam Chong
Accounts Assistant.

Write about all probs!

ANSWERS (Tasks 2 and 3)

CREDIT NOTE

HAMBURG PRINT PLATES LTD
Highgrove Road
Newbury
Berks NY9 4BW
T: 01461 476431
F: 01461 547643

To: Amica Printing Company
McLaren Trading Estate
Wantage OX12 8SD

VAT Registration: 0547351034

Date/tax point: 22 September 2006

Description	Quantity	Rate £	Total £
Hamburg 500 print press plates **Reason for credit** Damaged (part of batch delivered and invoiced 15 September 2006)	5	30.00	150.00

Goods total	150.00
Trade discount @ 0%	0.00
Sub-total	150.00
VAT @ 17.5%	25.46
Credit note total	175.46

Reduce cash (settlement) discount on original invoice by £4.50

Errors or discrepancies:

None

Action to be taken:

Process as normal

Credit note number:

277

ANSWERS (Tasks 2 and 3, continued)

CREDIT NOTE

Ilsley Inks Ltd
Ridgeway House
East Ilsley
Berks NY7 1LS
T: 01461 7576764
F: 01461 343463

To: Amica Printing Company
McLaren Trading Estate
Wantage OX12 8SD

VAT Registration: 0917757537

Date/tax point: 22 September 2006

Description		Unit price £	Total £
Special order pigment 291 – 10 kilos		25.00	250.00
Reason for credit Incorrect pigment delivered and invoiced 15 September 2006			

Goods total		250.00
Trade discount @ 5%		12.50
Sub-total		237.50
VAT @ 17.5%		41.56
Credit note total		279.06

Errors or discrepancies:

None

Action to be taken:

Process as normal

Credit note number:

2.73

ANSWERS (Task 2)

AMICA PRINTING COMPANY

McLaren Trading Estate, Wantage OX12 8SD

Tel: 01235 687465 Fax: 01235 687412

....

....

....

....

....

....

....

....

....

....

....

....

....

....

....

....

....

ANSWERS (Tasks 3 and 4)

PURCHASE DAY BOOK

Folio: PDB 30

Invoice number	Supplier	Subsidiary (purchases) ledger code	Date 2006	Total £	VAT £	Purchases £	Stationery £
6070	Abingdon Paper Ltd	1101	22/09/06	2679.00	399.00	2280.00	
6071	Hamburg Print Plates	1103	22/09/06	8042.03	1161.03	6875.00	
6072	Schay Stationers	1105	22/09/06	350.15	52.15		298.00
Total				1611.15	16/3.18	9155.00	298.00
Main ledger codes				110 CR	220 DR	190 DR	210 DR

ANSWERS (Tasks 3 and 4, continued)

PURCHASE RETURNS DAY BOOK

Folio: PRDB 6

Credit note number	Supplier	Subsidiary (purchases) ledger code	Date 2006	Total £	VAT £	Purchases Returns £	Stationery £
277	Hamburg Print Pals	1103	22/09/06	176.46	26.46	150.00	
278	Inkey Inks Ltd	1104	22/09/06	279.06	41.56	237.50	
Total				454.52	67.02	387.50	
Main ledger codes				110 DR	220 CR	200 CR	210 CR

ANSWERS (Tasks 4 and 10)

MAIN LEDGER

090 ADMINISTRATION

Date 2006	Details	Folio	Amount £	Date 2006	Details	Folio	Amount £
23 Sept	CB po	CB30	3000.00 ✓				

110 PURCHASE LEDGER CONTROL ACCOUNT

Date 2006	Details	Folio	Amount £	Date 2006	Details	Folio	Amount £
22 Sept	PRDB 6		454.52	22 Sept	Balance b/d		7,186.79 ✓
23 Sept	Cash book	CB30	12008.68	22 Sept	PDB 30		11071.18 ✓
23 Sept	Discounts	CB 30	201.75		batch		
	Bal b/d		5893.05				
			18257.97				18257.97
24 Sept	Bal b/d						5893.05 ✓

120 DISCOUNT RECEIVED

Date 2006	Details	Folio	Amount £	Date 2006	Details	Folio	Amount £
				23 Sept	Cash book	CB30	201.75 ✓

ANSWERS (Tasks 4 and 10, continued)

MAIN LEDGER

130 FACTORY WAGES CONTROL

Date 2006	Details	Folio	Amount £	Date 2006	Details	Folio	Amount £
23 Sept	Cash book	CB30	4569.53	26 Sept	Payroll		6198.21
26 Sept	Payroll		1206.65				
26 Sept	Payroll		422.03				

140 FACTORY WAGES EXPENSE

Date 2006	Details	Folio	Amount £	Date 2006	Details	Folio	Amount £
26 Sept	Payroll	6	6198.21				
26 Sept	Payroll		426.55				

150 PAYE/NIC CREDITOR

Date 2006	Details	Folio	Amount £	Date 2006	Details	Folio	Amount £
				26 Sept	Payroll		1206.65
				26 Sept	Payroll		422.03
				26 Sept	Payroll		426.55

ANSWERS (Tasks 4 and 10, continued)

MAIN LEDGER

170 POSTAGE

Date 2006	Details	Folio	Amount £	Date 2006	Details	Folio	Amount £

180 PRODUCTION EXPENSES

Date 2006	Details	Folio	Amount £	Date 2006	Details	Folio	Amount £
23 Sept	Petty cash	PCB30	13 61 ✓				

190 PURCHASES

Date 2006	Details	Folio	Amount £	Date 2006	Details	Folio	Amount £
22 Sept	PBB - 30		9155 00 ✓				

ANSWERS (Tasks 4 and 10, continued)

MAIN LEDGER

200 PURCHASES RETURNS

Date 2006	Details	Folio	Amount £	Date 2006	Details	Folio	Amount £
				22 Sept	PRDB 6		387.50

210 STATIONERY

Date 2006	Details	Folio	Amount £	Date 2006	Details	Folio	Amount £
22 Sept	PDB 30		298.00				
23 Sept	Petty cash	RCB 30	5.95				

220 VAT

Date 2006	Details	Folio	Amount £	Date 2006	Details	Folio	Amount £
22 Sept	PDB 30		1618.18	22 Sept	PRDB 6		67.02
23 Sept	Petty cash	RCB 30	3.42				

ANSWERS (Tasks 4, 5 and 10)

SUBSIDIARY (PURCHASES) LEDGER

1101 ABINGDON PAPER LTD

Date 2006	Details	Folio	Amount £	Date 2006	Details	Folio	Amount £
23 Sept	Cash book Bal c/d		2511.56 2679.00 5190.56	2 Sept 22 Sept	Invoice 5980 Invoice 6070	PDB27 PDB30	2,511.56 ✓ 2679.00 ✓ 5190.56
24 Sept	Bal b/d		2679.00				2679.00

1102 FELTHAM BINDERY LTD

Date 2006	Details	Folio	Amount £	Date 2006	Details	Folio	Amount £

1103 HAMBURG PRINT PLATES LTD

Date 2006	Details	Folio	Amount £	Date 2006	Details	Folio	Amount £
22 Sept 23 Sept 23 Sept	Credit Note 277 Cash book Discounts Bal c/d	PPDB6	175.46 ✓ 8682.50 201.75 1754.62 10814.33	5 Sept 15 Sept 22 Sept	Invoice 5982 Invoice 6040 Invoice 6071	PDB27 PDB29 PDB30	1,017.68 ✓✓ 1,754.62 ✓ 8042.03 ✓ 10814.33

24 Sept Bal b/d 1754.62

ANSWERS (Tasks 4, 5 and 10, continued)

SUBSIDIARY (PURCHASES) LEDGER

1104 ILSLEY INKS LTD

Date 2006	Details	Folio	Amount £	Date 2006	Details	Folio	Amount £
22 Sept	Credit Note 278	PRDB6	279.06	2 Sept	Invoice 5985	PDB27	726.46
23 Sept	Cashbook		726.46	15 Sept	Invoice 6042	PDB29	1,088.34
	Bal c/d		809.28				
			1814.80				1814.80
				24 Sept	Bal b/d		809.28

1105 SIDNEY STATIONERS LTD

Date 2006	Details	Folio	Amount £	Date 2006	Details	Folio	Amount £
29 Aug	Credit note 250	PRDB5	17.62	28 Aug	Invoice 5965	PDB26	105.75
				22 Sept	Invoice 6072	PDB30	350.18
23 Sept	Cashbook		88.13				
	Bal c/d		350.18				
			455.90				455.18
				24 Sept	Bal b/d		350.18

1106 WANTAGE ENGINEERING LTD

Date 2006	Details	Folio	Amount £	Date 2006	Details	Folio	Amount £

ANSWERS (Task 5)

STATEMENT

Lam,
Please pay ticked item.
Alex Cook

Abingdon Paper Ltd
Milton Park
Abingdon
Oxon OX13 9AS
T: 01235 412233
F: 01235 412866

To: Amica Printing Company
McLaren Trading Estate
Wantage OX12 8SD

VAT Registration: 9175698745

Date: 22 September 2006

Date	Transaction reference	Amount
1 Sept 2006	Invoice	2,511.56 ✓
22 Sept 2006	Invoice	2,679.00

Balance outstanding | 5,190.56

Our terms are strictly net 30 days

Discount to be taken:
None ✓

Discrepancies:
None ✓

Action to be taken about discrepancies:
N/A.

ANSWERS (Task 5, continued)

STATEMENT

HAMBURG PRINT PLATES LTD
Highgrove Road
Newbury
Berks NY9 4BW
T: 01461 476431
F:01461 547643

Lam,
Please pay ticked items.
Cash discount of £201.75 to be
taken on invoice and credit note
dated 22 September 06.
Alex Cook

To: Amica Printing Company
McLaren Trading Estate
Wantage OX12 8SD

VAT Registration: 0547351034

Date: 22 September 2006

Date	Transaction reference		Amount
4 Sept 2005	Invoice		1,017.68 ✓
15 Sept 2006	Invoice		1,754.62
22 Sept 2006	Credit note	170.96	-175.46 ✓
22 Sept 2006	Invoice	7835.8	8,042.03 ✓

Balance outstanding 10,638.87

3% settlement (cash) discount is available for payment within 7 days. Otherwise, our terms are strictly net 30 days.

Discount to be taken:

£206.25 off invoice 22nd Sept, £4.50 taken off CN - total invoice - 7835.78, CN - 140.96

Discrepancies:

None

Action to be taken about discrepancies:

N/A.

ANSWERS (Task 5, continued)

STATEMENT

Lam,
Please pay ticked item.
Alex Cook

Ilsley Inks Ltd
Ridgeway House
East Ilsley
Berks NY7 1LS
T: 01461 7576764 F: 01461 343463

To: Amica Printing Company
McLaren Trading Estate
Wantage OX12 8SD

VAT Registration: 0917757537

Date: 22 September 2006

Date	Transaction reference	Amount
1 Sept 2006	Invoice	726.46 ✓
22 Sept 2006	Invoice	1,088.34
22 Sept 2006	Credit note	-279.06

Balance outstanding | 1,535.74

Our terms are strictly net 30 days

Discount to be taken:
None ✓

Discrepancies:
None ✓

Action to be taken about discrepancies:
N/A ✓

ANSWERS (Task 5, continued)

STATEMENT

Lam,
Please pay ticked items.
Alex Cook

Sidney Stationers Ltd
40 Market Square
Wantage
OX12 5KK
T: 01235 497611
F: 01235 576643

To: Amica Printing Company
McLaren Trading Estate
Wantage OX12 8SD

VAT Registration: 1473658734

Date: 22 September 2006

Date	Transaction reference	Amount
27 Aug 2006	Invoice	105.75 ✓
28 Aug 2006	Credit note	−17.62 ✓
22 Sept 2006	Invoice	350.15

Balance outstanding | 438.28

Our terms are strictly net 30 days

Discount to be taken:
None ✓

Discrepancies:
None ✓

Action to be taken about discrepancies:
N A ✓

ANSWERS (Task 5, continued)

REMITTANCE ADVICE

Amica Printing Company, McLaren Trading Estate, Wantage OX12 8SD
Tel: 01235 687465 Fax: 01235 687412

Supplier: Abingdon Paper Ltd

Subsidiary (purchase) ledger code: 1101

Date	Transaction reference	Amount (£)
1 Sept	Invoice 5980	2511.56
23 Sept	Cheque Enclosed	-2511.56 ✓

REMITTANCE ADVICE

Amica Printing Company, McLaren Trading Estate, Wantage OX12 8SD
Tel: 01235 687465 Fax: 01235 687412

Supplier: Hamburg Print Plates Ltd

Subsidiary (purchase) ledger code: 1103

Date	Transaction reference	Amount (£)
4 Sept	Invoice 5982	1017.68
22 Sept	Invoice 6071	7835.78
22 Sept	Credit Note 277	-10.96
23 Sept	Cheque Enclosed	-8682.50

snap! discount!

ANSWERS (Task 5, continued)

REMITTANCE ADVICE

Amica Printing Company, McLaren Trading Estate, Wantage OX12 8SD
Tel: 01235 687465 Fax: 01235 687412

Supplier: Ilsley Inks Ltd

Subsidiary (purchase) ledger code: 1104

Date	Transaction reference	Amount (£)
2 Sept	Invoice 5985.	726.46.
23 Sept	Cheque Enclosed	-726.46 ✓

REMITTANCE ADVICE

Amica Printing Company, McLaren Trading Estate, Wantage OX12 8SD
Tel: 01235 687465 Fax: 01235 687412

Supplier: Sidney Stationers Ltd

Subsidiary (purchase) ledger code: 1105

Date	Transaction reference	Amount (£)
28 Aug	Invoice 5965	105.75
29 Aug	Credit Note 250	-17.62
23 Sept	Cheque Enclosed	-88.13 ✓

ANSWERS (Task 5, continued)

REMITTANCE ADVICE

Amica Printing Company, McLaren Trading Estate, Wantage OX12 8SD
Tel: 01235 687465 Fax: 01235 687412

Supplier:

Subsidiary (purchase) ledger code:

Date	Transaction reference	Amount (£)

REMITTANCE ADVICE

Amica Printing Company, McLaren Trading Estate, Wantage OX12 8SD
Tel: 01235 687465 Fax: 01235 687412

Supplier:

Subsidiary (purchase) ledger code:

Date	Transaction reference	Amount (£)

ANSWERS (Task 5, continued)

Cheque requisition to Yarton Estates
Ltd has no supporting documentation.
wait for this before approval of
cheque.

Cheque requisition to Children in Need-
issue cheque.

ANSWERS (Tasks 5, 6, 9 and 10)

MAIN LEDGER

100 CASH BOOK (PAYMENTS) — CB 30

Date 2006	Details	Cheque number/ BACS ref	Folio	Payment £	Admin £	Factory wages £	Petty cash £	Suppliers £	Discount received £	Subsidiary (purchases) ledger codes
23 Sept	Abingdon Paper	346612	Remittance	2511.56				2511.56		1101
25 Sept	Hamburg Print Plates	Remit-	882.50					882.50	201.75	1103
23 Sept	Ilsley Inks Ltd	346614	-11-	726.46				726.46		1104
23 Sept	Sidney Stationers	346615	-11-	88.13				88.13		1105
23 Sept	Children in need	346613	cheq req	300.00	300.00					
26 Sept	Pippa Allen	346616	Payroll	732.73		732.73				
26 Sept	Usha Gupta	346617	Payroll	175.87		175.87				
26 Sept	Factory Payroll	-11-		3660.93		3660.93				
26 Sept	Top-up PC	346618	PC	242.10			242.10			
				9120.28	300.00	4569.53	242.10	4208.65	201.75	
		DR			690 130			110	110	
		CR							120	

Main ledger codes

ANSWERS (Task 6)

Amica Printing Company				
Employee: Pippa Allen	Employee no: FT683			
NI No: KS 82 01 92 M	Tax code: 475L	Date: 26 Sept 2006	Tax period: Mth 6	
Pay for FOUR weeks ending: 19 September 2006	Hours	Rate (£)	AMOUNT (£)	YEAR TO DATE (£)
Basic hours	150.00	5.50	825.00	
Time and a half	12.00	8.25	99.00	
Bonus		15.00	15.00	
PAY FOR PERIOD			939.00	4,695.00
PAYE			149.93	899.57
Employees' NI (Employer's NI £61.28)			56.34	
TOTAL DEDUCTIONS			206.27	
NET PAY			732.73	

Errors or discrepancies:

........None........

....

Action to be taken:

........N/A........

....

Amica Printing Company				
Employee: Usha Gupta	Employee no: FT685			
NI No: WL 29 30 48 P	Tax code: BR	Date: 26 Sept 2006		Tax period: Mth 6
Pay for FOUR weeks ending: 19 September 2006	Hours	Rate (£)	AMOUNT (£)	YEAR TO DATE (£)
Basic hours	37.50	5.50	206.25	
Time and a half	4.00	8.25	33.00	
Bonus		5.00	5.00	
PAY FOR PERIOD			244.25	244.25
PAYE			53.73	53.73
Employees' NI (Employer's NI £17.50)			14.65	
TOTAL DEDUCTIONS			68.38	
NET PAY			175.87	

Errors or discrepancies:

None ✓

Action to be taken:

N/A

ANSWERS (Tasks 6 and 10)

FACTORY PAYROLL MONTH 6

Employee:	Employee number	Pay for period £	PAYE £	Employee's NIC £	Net pay £	Employer's NIC £
Pippa Allen	FT683	939.00	149.93	56.34	732.73	61.28
Usha Gupta	FT685	244.25	53.73	14.65	175.87	17.50
Temporary factory payroll total		1183.25	203.66	70.99	908.60	78.78
Permanent factory payroll total		5,014.96	1,002.99	351.04	3,660.93	347.77
Total factory payroll		6198.21	1206.65	422.03	4569.53	426.55
Main ledger codes DR		140	130	130		140
CR		130	150	150		150
Payment by BACS - permanent					3660.93	
Payment by cheque					908.60	

279

ANSWERS (Task 7)

EMAIL

To: henrylynch@amica.co.uk

From: heilamcheng@amica.co.uk

CC:

Subject: Larry Haynes

Date: 23 September 2006

Message:

Henry,

Thankyou for your message regarding Larry Haynes. However as the information requested is highly confidential I could not leave it on your desk as I am worried about its security

I would suggest that Larry Haynes comes to my office, with you if he wishes, so that I can hand the documents to him in person.

With best wishes,

Lam.

ANSWERS (Task 8)

PETTY CASH VOUCHER	
Number: *099*	Date: 22 Sept
Expenditure	*Amount*
Larkhill Stationers – Stapler	5.95
	rAT – 1.04
Total	6.99.
Supporting documentation: Receipt	
Paid to: Edward Hunt. ✓	

PETTY CASH VOUCHER	
Number: *100*	Date: 22 Sept
Expenditure	*Amount*
Spanner	13.61
VAT	2.38
Total	15.99
Supporting documentation: receipt	
Paid to: Larry Haynes. ✓	

PETTY CASH VOUCHER	
Number: *101*	Date:
Expenditure	*Amount*
Total	
Supporting documentation:	
Paid to:	

ANSWERS (Task 8, continued)

Claim by Martha Collins for payments made at the Post office totals £50.90, this is higher than the maximum claim on £40. An expense claim must be made. ✓

ANSWERS (Task 8, continued)

PETTY CASH LISTING

Notes and coin in box	In petty cash box as at 22-Sept-06 £	To be paid out 23-Sept-05			In petty cash box as at 23-Sept-06 £
		Voucher number: 099 £	Voucher number: 100 £	Voucher number: £	
£50	0.00				0.00
£20	40.00				40.00
£10	20.00		10.00		10.00
£5	15.00	5.00	5.00		5.00
£2	0.00				0.00
£1	3.00	1.00			2.00
50p	1.50	0.50	0.50		0.50
20p	1.00	0.40	0.40		0.20
10p	0.20				0.10
5p	0.10	0.05	0.05		0.00
2p	0.04	0.04			0.00
1p	0.04		0.04		0.00
Total	83.88	6.99	15.99		57.90

ANSWERS (Tasks 8 and 10)

160 PETTY CASH BOOK PCB 30

Date 2006	Details	Receipts £	Date 2006	Voucher number	Payments £	Postage £	Production expenses £	Stationery £	VAT £
22 Sept	Balance b/d	80.88							
			22 Sept	099	6.99			5.95	1.04
			22 Sept	100	15.99		13.61		2.38
				Totals	22.98		13.61	5.95	3.42
				Balance c/d	57.90				
					80.88				
23 Sept	Balance b/d	57.90							
23 Sept	Topup RC	242.10							
23 Sept	End of day balance	300.00							
Main ledger codes					DR	170	180	216	220
					CR				

ANSWERS (Task 9)

OXBANK PLC
13 - 45 - 65

Date 23rd Sept

Abingdon

Paper

£ 2511.56

Cornmarket, Oxford OX1 4FG

Date 23rd September 06

Pay Abingdon Paper Ltd

Two thousand, five hundred +

eleven pounds 56p

£ 2511.56

Account Payee

Cheque No.	Sort Code	Account No.
546612	546612	13—45—65	63500671

Amica Printing Company

OXBANK PLC
13 - 45 - 65

23/09/06
Date 23rd Sept
Children in
Hamburg
need
Print Plates

300.00
£ 86875O

Cornmarket, Oxford OX1 4FG

23rd September 06
Date 23rd September 06

Pay Children in need
Hamburg Print Plates Ltd

Three hundred
Eight thousand, six hundred +
pounds only
eighty two pounds 50p

£ 300.00
8682.50

Account Payee

Cheque No.	Sort Code	Account No.
546613	546613	13—45—65	63500671

Amica Printing Company

ANSWERS (Task 9, continued)

OXBANK PLC   13 - 45 - 65

Cornmarket, Oxford OX1 4FG

Date 23/09/06   Date 23rd September 06

Isley   Pay Isley Inks Ltd

Inks   Seven hundred + twenty six

£ 726 46   pounds 46p   £ 726.46

Cheque No.   Sort Code   Account No.

546614   546614   13-45-65   63500671   Amica Printing Company

---

OXBANK PLC   13 - 45 - 65

Cornmarket, Oxford OX1 4FG

Date 23/09/06   Date 23rd September 06

Sidney   Pay Sidney Stationers Ltd

Stationers   Eighty eight pounds +   £ 88.13

£ 88.13   thirteen pence

Cheque No.   Sort Code   Account No.

546615   546615   13-45-65   63500671   Amica Printing Company

---

OXBANK PLC   13 - 45 - 65

Cornmarket, Oxford OX1 4FG

Date 26/09/06   Date 26th September 06

Pippa   Pay Pippa Allen

Allen   Seven hundred + thirty two pounds   £ 732.73

£ 732.73   seventy three pence

Cheque No.   Sort Code   Account No.

546616   546616   13-45-65   63500671   Amica Printing Company

OXBANK PLC
13 - 45 - 65

Cornmarket, Oxford OX1 4FG

Date 26/09/06

Osha

Gupta

£ 175.87

Date 26th September 06

Pay Usha Gupta

One hundred + seventy

five pounds 87p

Account Payee

£ 175.87

Cheque No.	Sort Code	Account No.

546617   546617   13-45-65   63500671

Amica Printing Company

OXBANK PLC
13 - 45 - 65

Cornmarket, Oxford OX1 4FG

Date 23/09/06

Cash

£ 242.10

Date 23rd September 06

Pay Cash

Two hundred + forty two

pounds ten pence

Account Payee

£ 242.10

Cheque No.	Sort Code	Account No.

546618   546618   13-45-65   63500671

Amica Printing Company

AAT

SAMPLE SIMULATION
UNIT 3

WEASLEY SUPPLIES LTD

This is the AAT's Sample Simulation for Unit 3. Its purpose is to give you an idea of what an AAT simulation looks like. It is not intended as a definitive guide to the tasks you may be required to perform.

Total time: 3 hours

Coverage of performance criteria and range statements

The following performance criteria are covered in this simulation.

Element	PC Coverage
3.1	**Balance bank transactions**
a)	Record details from the relevant **primary documentation** in the **cashbook and ledgers**.
b)	Correctly calculate totals and balances of receipts and payments.
c)	Compare individual items on the bank statement and in the **cashbook** for accuracy.
d)	Identify discrepancies and prepare a bank reconciliation statement.
3.2	**Prepare ledger balances and control accounts**
a)	Make and **record** authorised **adjustments**.
b)	Total relevant accounts in the main ledger.
c)	Reconcile **control accounts** with the totals of the balance in the subsidiary ledger.
d)	Reconcile petty cash control account with the cash in hand and subsidiary records.
e)	Identify **discrepancies** arising from the reconciliation of **control accounts** and either resolve or refer to the appropriate person.
3.3	**Draft an initial trial balance**
a)	Prepare the draft **initial trial balance** in line with the organisation's policies and procedures.
b)	Identify **discrepancies** in the balancing process.
c)	Identify reasons for imbalance and **rectify** them.
d)	Balance the trial balance.

The following performance criterion is not covered in this simulation and should be assessed separately.

3.2 f)	Ensure documentation is stored securely and in line with the organisation's confidentiality requirements.

The following range statements are not covered in this simulation and should be assessed separately.

Element	Range Statement
3.1	**Cash book and ledgers:** computerised
	Bank reconciliation statement: computerised
3.2	**Record:** computerised
	Control accounts: computerised; non-trade debtors
	Discrepancies: cash in hand not agreeing with subsidiary record and control record
3.3	**Trial balance:** computerised

DATA AND TASKS

INSTRUCTIONS

This simulation is designed to let you show your ability to prepare ledger balances and an initial trial balance.

You should read the whole simulation before you start work, so that you are fully aware of what you will have to do.

You are allowed **three hours** to complete your work.

Write your answers in the Answer Booklet provided on pages 303 to 312. If you need more paper for your answers, ask the person in charge.

You should write your answers in blue or black ink, **not** pencil.

You may use correcting fluid, but in moderation. You should cross out your errors neatly and clearly.

You may pull apart and rearrange your booklets if you wish to do so, but you must put them back in their original order before handing them in.

Your work must be accurate, so check your work carefully before handing it in.

You are not allowed to refer to any unauthorised material, such as books or notes, while you are working on the simulation. If you have any such material with you, you must hand it to the person in charge before you start work.

Any instances of misconduct will be reported to the AAT, and disciplinary action may be taken.

Coverage of performance criteria and range statements

It is not always possible to cover all performance criteria and range statements in a single simulation. Any performance criteria and range statements not covered must be assessed by other means by the assessor before a candidate can be considered competent.

Performance criteria and range statement coverage for this simulation is shown on page 290.

THE SITUATION

Your name is Kim Wendell. You are a qualified accounting technician working for Weasley Supplies. You report to the manager, Ari Pottle.

All of the company's sales and purchases are on credit terms.

The books of account are maintained in manual form.

Today's date is Monday 7 July 2006, and you will be dealing with transactions taking place in June 2006.

Ledgers

A sales ledger control account and a purchases ledger control account are maintained in the main (general) ledger. There is a subsidiary (sales) ledger for customers and a subsidiary (purchases) ledger for suppliers.

Bank account and cash book

A bank statement is received monthly. Entries on the bank statement are compared with:

- entries in the cash book:
- a schedule of standing orders, direct debits and credit transfers.

The cash book is updated as appropriate in the light of the bank statement and the schedule of standing orders, direct debits and credit transfers. The main items paid for by standing order, direct debit and credit transfer are:

- business rates;
- insurance and leasing payments;
- staff salaries;
- the company's credit card bill.

These items are analysed as 'Other payments' in the cash book.

THE TASKS TO BE COMPLETED

Task 1

Refer to the schedule of standing orders, direct debits and credit transfers on page 295, and the bank statement for June 2006 on page 296 of this book.

- Enter the appropriate details from the schedule in the cash book for June 2006 on page 303 of the Answer Booklet.

- Also enter any other items on the bank statement not so far recorded in the cash book.

Note: You must complete both the total columns and the analysis columns in the cash book.

Task 2

Total all columns of the cash book and bring down a balance as at close of business on 30 June 2006.

Task 3

Prepare a bank reconciliation statement as at 30 June 2006, clearly identifying all discrepancies between the cash book and the bank statement. Use the blank page 304 of the Answer Booklet.

Task 4

Refer to the email from Ari Pottle on page 297 of this book.

- Prepare the journals referred to in the email, including appropriate narrative, using the journal vouchers on page 305 of the Answer Booklet.

Task 5

- Post from the cash book (Task 2) and the journals (Task 4) to the sales ledger control account and the purchases ledger control account on page 306 of the Answer Booklet. (You are not required to make entries in the subsidiary ledgers in respect of these journals.)

- Total the two control accounts and bring down balances as at close of business on 30 June 2006.

Task 6

Refer to the list of balances on page 298 of this book, which have been taken from the subsidiary (purchases) ledger on 30 June 2006.

- Total the list of balances and reconcile the total with the balance on the purchases ledger control account.

- Suggest a reason for any discrepancy you observe.

Present your work on the blank page 307 of the Answer Booklet.

Task 7

The petty cash book has been written up for the month of June 2006; see page 308 of the Answer Booklet. On page 309 of the Answer Booklet you will see a list of the notes and coins in the petty cash tin at close of business on 30 June 2006, and a reconciliation schedule.

- Total the petty cash book and bring down a balance at close of business on 30 June 2006.

- Complete the reconciliation schedule, including a note of any discrepancy.

Task 8

Refer to the list of ledger balances prepared by Ari Pottle as at 30 June 2006 (page 298 of this book).

- Enter Ari's balances, and also the control account balances computed in Tasks 2, 5 and 7, onto the trial balance on page 310 of the Answer Booklet. Note that the balance to be entered for cash at bank should reflect the journal entries drafted in Task 4.

- Total the trial balance, and ensure that it balances by entering a suspense account balance.

Task 9

After informing Ari Pottle of the suspense account balance, you have now received the email on page 301 of this book.

- Prepare the journals referred to in the email, including appropriate narrative, using the journal vouchers on page 311 of the Answer Booklet.

Task 10

Enter the journals prepared in Task 9 into the suspense account on page 311 of the Answer Booklet and ensure that the closing balance on this account is zero.

Task 11

Reply to Ari's email explaining how the journals prepared in Task 9 will affect the trial balance and confirming that it will now balance. Use the blank email form on page 312 of the Answer Booklet.

Schedule of standing orders, direct debits and credit transfers (extract)

Standing orders	Amount	When payable
Standing orders		
Medwith Borough Council (business rates)	£600	Monthly from April to January inclusive; no payment in February, March
Safeguard Insurance	£310	Monthly
Finance Leasing plc	£425	March, June, September, December
Direct debits		
Purchasecard plc	Variable	Monthly
Credit transfers		
Staff salaries	Variable	Monthly

STATEMENT

Northern Bank plc
27 High Street, Malliton FR5 6EW   **27-76-54**

Account: Weasley Supplies   **Statement number:** 226

Account number: 22314561

Date	Details		Payments £	Receipts £	Balance £
2006					
1 June	Balance from previous sheet				5,267.88
6 June	Cash/cheques received	CC		4,776.15	10,044.03
10 June	Cheque 331174		781.03		9,263.00
13 June	Cheque 331175		1,456.91		
13 June	Cash/cheques received	CC		7,715.96	15,522.05
17 June	Safeguard Insurance 30056561	SO	310.00		15,212.05
20 June	Cash/cheques received	CC		15,901.22	31,113.27
23 June	Medwith BC 4412341125	SO	600.00		30,513.27
24 June	Cheque 331176		9,912.75		
24 June	Cash/cheques received	CC		2,816.55	23,417.07
25 June	Cheque 331177		3,901.25		19,515.82
26 June	Bank interest and charges	CHGS	107.33		
26 June	Finance Leasing plc 771233115	SO	425.00		
26 June	Salaries		8,215.50		10,767.99
27 June	Purchasecard plc	CT	2,341.89		8,426.10
30 June	Cash/cheques received	DD		2,451.88	
30 June	Cheque 331179	CC	3,126.99		7,750.99

**Key SO Standing order   CC Cash and/or cheques   CT Credit transfer
O/D Overdrawn   D/D Direct Debit   CHGS Bank charges**

EMAIL

From:	Ari Pottle
To:	Kim Wendell
CC:	
Subject:	Journal entries
Date:	7 July 2006

Message:

Hi Kim

Please could you draw up two journal entries for me please?

The first concerns our cheque number 331179. This has been logged in the cash book at an amount of £3,216.99, but in fact was for £3,126.99. The wrong amount has also been posted to the purchases ledger control account.

The second concerns our customer Driftway Limited. They owe us £1,233.75, but have gone into liquidation so we have no chance of recovering the debt. Later on we may be able to recover the VAT included in this amount, but for the moment please write off the whole balance and ignore VAT.

Both of these matters should be dealt with by means of journals dated 30 June 2006.

Thanks

Ari

Creditors' balances at 30 June 2006

	£
Earley and Partners	3,990.65
Horsfall Limited	2,561.22
James Ross	4,016.73
Peters Limited	2,351.67
Pickard Newton (debit balance)	(90.00)
Stainton and Co	3,109.81
Other creditors	5,667.54

Main (general) ledger: balances at 30 June 2006

	£
Administration expenses	3,276.88
Bad debts	2,010.76
Bank	Own figure
Business rates	1,800.00
Capital	46,745.76
Fixed assets	25,219.05
HMRC	4,003.51
Insurance	930.00
Leasing costs	1,275.00
Petty cash	Own figure
Purchases	64,016.83
Purchases ledger control	Own figure
Purchases returns	1,125.31
Salaries expense	35,211.81
Sales	96,558.43
Sales and distribution expenses	2,006.81
Sales ledger control	Own figure
Sales returns	1,327.44
Stock	7,270.00
VAT control (credit balance)	3,995.20

EMAIL

From:	Ari Pottle
To:	Kim Wendell
CC:	
Subject:	Correcting the trial balance
Date	7 July 2006

Message:

Hi Kim

I've looked into the discrepancy on the initial trial balance, and I've found two items that cause the problem.

First, we returned goods to a supplier to the value of £200. We correctly entered this in the subsidiary (purchases) ledger, and in the purchases ledger control account.

However, in the purchases returns account we mistakenly entered it as a debit.

Second, we received a cheque for £3,000 which was correctly debited to bank account. However, no credit entry was made. The double entry should have been completed in the capital account.

Please could you draft journals dated 30 June 2006 to deal with both of these items, and then let me have a reply to this message confirming that the trial balance will now balance.

Thanks

Ari

ANSWER BOOKLET

ANSWERS (Tasks 1 and 2)

CB 241

Date 2006	Details	RECEIPTS Sales ledger £	Other receipts £	Total £	Cheque number	PAYMENTS Total £	Purchases ledger £	Other payments £
1 June	Balance b/f			4,486.85				
5 June	Metrix plc	4,776.15		4,776.15				
6 June	Horsfall Limited				331175	1,456.91	1,456.91	
12 June	Plympton Limited	7,715.96		7,715.96				
16 June	Stainton and Co				331176	9,912.75	9,912.75	
16 June	Inland Revenue				331177	3,901.25		3,901.25
19 June	Maidstone plc	15,901.22		15,901.22				
23 June	Earley and Partners				331178	3,341.20	3,341.20	
23 June	Stenshaw Limited	2,816.55		2,816.55				
25 June	Pickard Newton				331179	3,216.99	3,216.99	
29 June	Fitzroy Limited	2,451.88		2,451.88				
30 June	Dove Ambleside	1926.34		1,926.34				
23 June	Medworth Borough Council				SO	600.00		600.00
17 June	Safeguard Insurance				SO	310.00		310.00
26 June	Finance leasing Plc				SO	45.00		45.00
27 June	Purchase cost Plc				DD	234.89		234.89
26 June	salaries				DD	8215.50		8215.50
30 June	Interest + Bank charges				CHGS	107.33		107.33

Handwritten totals:

48,074.95   197.33   22,746.13

306 Bal b/d   6246.13.

ANSWERS (Task 3)

Bank reconcilliation for Weasley Supplies
as at 30 June 2006.

	£	£
Balance per bank statement		750.99
Add deposits paid in, not yet on bank statement		
30/6 Dove Ambleside		1926.34
		9677.33
Less unpresented cheques		
23/6 331178	3341.20	
25/6 331179-discrep.	90.00	3431.20
		6246.13
Balance as per cash book		6246.13

ANSWERS (Task 4)

JOURNAL

Date 2006	Account names and narratives	Debit £	Credit £
1. 30/06	Bank account	90.00	
	Purchase ledger control		90.00.
	Error of transposition.		
	Chq #33117? logged		
	as £3216.99 instead		
	of £3126.99 in error.		
2. 30/06.	Bad debts written off	1233.75	
	Sales ledger control		1233.75.
	Being bad debt		
	write off		

305

ANSWERS (Task 5)

MAIN (GENERAL) LEDGER

Account Sales ledger control account

Debit			Credit		
Date 2006	Details	Amount £	Date 2006	Details	Amount £
1 June	Balance b/f	30,914.66	30 June	Receipts	3588.10
30 June	Invoices in month	32,617.80	30 June	Journal 2	1233.75
			30 June	Bal c/d.	26710.61
		63532.46			63532.46

30 June Bal b/d 26710.61

Account Purchases ledger control account

Debit			Credit		
Date 2006	Details	Amount £	Date 2006	Details	Amount £
30 June	payments	17927.85	1 June	Balance b/f	19,334.02
30 June	Journal 1	90.00	30 June	Invoices in month	20,201.45
30 June	Bal c/d	21517.62	~~30 June~~ → muppet!!		
		39535.47			39535.47
			30 June	Bal b/d	21517.62

ANSWERS (Task 6)

Total of Balances = 21607.62

Purchases ledger control = 21517.62

Diff. = 90.00

It is possible there has been an error of transposition in one of the entries to the purchase ledger control account. This is suggested by the fact that the difference between the balances is a multiple of 9 — journal not actioned!!

ANSWERS (Task 7)

PETTY CASH BOOK	Date 2006	Details	Voucher number	Total £	VAT £	Postage £	Stationery £	Other expenses £	PCB 52
Receipts £									
200.00	1 June	Balance b/f							
	5 June	Postage	358	4.26		4.26			
	9 June	Stationery	359	12.87	1.91		10.96		
	12 June	Tea, coffee etc	360	7.02				7.02	
	16 June	Postage	361	3.12		3.12			
	18 June	Stationery	362	13.51	2.01		11.50		
	23 June	Stationery	363	6.58	0.98		5.60		
	26 June	Stationery	364	5.73	0.85		4.88		
	27 June	Postage	365	5.90		5.90			
	30 June	Tea, coffee etc	366	6.50				6.50	

Handwritten notes: Badd — 65.47 | 5.75 | 13.28 | 32.94 | 13.52 ; Bal c/d Bal.Si. 134.51 ; 200.00 ; Bal c/d Bal.Si. 200.00

ANSWERS (Task 7, continued)

Notes and coin in the petty cash tin, 30 June 2006

Value	Number	Total value £
£20	4	80.00
£10	3	30.00
£5	2	10.00
£1	8	8.00
50p	8	4.00
20p	8	1.60
10p	8	0.80
5p	1	0.05
2p	2	0.04
1p	2	0.02
		134.51

Petty cash reconciliation

Date: 30 June 2006.

£

Balance per petty cash book   134.51
Total of notes and coin   134.51.
Discrepancy (if any)   – None.

Explanation of discrepancy (if any)
  N/A.

309

ANSWERS (Task 8)

Trial balance at 30 June 2006

DESCRIPTION	Dr £	Cr £
Administration expenses	3276.88	
Bad debts	2010.76	
Bank	~~6246.13~~ *6 336.13*	
Business rates	1800.00	
Capital		46745.78
Fixed assets	25219.05	
HMRC		4003.51
Insurance	930.00	
Leasing costs	1275.00	
Petty cash	134.51	
Purchases	64016.83	~~21807.62~~ *21807.62*
Purchases ledger control		~~21807.62~~
Purchases returns		1125.31
Salaries expense	35211.81	
Sales		96558.43
Sales and distribution expenses	2006.81	
Sales ledger control	~~26710.61~~	
Sales returns	1327.44	
Stock	7270.00	
VAT control		3995.20
Suspense account		34~~90.00~~
Totals	177435.83	~~177435.83~~ ~~177435.83~~

177525.83   17752~~5.83~~

ANSWERS (Tasks 9 and 10)

JOURNAL

Date 2006	Account names and narrative	Dr £	Cr £
1.30/06 30/06.	Suspense account Purchases return. Purchase return posted as debit in error.	400.00	400.00
2.30/06 30/06	Suspense account Capital account cheque not entered onto capital account	3000.00	3000.00

Account Suspense

Debit   Credit

Date 2006	Details	Amount £	Date 2006	Details	Amount £
30/06 30/06.	Purchases return Capital	400.00 3000.00	30/06	Bal b/d	3400.00 3400.00
		3400.00			3400.00

311

ANSWERS (Task 11)

EMAIL

From:	Kim Wendell
To:	Ari Pottle
CC:	
Subject:	Re: Correcting the trial balance
Date:	7 July 2006

Message:

Ari

I have prepared the journals as per your email.

This it will increase the balance of the purchase returns account to £15253) and increase the capital account balance to £49745.76. This will clear the suspense account balance and the trial balance will agree.

Best wishes.

Kim,

AAT

SAMPLE SIMULATION
UNIT 4

AVONTREE LTD

This is the AAT's Sample Simulation for Unit 4. Its purpose is to give you an idea of what an AAT simulation looks like. It is not intended as a definitive guide to the tasks you may be required to perform.

Total time: 2 hours 30 minutes

SIMULATION

Coverage of performance criteria and range statements

The following performance criteria are covered in this simulation.

Element	PC Coverage
4.1	**Code and extract information**
a)	Recognise appropriate cost centres and **elements of costs**.
b)	Extract income and expenditure details are from the relevant sources.
c)	Code income and expenditure correctly.
d)	Refer any problems in obtaining the necessary **information** to the appropriate person.
e)	Identify and report **errors** to the appropriate person.
4.2	**Provide comparisons on costs and income**
b)	Compare **information** extracted from a particular source with actual results.
c)	Identify discrepancies.
d)	Provide comparisons to the appropriate person in the required **format**.

The following performance criteria are not covered in this simulation and should be assessed separately.

4.2 a)	Clarify **information** requirements with the appropriate person.
4.2 e)	Follow organisational **requirements for confidentiality** strictly.

The following range statements are not covered in this simulation and should be assessed separately.

Element	Range Statement
4.1	**Sources:** sales orders
4.2	**Sources:** previous period's data; forecast data; ledgers
	Format: letter; memo; note
	Confidentiality requirements: sharing of information; storage of documents

DATA AND TASKS

INSTRUCTIONS

This simulation is designed to let you show your ability to supply information for management control.

You should read the whole simulation before you start work, so that you are fully aware of what you will have to do.

You are allowed two hours and 30 minutes to complete your work.

Write your answers in the Answer Booklet provided on pages 331 to 336. If you need more paper for your answers, ask the person in charge.

You should write your answers in blue or black ink, not pencil.

You may use correcting fluid, but in moderation. You should cross out your errors neatly and clearly.

You may pull apart and rearrange your booklets if you wish to do so, but you must put them back in their original order before handing them in.

Your work must be accurate, so check your work carefully before handing it in.

You are not allowed to refer to any unauthorised material, such as books or notes, while you are working on the simulation. If you have any such material with you, you must hand it to the person in charge before you start work.

Any instances of misconduct will be reported to the AAT, and disciplinary action may be taken.

Coverage of performance criteria and range statements

It is not always possible to cover all performance criteria and range statements in a single simulation. Any performance criteria and range statements not covered must be assessed by other means by the assessor before a candidate can be considered competent.

Performance criteria and range statement coverage for this simulation is shown on page 314.

THE SITUATION

Your name is Parfraz Mehdi, and you are an Accounts Assistant working for Avontree Limited, Unit 5, Burberry Business Park, Newfields NF8 2PR. Avontree is a publisher of textbooks used in primary, secondary and higher education. You report to the Accounts Supervisor, Emily Padden.

Coding of original documents

Avontree's accounts are maintained on a simple computerised system. One of your responsibilities is to code original documents for entry onto this system. For example, you code both sales and purchase invoices and enter relevant details onto data input sheets, which are then used for entering data into the computer system. In some cases you delegate the original coding to a colleague.

Payroll is maintained by Emily Padden on a computerised system separate from the accounts system. Each month she provides you with a payroll printout. Your task is to enter the appropriate codes for posting to the accounts system.

When doing your coding, you will need to refer to the company's policy manual; see page 318 of this book for relevant extracts. The purpose of the coding is to allocate costs and revenues to the appropriate cost and revenue centres, and also to distinguish between different types of costs and revenues.

VAT

Coding of VAT is performed automatically by the computerised accounts system, and therefore it is the amount **before** VAT on a purchase invoice that needs to be coded. There is no VAT on Avontree's sales invoices because textbooks are zero-rated.

The date

In this simulation you will be dealing with transactions arising in May and June 2006. Today's date is 9 June 2006.

THE TASKS TO BE COMPLETED

Task 1

On pages 319-322 of this book you will find eight sales invoices.

- Enter relevant details of the sales invoices, including appropriate codes, on the data input sheet on page 331 of the Answer Booklet. You will need to refer to the extract from the company's policy manual on page 318 of this book.

Task 2

On pages 323-327 of this book you will find purchase invoices received from Avontree's suppliers, and related purchase orders raised by Avontree. The purchase invoices have already been coded by one of your colleagues.

- Check the purchase invoices to ensure that they match the purchase orders, and also check that your colleague has entered the correct codes on the invoices. You will need to refer to the extract from the company's policy manual on page 318 of this book.

- Your checks should reveal discrepancies. Draft an email to Emily Padden describing these discrepancies. Use the blank email on page 332 of the Answer Booklet.

Task 3

The payroll printout for May 2006 is on page 327 of this book.

- Enter the appropriate amounts and codes on the input sheet on page 333 of the Answer Booklet, ready for inputting the payroll details to the accounts system.

Task 4

Refer to the report on page 334 of the Answer Booklet. This has been extracted from the accounts system and shows the year-to-date (YTD) totals for certain revenue and expenditure accounts up to the end of May 2006, along with comparative figures for the previous year.

- In the column headed 'Variance (£)', enter the monetary amount of the variance between this year and last, using the symbol '+' to indicate an increase over last year and the symbol '–' to indicate a decrease compared with last year.

- In the column headed 'Variance (%)' enter each variance as a percentage of last year's total, again using the symbols '+' and '–' and expressing the percentages to one decimal place.

(To guide you, the first line of the schedule has already been completed.)

Task 5

Draft a brief report to Emily Padden, to which you will attach the schedule you prepared in Task 4. Draw her attention to any instances where the calculated variance exceeds 5%. Use page 335 of the Answer Booklet and date your report 9 June 2006.

Policy manual (extracts)

Coding of sales revenue

Each item of sales revenue must be coded with two pieces of information:

- the revenue centre (see below);
- the type of revenue (see below).

The type of revenue is indicated by the product code. Textbooks for primary education have codes beginning with P. Textbooks for secondary education have codes beginning with S. Textbooks for higher education have codes beginning with H.

Only the net goods value is coded (ie the value of goods after deduction of trade discount).

Revenue centres

UK sales	100
Overseas sales	200

Types of revenue

Textbook sales: primary education	300
Textbook sales: secondary education	400
Textbook sales: higher education	500

Coding of expenditure

Each item of expenditure must be coded with two pieces of information:

- the cost centre (see below);
- the type of expenditure (see below).

Cost centres

Typesetting costs	610
Editing costs	620
Printing and binding costs	630
Distribution and despatch costs	640
Marketing costs	650
Establishment costs	660

Types of cost

Materials	710
Expenses	720
Salaries	730

The costs of services performed by external individuals or organisations are classified as 'expenses'. The costs of paying internal staff are classified as 'salaries'. All salaries are classified to the 'establishment costs' cost centre.

SALES INVOICES

INVOICE

Avontree Limited
Unit 5, Burberry Business Park, Newfields NF8 2PR

To: Megabooks Limited
33 High Street
Maidenhead SL6 1PQ

VAT Registration: 225 6712 89
Date/tax point: 5 June 2006
Invoice number: 52711

Titles supplied	Item code	Quantity	List price £	Total £
GCSE Mathematics	S2251	10	12.50	125.00
Intermediate Mathematics	S1201	12	5.50	66.00

Total at list price		191.00
Less trade discount @ **35%**		66.85
Net goods value		124.15
VAT @ **0%**		0.00
Total due		124.15

100400

Terms: net 30 days

INVOICE

Avontree Limited
Unit 5, Burberry Business Park, Newfields NF8 2PR

To: Books Plus
102 Lampard Avenue
Bristol BS3 5EW

VAT Registration: 225 6712 89
Date/tax point: 5 June 2006
Invoice number: 52712

Titles supplied	Item code	Quantity	List price £	Total £
Applications of Electronics	H3141	4	27.00	108.00
Thermodynamics	H2278	2	32.50	65.00

Total at list price		173.00
Less trade discount @ **40%**		69.20
Net goods value		103.80
VAT @ **0%**		0.00
Total due		103.80

100500

Terms: net 30 days

INVOICE

Avontree Limited
Unit 5, Burberry Business Park, Newfields NF8 2PR

To: Empstone Books Ltd
14 Cygnet Street
Holyport SO13 7KK

VAT Registration: 225 6712 89
Date/tax point: 5 June 2006
Invoice number: 52713

Titles supplied	Item code	Quantity	List price £	Total £
The Metres of English Poetry	S1190	3	16.00	48.00
Tudor History for Teenagers	S3124	6	14.00	84.00
The Stuarts: a Brief Survey	S5155	6	14.00	84.00

Total at list price	216.00
Less trade discount @ 32.5%	70.20
Net goods value	145.80
VAT @ 0%	0.00
Total due	145.80

Terms: net 30 days

INVOICE

Avontree Limited
Unit 5, Burberry Business Park, Newfields NF8 2PR

To: Win Hong Books
17 Swire Street
Central
HONG KONG

VAT Registration: 225 6712 89
Date/tax point: 5 June 2006
Invoice number: 52714

Titles supplied	Item code	Quantity	List price £	Total £
Daily Life in Ancient Egypt	P9124	20	6.20	124.00
Daily Life in Ancient Rome	P9130	20	6.20	124.00

Total at list price	248.00
Less trade discount @ 35%	86.80
Net goods value	161.20
VAT @ 0%	0.00
Total due	161.20

Terms: net 30 days

INVOICE

Avontree Limited
Unit 5, Burberry Business Park, Newfields NF8 2PR

To: Tradesales Limited
65 Limetree Avenue
Birkenhead WA12 5TR
UK

VAT Registration: 225 6712 89
Date/tax point: 5 June 2006
Invoice number: 52715

Titles supplied	Item code	Quantity	List price £	Total £
GCSE Mathematics	S2251	4	12.50	50.00
A level Mathematics	S1452	10	15.00	150.00

Total at list price		200.00
Less trade discount @ 40%		80.00
Net goods value		120.00
VAT @ 0%		0.00
Total due		120.00

100400

Terms: net 30 days

INVOICE

Avontree Limited
Unit 5, Burberry Business Park, Newfields NF8 2PR

To: Palmer and Company
18 Ambleden Avenue
Rystone
UK

VAT Registration: 225 6712 89
Date/tax point: 5 June 2006
Invoice number: 52716

Titles supplied	Item code	Quantity	List price £	Total £
GCSE French	S4123	20	12.80	256.00
GCSE Spanish	S4145	16	12.80	204.80

Total at list price		460.80
Less trade discount @ 35%		161.28
Net goods value		299.52
VAT @ 0%		0.00
Total due		299.52

100400

Terms: net 30 days

INVOICE

Avontree Limited
Unit 5, Burberry Business Park, Newfields NF8 2PR

To: Business Books
18 High Street
Hensham CV28 5AP
UK

VAT Registration: 225 6712 89
Date/tax point: 5 June 2006
Invoice number: 52717

Titles supplied	Item code	Quantity	List price £	Total £
Management Principles and Practice	H3121	8	26.50	212.00

Total at list price		212.00
Less trade discount @ 30%		63.60
Net goods value		148.40
VAT @ 0%		0.00
Total due		148.40

100500

Terms: net 30 days

INVOICE

Avontree Limited
Unit 5, Burberry Business Park, Newfields NF8 2PR

To: Megabooks Limited
33 High Street
Maidenhead SL6 1PQ
UK

VAT Registration: 225 6712 89
Date/tax point: 5 June 2006
Invoice number: 52718

Titles supplied	Item code	Quantity	List price £	Total £
En Avant: French for Beginners	S2234	22	16.00	352.00

Total at list price		352.00
Less trade discount @ 35%		123.20
Net goods value		228.80
VAT @ 0%		0.00
Total due		228.80

100400

Terms: net 30 days

PURCHASE INVOICES

SALES INVOICE

The Boxshop
25 Lyme Street, Taunton, TA2 4RP

To: Avontree Limited
Unit 5
Burberry Business Park
Newfields NF8 2PR

VAT Registration: 254 1781 26
Date/tax point: 5 June 2006
Invoice number: 288712
Your order: 2305

Description of goods/services	Total £
2,000 postal despatch boxes, PDB126	765.00

Amount (£)	Cost centre/ revenue centre	Expenditure/ revenue type
765.00	640	710

Goods total	765.00
VAT @ 17.5%	133.87
Total due	898.87

Terms: net 30 days

SALES INVOICE

Editype Limited
28 Wakeland Road, Newfields NF4 7LK

To: Avontree Limited
Unit 5
Burberry Business Park
Newfields NF8 2PR

VAT Registration: 267 9912 46
Date/tax point: 5 June 2006
Invoice number: 2511

Description of goods/services	Total £
Editorial work to your specification on Corporate Strategy	400.00

Amount (£)	Cost centre/ revenue centre	Expenditure/ revenue type
400.00	640	720

Total at list price	400.00
VAT @ 17.5%	70.00
Total due	470.00

Terms: net 30 days

SALES INVOICE

Education Magazine
17 Britton Street, London EC1M 5TP

To: Avontree Limited
Unit 5
Burberry Business Park
Newfields NF8 2PR

VAT Registration: 315 8123 49
Date/tax point: 5 June 2006
Invoice number: 22111098
Your order: 2259

Description of goods/services	Total £
Sales advertisement in June 2005 issue	870.00

Amount (£)	Cost centre/ revenue centre	Expenditure/ revenue type
870.00	650	720

Total at list price	870.00
VAT @ 17.5%	152.25
Total due	1,022.25

Terms: net 30 days

SALES INVOICE

Litho Printing Limited
Rosina Street, London E8 7RT

To: Avontree Limited
Unit 5
Burberry Business Park
Newfields NF8 2PR

VAT Registration: 412 5512 38
Date/tax point: 5 June 2006
Invoice number: 217765
Your order: 2271

Description of goods/services	Total £
Printing and binding 5,000 copies of The War of the Roses	16,410.00

Amount (£)	Cost centre/ revenue centre	Expenditure/ revenue type
16,410.00	630	710

Total at list price	16,410.00
VAT: zero-rated	0.00
Total due	16,410.00

Terms: net 30 days

SALES INVOICE

Typetext Limited
21 Ashton Lane, Newfields NF2 7UT

To: Avontree Limited
Unit 5
Burberry Business Park
Newfields NF8 2PR

VAT Registration: 251 7171 34
Date/tax point: 5 June 2006
Invoice number: 276
Your order: 2286

Description of goods/services	Total £
Typesetting of *GCSE Geography* to agreed specification	1,200.00

Amount (£)	Cost centre/ revenue centre	Expenditure/ revenue type
1,200.00	610	720

Total at list price	1,200.00
VAT @ 17.5%	210.00
Total due	1,410.00

Terms: net 30 days

SALES INVOICE

Decofix Limited
Panton Close, Newfields NF8 2PR

To: Avontree Limited
Unit 5
Burberry Business Park
Newfields NF8 2PR

VAT Registration: 381 5512 60
Date/tax point: 5 June 2006
Invoice number: 198
Your order: 2268

Description of goods/services	Total £
Repainting of accounts office to agreed specification	312.00

Amount (£)	Cost centre/ revenue centre	Expenditure/ revenue type
312.00	660	710

Total at list price	312.00
VAT @ 17.5%	54.60
Total due	366.60

Terms: net 30 days

PURCHASE ORDER

Avontree Limited
Unit 5, Burberry Business Park,
Newfields NF8 2PR

To:
Litho Printing
Limited
Rosina Street
London E8 7RT

Date: 13 May 2006
Order no: 2271

Please supply the items/services below on the agreed terms

Quantity	Description	Item code
500	Bound copies of *The War of the Roses*	N/A

On behalf of Avontree Limited   *Emily Padden*

PURCHASE ORDER

Avontree Limited
Unit 5, Burberry Business Park,
Newfields NF8 2PR

To:
The Boxshop
25 Lyme Street
Taunton TA2 4RP

Date: 20 May 2006
Order no: 2305

Please supply the items/services below on the agreed terms

Quantity	Description	Item code
2,000	Postal despatch boxes	PDB126

On behalf of Avontree Limited   *Emily Padden*

PURCHASE ORDER

Avontree Limited
Unit 5, Burberry Business Park,
Newfields NF8 2PR

To:
Decofix Limited
Panton Close
Newfields NF6 3QT

Date: 12 May 2006
Order no: 2268

Please supply the items/services below on the agreed terms

Quantity	Description	Item code
1	Repainting of accounts office to agreed specification	N/A

On behalf of Avontree Limited   *Emily Padden*

PURCHASE ORDER

Avontree Limited
Unit 5, Burberry Business Park,
Newfields NF8 2PR

To:
Typestext Limited
21 Ashton Lane
Newfields NF2 7UT

Date:
16 May 2006
Order no:
2286

Please supply the items/services below on the agreed terms

Quantity	Description	Item code
1	Typesetting of GCSE Geography to agreed specification	N/A

On behalf of Avontree Limited   *Emily Padden*

PURCHASE ORDER

Avontree Limited
Unit 5, Burberry Business Park,
Newfields NF8 2PR

To:

Education Magazine
17 Britton Street
London EC1M 5TP

Date: 9 May 2006
Order no: 2259

Please supply the items/services below on the agreed terms

Quantity	Description	Item code
1	Sales advertisement in June 2006 issue	N/A

Salaries summary

Month: May 2006

Employee name	Gross pay (£)	PAYE tax (£)	Employee NIC	Net pay (£)	Employer NIC (£)
James Bailey	850.00	91.00	46.60	712.40	54.99
Laura Drinkwater	3,000.00	572.00	215.00	2,213.00	308.57
Allan Holmes	1,250.00	189.00	86.60	974.40	102.19
Caroline Johnson	1,000.00	139.00	61.40	799.60	72.45
Parfraz Mehdi	1,400.00	225.00	101.40	1,073.60	119.65
Emily Padden	2,300.00	418.00	191.40	1,690.60	225.85
Roland White	1,100.00	157.00	71.40	871.60	84.25
	10,900.00	1,791.00	773.80	8,335.20	967.95

ANSWER BOOKLET

ANSWERS (Task 1)

DATA INPUT SHEET				
Sales invoices		Date: _____		
			Coding	
Invoice number	Customer	Amount £	Revenue centre	Type of revenue
52711	Megabooks Limited	124.15	100	400
52712	Books Plus	103.50	100	500
52713	Empstone Books Ltd	145.80	100	400
52714	Wun Hong Books	161.20	200	300
52715	Tradesales Limited	120.00	100	400
52716	Palmer + Company	299.52	100	400
52717	Business Books	148.40	100	500
52718	Megabooks Limited	228.80	100	400

ANSWERS (Task 2)

EMAIL

From: Parfraz Mehdi

To: Emily Padden.

CC:

Subject: Purchase invoices

Date: 9 June 2006

Message:

Emily,
I looked at the purchase invoices for today and I found a number of problems.

• Editype Limited – there is no purchase order to match this invoice, there is also a problem in the coding it should be coding costs not dispatch costs.

• education magazine – coding is fine but description says advert June 2005, purchase order says 2006. – not needed.

• Litho Printing Limited – should be expenses not materials, also purchase order says 500 copies invoice is for 5000. ✓

• Decofix Limited – should be expenses not materials. ✓

ANSWERS (Task 3)

DATA INPUT SHEET

Payroll

Date: 9 June 2006

Detail	Amount £	Cost centre	Type of expenditure
Gross pay	10900	660	730. ✓
~~PAYE~~	~~1741~~		
~~Employee PAYE~~	~~773.80~~		
~~Net pay~~	~~8385.20~~		
Employer NIC	967.95	660	730. ✓

ANSWERS (Task 4)

AVONTREE LIMITED
PROFIT AND LOSS ACCOUNT

Date: 31 May 2006

Account code	Account name	YTD This year	Last year	Variance £	Variance %
100-300	UK sales: primary	75,600	74,100	+1,500	✓ +2.0
100-400	UK sales: secondary	100,900	108,700	–7800	–7.1%
100-500	UK sales: higher	98,700	95,000	+3700	+3.9%
610-720	Typesetting: expenses	15,300	16,000	–700	–4.4%
620-720	Editing: expenses	16,400	15,700	+700	+4.5%
630-710	Printing & binding: materials	40,100	36,500	+3600	+9.9%
640-710	Distribution: materials	4,600	6,100	–1500	–24.6%
650-720	Marketing: expenses	16,400	15,900	+500	+3.1%
660-720	Establishment: expenses	5,600	5,200	+400	+7.7%
660-730	Establishment: salaries	34,200	33,000	+1200	+3.6%

ANSWERS (Task 5)

REPORT

To: Emily Padden.

From: Parfraz Mehdi.

Subject: Profit + Loss

Date: 9 June 2006

I attach a profit + loss schedule comparing current figures with last year.

I would like to bring your attention to the following where the variance exceeds 5%:

- U.K. sales-secondary -7.1% adv (7800)
- Printing + binding-materials -9.9% fav (3600)
- Distribution materials -24.6% adv (1500)
- Establishment: expenses -7.1% fav (400)

If you have any queries do not ✓ hesitate to ask.

If using this page, please state clearly which task you are answering.

UNIT 3

PRACTICE EXAM 1

WM PRINTING

These tasks were set by the AAT in June 2004.

This exam paper is in two sections.

You have to show competence in both sections, so attempt and aim to complete EVERY task in BOTH sections.

Section 1   Processing exercise
              Complete all six tasks

Section 2   10 tasks and questions
              Complete all tasks and questions

You should spend about 90 minutes on each section.

Include all essential workings within your answers, where appropriate.

Sections 1 and 2 both relate to the business described below.

INTRODUCTION

Wendy Mason is the owner of a printing business which trades as WM Printing.

You are employed by the business as a bookkeeper.

The business uses a manual accounting system.

Double entry takes place in the main (general) ledger. Individual accounts of debtors and creditors are kept in subsidiary ledgers as memorandum accounts.

Bank payments and receipts are recorded in the cash book, which is part of the double entry system.

Assume today's date is 30 June 2006 unless you are told otherwise.

SECTION 1 – PROCESSING EXERCISE

You should spend about 90 minutes on this section.

DATA

Balances at the start of the day on 30 June 2006

The following balances are relevant to you at the start of the day on 30 June 2006:

	£
Credit suppliers	
TGB Ltd	3,000
Compton & Company	8,600
Rowley Associates	10,432
Elton & Lowe Ltd	1,750
Purchases	285,200
Purchases returns	3,000
Purchases ledger control	40,698
Motor vehicles	5,000
General repairs	200
Insurance	2,900
Motor tax	180
VAT (credit balance)	15,560

Task 1.1

Enter these opening balances into the following accounts given on pages 340 to 343.

Subsidiary (Purchases) ledger
    TGB Ltd
    Compton & Company
    Rowley Associates
    Elton & Lowe Ltd

Main (General) ledger
    Purchases
    Purchases returns
    Purchases ledger control
    Motor vehicles
    General repairs
    Insurance
    Motor tax
    VAT

DATA

Transactions

The following transactions all took place on 30 June 2006 and have been entered into the relevant books of prime entry as shown below. No entries have yet been made into the ledger system. The VAT rate is 17½%.

Purchases day book

Date 2006	Details	Invoice number	Total £	VAT £	Net £
30 June	TGB Ltd	1602	5,875	875	5,000
30 June	Compton & Company	1011	1,175	175	1,000
30 June	Rowley Associates	P/101	10,575	1,575	9,000
30 June	Elton & Lowe Ltd	1974	2,350	350	2,000
	Totals		19,975	2,975	17,000

Purchases returns day book

Date 2006	Details	Credit note no	Total £	VAT £	Net £
30 June	TGB Ltd	C042	47	7	40
30 June	Rowley Associates	336	94	14	80
	Totals		141	21	120

Cash book

Date 2006	Details	Bank £	Date 2006	Details	VAT £	Bank £
30 June	Balance b/f	21,642	30 June	Motor vehicle		6,000
			30 June	General repairs	28	188
			30 June	Insurance		150
			30 June	Motor tax		90
			30 June	Compton & Co (creditor)		3,000
			30 June	Balance c/f		12,214
	Total	21,642			28	21,642

Task 1.2

From the day books and cash book shown above, make the relevant entries into the accounts in the subsidiary (purchases) ledger and main (general) ledger.

Task 1.3

Balance the accounts showing clearly the balances carried down at 30 June (closing balance).

Task 1.4

Now show the balances brought down at 1 July (opening balance).

SUBSIDIARY (PURCHASES) LEDGER

TGB Ltd

Date 2006	Details	Amount £	Date 2006	Details	Amount £
30 June	PRDB	47	30 June	O/bal	3000
30 June	Bal c/d	8828	30 June	PDB	5875
		8875			8875
			1 Jul	O/bal	8828

Compton & Co

Date 2006	Details	Amount £	Date 2006	Details	Amount £
30 June	Cash book	3000	30 June	O/bal	8600
30 June	Bal c/d	6775	30 June	PDB	1175
		9775			9775
			1 Jul	O/bal	6775

Rowley Associates

Date 2006	Details	Amount £	Date 2006	Details	Amount £
30 June	PRDB	94	30 June	O/bal	10432
30 June	Bal c/d	20913	30 June	PDB	10575
		21007			21007
			1 Jul	O/bal	20913

Elton & Lowe Ltd

Date 2006	Details	Amount £	Date 2006	Details	Amount £
30 June	Bal c/d	4100	30 June	O/bal	1750
			30 June	PDB	2350
		4100			4100
			1 Jul	O/Bal	4100

MAIN (GENERAL) LEDGER

Purchases

Date 2006	Details	Amount £	Date 2006	Details	Amount £
30 June	O/bal	285200	30 June	Bal c/d	302200
30 June	Cash Book PDB	17000			
		302200			302200
1 Jul	O/bal	302200			

Purchases returns

Date 2006	Details	Amount £	Date 2006	Details	Amount £
30 June	Bal c/d	3120	30 June	O/bal	3000
			30 June	PRDB	120
		3120			3120
			1 Jul	O/Bal	3120

Purchases ledger control

Date 2006	Details	Amount £	Date 2006	Details	Amount £
30 June	PRDB	141	30 June	O/bal	40698
30 June	Cashbook	3000	30 June	Cash Book PRDB	19975
30 June	Bal c/d	57532			
		60673			60673
			1 Jul	O/bal	57532

Motor vehicles

Date 2006	Details	Amount £	Date 2006	Details	Amount £
30 June	O/bal	5000	30 June	Bal c/d	11000
30 June	Cashbook	6000			
		11000			11000
1 Jul	O/Bal	11000			

General repairs

Date 2006	Details	Amount £	Date 2006	Details	Amount £
30 June	O/bal	200	30 June	Bal c/d	360
30 June	Cashbook	160			
		360			360
1 Jul	O/Bal	360			

Insurance

Date 2006	Details	Amount £	Date 2006	Details	Amount £
30 June	O/bal	2900	30 June	Bal c/d	3050
30 June	Cashbook	150			
		3050			3050
1 Jul	O/Bal	3050			

Motor tax

Date 2006	Details	Amount £	Date 2006	Details	Amount £
30 June	O/bal	180	30 June	Bal c/d	270
30 June	Cash book	90			
		270			270
1 Jul	O/Bal	270.			

VAT

Date 2006	Details	Amount £	Date 2006	Details	Amount £
30 June	Purchase Daybook	2975	30 June	O/bal	15560
30 June	Cash book	28.	30 June	PRDB	21
30 June	Bal c/d	12578			
		15581			15581
			1 Jul	O/Bal	12578

DATA

Other balances to be transferred to the trial balance.

	£
Office equipment	15,000
Stock	17,500
Cash	186
Sales ledgers control	106,842
Capital	30,710
Sales	418,200
Sales returns	2,605
Discounts allowed	350
Wages	42,181
Rent	3,000
Rates	2,100
Stationery	620
Telephone	800
Heat and light	1,300
Miscellaneous expenses	562

Task 1.5

Transfer the balances that you calculated in Task 1.3, and the bank balance, to the trial balance on page 344.

Task 1.6

Transfer the remaining balances shown above to the trial balance, and total each column.

Trial balance as at 30 June 2006

	Debit £	Credit £
Motor vehicles	11000	
Office equipment	15000	
Stock	17500	
Bank	12214	
Cash	186.	
Sales ledger control	106842	
Purchases ledger control		57532
VAT		12578
Capital		30710
Sales		478200
Sales returns	2605	
Purchases	302200	
Purchases returns		3120
Discounts allowed	350	
Motor tax	270	
General repairs	360	
Wages	42181	
Insurance	3050	
Rent	3000	
Rates	2100	
Stationery	620	
Telephone	800	
Heat and light	1300	
Miscellaneous expenses	562	
Total	522140	522140

SECTION 2 – TASKS AND QUESTIONS

You should spend about 90 minutes on this section.

Answer all of the following questions on pages 345 to 351.

Write your answers in the spaces provided.

Note. You do not need to adjust the accounts in Section 1 as part of any of the following tasks.

Task 2.1

The cheque below has been received today.

Western Bank plc			65 - 29 - 38
Bedford Branch High Street, Bedford, BF15 8ZX		Date *25 June 2006*	
Pay *WM Printing*			
One hundred and five pounds only		**£**	*150.00*
		Design Data Ltd	
Cheque No.	Sort code	Account No.	
			Director
00−04−93	65−29−38	82157802	

a) Give TWO reasons why the cheque will not be honoured by the bank.

1. The cheque has not been signed.
2. The amount in figures does not match the amount in words.

b) What would you do in this situation?

Send the cheque back and request a new one.

Task 2.2

WM Printing buys goods from and sells goods to Haven Stationers Ltd. It has been agreed to set off a debt of £50 owing between them by a contra entry.

What accounts in the main (general) ledger of WM Printing would be adjusted to record this set off?

Debit	£	Credit	£
Purchase ledger	50	sales ledger	50

Task 2.3

During the last VAT quarter sales amounted to £122,000 **plus VAT**. Purchases totalled £9,870 **including VAT**. What would have been the amount payable to H M Revenue & Customs at the end of that quarter? Show workings.

122000 × 1.175 = 143350   VAT = 21350
Net = ~~8400~~   VAT = 1470
21350 − 1470 = 19880 due to HMRC

Task 2.4

WM Printing offers its customers both trade and cash settlement discounts. Briefly explain the reason why each of these discounts is offered.

A trade discount is offered: to encourage regular buying from the company & to encourage bulk purchases.

A cash settlement discount is offered: to ensure that invoices are paid quickly.

Task 2.5

Wendy Mason is considering purchasing some new office furniture. The seller is not willing to accept a cheque because of the time it would take to clear.

Briefly explain why it takes time for a cheque to clear.

The cheque must pass through a clearing system before funds can pass from one account to another.

Task 2.6

WM Printing's transactions in June included the items listed below.

Show whether each is a capital transaction or a revenue transaction by circling the correct answer.

a) Purchase of office stationery — Capital/**Revenue** R

b) Decoration of offices — Capital/**Revenue** R

c) Purchase of a delivery van — **Capital**/Revenue C

d) Purchase of fuel for the delivery van — Capital/**Revenue** R

Task 2.7

Wendy Mason is considering introducing a computerised accounting system. She has been advised to purchase integrated accounting software.

Briefly explain the meaning of integrated accounting software.

Integrated accounting software automatically enters figures from the cash book etc unto the relevant subsidiary accounts etc, so figures only need to be entered once.

Task 2.8

You are reminded that you do NOT need to adjust, or refer to, the accounts in Section 1 or Section 2.

The following information has become available.

a) An amount of £78 has been debited to the miscellaneous expenses account instead of the heat and light account.

b) An amount paid by cheque for rent has been recorded as £50 instead of the correct amount of £500.

c) An amount of £75 has been credited to the suspense account. The following two errors have now been discovered.

    i) A payment of £1,000 has been recorded as £1,100 in the insurance account.

    ii) An amount of £25 has been omitted from the stationery account.

Record the journal entries needed in the Main (General) ledger, to deal with the above. Narratives are not required.

THE JOURNAL

Details	Dr £	Cr £
a) Heat + light	78	
Miscellaneous expenses		78.
Amount debited to miscellan		
eous expenses account in		
error.		
b) Rent	450	
Bank. bank.		450
£500 rent misposted as		
£50 in error.		
c) Stationery account	25	
Suspense account.	100	
Suspense account		25
Insurance account		100
To clear errors.		

Task 2.9

This is a summary of transactions with customers during the month of June.

	£
Balance of debtors at 1 June 2006	100,102
Goods sold on credit	40,140
Money received from credit customers	32,250
Discounts allowed	150
Goods returned by credit customers	1,000

a) Prepare a sales ledger control account from the above details. Show clearly the balance carried down at 30 June (closing balance) and brought down at 1 July (opening balance).

Sales ledger control

Date 2006	Details	Amount £	Date 2006	Details	Amount £
1 June	O/Bal	100102	30 June	money received	32250
3 June	Goods sold	40140	30 June	Discounts allowed	150
			30 June	Goods returned	1 000
			30 June	Bal c/d	106842
		140242			140242
1 Jul	O/Bal	106842			

The following closing debit balances were in the Subsidiary (sales) ledger on 30 June.

	£
PDG Commercials	28,333
A B Smith Ltd	15,020
South and Attwood	235
Francis & Company	18,212
Langley & Law	22,400
IJB Ltd	22,792

b) Reconcile the balances shown above with the sales ledger control account balance you have calculated in part a).

	£
Sales ledger control account balance as at 30 June 2006	106842
Total of subsidiary (sales) ledger accounts as at 30 June 2006	106992
Difference	150

c) What may have caused the difference you calculated in part b)?

It is likely the discounts allowed have not been posted to the subsidiary ledgers.

Task 2.10

On 28 June WM Printing received the following bank statement as at 21 June:

	CENTREPOINT BANK plc			
	High Street, Bedford, BF13 8RF			

To: Special Events   Account No 54387299   21 June 2006

STATEMENT OF ACCOUNT

Date	Details	Paid out	Paid in	Balance
2005		£	£	£
2 June	Balance b/f			21,421 C
9 June	Cheque No 300175	3,550		17,871 C
10 June	Cheque No 300176	368		17,503 C
11 June	Cheque No 300178	412		17,091 C
14 June	Bank Giro Credit			
	Law & Lodge		12,100	29,191 C
21 June	Cheque No 300180	158		29,033 C
21 June	Direct Debit			
	Bedford MBC	210		28,823 C
21 June	Direct Debit			
	LTM Ltd	4,800		24,023 C
21 June	Bank charges	97		23,926 C
21 June	Bank Giro Credit			
	BGC Ltd		1,569	25,495 C

D = Debit C = Credit

The cash book as at 28 June 2006 is shown below.

Cash book

Date 2006	Details	Amount £	Date 2006	Cheque number	Details	Amount £
1 June	Balance b/f	21,421	3 June	300175	Mills Ltd	3,550
25 June	Paper Design	1,500	3 June	300176	Baker & Brown	368
27 June	Bate Ltd	2,000	4 June	300177	Legge Ltd	100
14 June	Law + Lodge	12100	6 June	300178	Parker Papers	412
21 June	BGC Ltd	1569	17 June	300179	Beta Ltd	300
			17 June	300180	Paper Unlimted	158
			20 June		Bedford MBC	210
			21 June	DD	LTM Ltd	4800
			21 June	DD	charges	97
		38	3 June		Bal c/d	28595
		38510				38510

30 June Bal b/d   28595

a) Check the items on the bank statement against the items in the cash book.

b) Update the cash book as needed.

c) Total the cash book and clearly show the balance carried down at 28 June and brought down at 29 June.

Note. You do not need to adjust the accounts in Section 1.

d) Using the information on page 364, complete the bank reconciliation statement as at 28 June.

Bank reconciliation statement as at 28 June 2006	
	£
Balance as per bank statement	25495
Add: Paper Design	1500
Bank Ltd	2000
Total	28995
Less: Legge Ltd	100
Beta Ltd	300
Total	28595
Balance as per the updated cash book	28595

UNIT 3

PRACTICE EXAM 2

THE GARDEN WAREHOUSE

These tasks were set by the AAT in June 2005.

This exam paper is in two sections.

You have to show competence in both sections, so attempt and aim to complete EVERY task in BOTH sections.

> Section 1   Processing exercise
> **Complete all six tasks**
>
> Section 2   10 tasks and questions
> **Complete all tasks and questions**

You should spend about 90 minutes on each section.

Include all essential workings within your answers, where appropriate.

Sections 1 and 2 both relate to the business described below.

INTRODUCTION

Marian Walker is the owner of a business that supplies gardening equipment, The Garden Warehouse.

You are employed by the business as a bookkeeper.

The business uses a manual accounting system.

Double entry takes place in the main (general) ledger. Individual accounts of debtors and creditors are kept in subsidiary ledgers as memorandum accounts.

Bank payments and receipts are recorded in the cash book, which is part of the double entry system.

Assume today's date is 30 June 2006 unless you are told otherwise.

SECTION 1 – PROCESSING EXERCISE

You should spend about 90 minutes on this section.

DATA

Balances at the start of the day on 30 June 2006

The following balances are relevant to you at the start of the day on 30 June 2006:

	£
Credit customers	
Creations Limited	8,756
Jackson and Company	4,814
Loxley Limited	6,320
PTT Limited	4,500
Office equipment	3,500
Sales	321,650
Sales returns	15,800
Sales ledger control	112,636
Discounts allowed	750
Motor expenses	1,225
Rent and rates	3,600
VAT (credit balance)	11,463

Task 1.1

Enter these opening balances into the following accounts given on pages 356 to 359.

Subsidiary (Purchases) ledger
Creations Limited
Jackson and Company
Loxley Limited
PTT Limited

Main (General) ledger
Office equipment
Sales
Sales returns
Sales ledger control
Discounts allowed
Motor expenses
Rent and rates
VAT

DATA

The following transactions all took place on 30 June 2006 and have been entered into the relevant books of prime entry as shown below. No entries have yet been made into the ledger system. The VAT rate is 17½%.

Sales day book

Date 2006	Details	Invoice number	Total £	VAT £	Net £
30 June	Creations Limited	849	2,115	315	1,800
30 June	Jackson and Company	850	9,870	1,470	8,400
30 June	Loxley Limited	851	3,055	455	2,600
30 June	PTT Limited	852	7,050	1,050	6,000
	Totals		22,090	3,290	18,800

Sales returns day book

Date 2006	Details	Credit note number	Total £	VAT £	Net £
30 June	Creations Limited	131	4,700	700	4,000
30 June	Loxley Limited	132	423	63	360
	Totals		5,123	763	4,360

Cash book

Date 2006	Details	Discount allowed £	Bank £	Date 2006	Details	Bank £
30 June	Balance b/f		8,190	30 June	Motor expenses	350
30 June	Jackson and Company	100	3,650	30 June	Rent and rates	1,200
				30 June	Office equipment	5,250
				30 June	Balance c/f	5,040
	Total	100	11,840			11,840
1 July	Balance b/d		5,040			

Task 1.2

From the day books and cash book shown above, make the relevant entries into the accounts in the subsidiary (sales) ledger and main (general) ledger.

Task 1.3

Balance the accounts showing clearly the balances carried down at 30 June (closing balance).

Task 1.4

Now show the balances brought down at 1 July (opening balance), showing clearly the date and details, as well as the amount.

SUBSIDIARY (PURCHASES) LEDGER

Creations Limited

Date 2006	Details	Amount £	Date 2006	Details	Amount £
30 Jun	O/Bal	8756	30 Jun	O/Bal	8756
30 Jun	SDB	2115	30 Jun	SRDB	4700
			30 Jun	balance c/d	6171
		10871			10871
1 Jul	Bal b/d	6171			

Jackson and Company

Date 2006	Details	Amount £	Date 2006	Details	Amount £
30 Jun	O/Bal	4814	30 Jun	O/Bal	4814
30 Jun	SDB	9870	30 Jun	Cash book	3650
			30 Jun	Discount	100
			30 Jun	Bal c/d	10934
		14684			14684
1 Jul	Bal b/d	10934			

Loxley Limited

Date 2006	Details	Amount £	Date 2006	Details	Amount £
30 Jun	O/Bal	6320	30 Jun	O/Bal	6320
30 Jun	SDB	3055	30 Jun	SRDB	423
			30 Jun	Bal c/d	8952
		9375			9375
1 Jul	Bal b/d	8952			

PTT Limited

Date 2006	Details	Amount £	Date 2006	Details	Amount £
30 Jun	O/Bal	4500	~~30 Jun~~	~~O/Bal~~	~~4500~~
30 Jun	SDB	7050	30 Jun	Bal c/d	11550
		11550			11550
1 Jul	Bal b/d	11550			

MAIN (GENERAL) LEDGER

Office equipment

Date 2006	Details	Amount £	Date 2006	Details	Amount £
30 Jun	O/Bal	3500	30 Jun	Bal c/d	8750
30 Jun	Cash book	5250			
		8750			8750
1 Jul	Bal b/d	8750			

Sales

Date 2006	Details	Amount £	Date 2006	Details	Amount £
30 Jun	Bal c/d	~~34830~~ 340450	30 Jun	O/Bal	~~321650~~
			30 Jun	SDB	18800
		3404 ~~340630~~			~~340630~~ 340450
			1 Jul	Bal b/d	340450 ~~340630~~

Sales returns

Date 2006	Details	Amount £	Date 2006	Details	Amount £
30 Jun	O/Bal	15800	30 Jun	Bal c/d	20160
30 Jun	SRDB	4360			
		20160			20160
1 Jul	Bal b/d	20160			

357

Sales ledger control

Date 2006	Details	Amount £	Date 2006	Details	Amount £
30 Jun	O/Bal	112636	30 Jun	SRDB	5123
30 Jun	SDB	22090	30 Jun	Cash book	3650
			30 Jun	Discounts.	100
			30 Jun	Bal c/d	125853
		134726			134726
1 Jul	Bal b/d	125853			

Discount allowed

Date 2006	Details	Amount £	Date 2006	Details	Amount £
30 Jun	O/Bal	750	30 Jun	Bal c/d	850
30 Jun	Cash book	100			
		850			850
1 Jul	Bal b/d	850			

Motor expenses

Date 2006	Details	Amount £	Date 2006	Details	Amount £
30 Jun	O/Bal	1225	30 Jun	Bal c/d	1575
30 Jun	Cash book	350			
		1575			1575
1 Jul	Bal b/d	1575			

Rent and rates

Date 2006	Details	Amount £	Date 2006	Details	Amount £
30 Jun	O/Bal	3600	30 Jun	Bal c/d	4800
30 Jun	Cash book	1200			
		4800			4800
1 Jul	Bal b/d	4800			

VAT

Date 2006	Details	Amount £	Date 2006	Details	Amount £
30 Jun	SRDB	763	30 Jun	O/Bal	11463
30 Jun	Bal c/d	13990	30 Jun	SDB	3290
		14753			14753
			1 Jul	Bal b/d	13990 ✓

DATA

Other balances to be transferred to the trial balance.

	£
Motor vehicles	5,200
Stock	17,000
Petty cash control	60
Purchases ledger control	56,713
Loan from bank	15,000
Capital	27,798
Purchases	206,511
Purchase returns	862
Discounts received	248
Wages	50,425
Heat and light	963
Travel expenses	1,650
Telephone	1,006
Accountancy fees	2,530
Miscellaneous expenses	2,688

Task 1.5

Transfer the balances that you calculated in Tasks 1.3 and 1.4, and the bank balance, to the trial balance on page 360.

455061
439971

Task 1.6

Transfer the remaining balances shown above to the trial balance, and total each column.

Trial balance as at 30 June 2006

	Debit £	Credit £
Motor vehicles	5200	
Office equipment	8750	
Stock	17000	
Bank	5040	
Petty cash control	60	
Sales ledger control	125853	
Purchases ledger control		56713
VAT		13990
Loan from bank		15000
Capital		27~~26054~~
Sales		340 ~~36045O~~
Sales returns	20160	
Purchases	~~862~~ 206511	
Purchases returns		862
Discounts received		248
Discounts allowed	850	
Wages	50425	
Heat and light	963	
Motor expenses	1575	
Rent and rates	4800	
Travel expenses	1650	
Telephone	1006	
Accountancy fees	2530	
Miscellaneous expenses	2686	
Total	455061	455061

SECTION 2 – TASKS AND QUESTIONS

You should spend about 90 minutes on this section.

Answer all of the following questions on pages 361 to 367.

Write your answers in the spaces provided.

Note. You do not need to adjust the accounts in Section 1 as part of any of the following tasks.

Task 2.1

The following purchase invoice has been received at The Garden Warehouse.

WENTWORTH SUPPLIES	
18 High Street, Droitwich, Worcestershire WR15 01W	
Tel: 01943 567392	

VAT Registration Number 374 8219 00

To: The Garden Warehouse   29 June 2006
2a Lower Parade
Droitwich
Worcestershire WR16 81S

INVOICE NO P/1674

	£
20 Garden spades	200.00
Less 10% trade discount	20.00
	180.00
VAT @ 17.5%	30.87
Total	**210.87**

Terms: 2% settlement discount for payment within 7 days

Marian Walker has asked you to pay this invoice immediately.

a)   What is the amount to be paid to Wentworth Supplies? (Show workings.)

180 x 0.02 = 3.6   180 - 36 = 176.4
176.4 + 30.87 = 207.27. ✓

b)   What is the purpose of a TRADE discount? Circle the correct answer.

i)   To reward customers who pay in cash
ii)   To offer a lower price to an organisation within the same trade ✓
iii)   To reduce the price of goods which are damaged

c) To which customers might The Garden Warehouse offer a BULK discount? Circle the correct answer.

    i)   (Those placing large orders)

    ii)   Those with many branches

    iii) Those who have been customers for many years

Task 2.2

If the VAT account showed a debit balance, what would this indicate?

More has been bought in the period than sold, usually an asset purchase, money is owed from HM Revenue + Customs to the company.

Task 2.3

The Garden Warehouse has just opened a credit account for a new supplier, Wright Brothers, which brings the total number of suppliers to 50.

a) Suggest an appropriate four-digit alphanumeric ledger code for this account.

WBS0.

b) In which ledger would you expect to see this account?

Subsidiary (purchases) ledger.

Task 2.4

The following errors have been made in the accounting records of The Garden Warehouse.

Show whether the errors cause an imbalance in the trial balance by circling the correct answer.

a) A purchase invoice is lost in the post and not received at The Garden Warehouse.

    (The trial balance will balance) / The trial balance will not balance

b) Discount allowed has not been taken by a customer.

    (The trial balance will balance) / The trial balance will not balance

c) A purchase invoice has been correctly entered in the main ledger but omitted from the subsidiary (purchases) ledger.

    (The trial balance will balance) / The trial balance will not balance

d)   An entry has been made to the purchases and VAT accounts but omitted from the purchases ledger control account.

The trial balance will balance / ~~The trial balance will not balance~~

Task 2.5

On 7 July you extract a trial balance, which does not balance. You are unable to find the error.

What bookkeeping action could you take to ensure the trial balance does balance until you are able to find and correct the error?

Post the amount to a suspense account until the error can be found. ✓

Task 2.6

Marian Walker is considering computerising the accounting system.

a)   Give TWO advantages of a computerised accounting system.

Entries are only made once - the computer does the entry. reports can be printed quickly + you will not have errors of single entry.

b)   Name TWO reports that can be produced more efficiently by a computerised accounting system.

Invoices   - VAT return
credit notes.   → Trial balance

c)   Name TWO precautions that can be taken to avoid the loss of data held within a computerised accounting system.

Back-up data regularly
Have virus scan software. ✓

Task 2.7

Marian Walker has decided to rent out surplus offices to a number of businesses and has asked you to open the relevant customer accounts in a separate subsidiary ledger. Marian does not wish the amounts due to be recorded in the existing sales ledger control account.

Name the TWO accounts that you will need to open in the main (general) ledger.

Rent received control account ✓

Rent received (income) account.

Non-trade debtors control.

Task 2.8

The following information has become available.

a)   An amount of £70 has been debited to the miscellaneous account instead of the motor tax account.

b)   Purchases of £500 have been credited to the purchases account and debited to the purchases ledger control account (ignore VAT).

c)   A credit customer, L G Whitburn, has ceased trading, owing The Garden Warehouse £200 plus VAT. The net amount and VAT must be written off in the the main (general) ledger.

Record the journal entries needed in the main (general) ledger, to deal with the above. Narratives are not required.

Note. You are reminded that you do NOT need to adjust, or refer to, the accounts in Section 1 or Section 2.

THE JOURNAL

Details	Dr £	Cr £
a) Motor tax	70	
Miscellaneous		70
b) Purchases	1000	
Purchase ledger control		1000
c) Bad debts	200	
VAT	35	
Sales ledger control		235

Task 2.9

This is a summary of transactions with suppliers during the month of June 2006.

	£
Balance of creditors at 1 June 2006	53,386
Goods bought on credit	20,500
Money paid to credit customers	16,193
Discounts received	380
Goods returned to credit suppliers	600

a) Prepare a purchases ledger control account from the above details. Show clearly the balance carried down at 30 June (closing balance) and brought down at 1 July (opening balance).

Purchases ledger control

Date 2006	Details	Amount £	Date 2006	Details	Amount £
1 Jun	O/Bal	53386	30 Jun	Money paid	16193
30 Jun	Goods Bought	20500	30 Jun	Discounts	380
			30 Jun	Goods returned	600
			30 Jun	Bal c/d	56713
		73886			73886
1 Jul	Bal b/d	56713 ✓			

The following closing credit balances were in the subsidiary (purchases) ledger on 30 June.

	£
Gardens Unlimited	15,620
P Lower	1,695
L Brown	23,000
White Brothers	16,200
Hoe and Dig	578

b) Reconcile the balances shown above with the purchases ledger control account balance you have calculated in part a).

	£
Purchases ledger control account balance as at 30 June 2006	56713
Total of subsidiary (purchases) ledger accounts as at 30 June 2006	57093
Difference	380 ✓

c) What may have caused the difference you calculated in part b)?

Discounts have not been posted to the subsidiary accounts ✓

Task 2.10

On 28 June The Garden Warehouse received the following bank statement as at 24 June:

MIDDLE BANK plc
12 High Street, Droitwich WR15 7LW

To: The Garden Warehouse   **Account No** 867287234   24 June 2006

STATEMENT OF ACCOUNT

Date 2006	Details	Paid out £	Paid in £	Balance £
01 June	Balance b/f			15,619 C
06 June	Cheque 008301	2,650		12,969 C
08 June	Cheque 008302	1,986		10,983 C
10 June	Bank Giro			
	A Parker		550	11,533 C
10 June	Bank Giro Credit			
	L Westwood		6,140	17,673 C
13 June	Cheque 008303	8,432		9,241 C
15 June	Direct debit			
	Droitwich CC	100		9,141 C
20 June	Direct debit			
	Cranston Insurance	250		8,891 C
22 June	Overdraft facility fee	50		8,841 C
22 June	Bank charges	16		8,825 C
22 June	Bank interest		26	8,851 C

D = Debit C = Credit

The cash book as at 28 June 2006 is shown below.

Cash book

Date 2006	Details	Bank £	Date 2006	Cheque number	Details	Amount £
01 June	Balance b/f	15,619	01 June	008301	Portman Bros	2,650
10 June	A Parker	550	01 June	008302	Tether & Tie	1,986
10 June	L Westwood	6,140	06 June	008303	D Price	8,432
15 June	CCC Limited	1,260	06 June	008304	Mundon Ltd	1,407
22 June	B Williams	142	22 June	008305	Hacket Ltd	350
22 June	Interest	26	15 June	DD	Droitwich	100
			20 June	DD	Cranston	250
			22 June	DD	O/Draft fee	50
			22 June	DD	Charges	16
			24 June		Bal c/d	8496
		23737				23737

24 June Bal b/d 8496

a) Check the items on the bank statement against the items in the cash book.

b) Update the cash book as needed.

c) Total the cash book and clearly show the balance carried down at 28 June and brought down at 29 June.

   Note. You do not need to adjust the accounts in Section 1.

d) Using the information on page 366, complete the bank reconciliation statement as at 28 June.

Bank reconciliation statement as at 28 June 2006

		£
Balance as per bank statement		8851
Add: CCC Ltd	1260	
B Williams	142	
	1402	10253
Less: Murdon Ltd	1407	
Hackett Ltd	350	
	1757	8496
Balance as per the updated cash book		8496.

UNIT 3

PRACTICE EXAM 3

PREMIER SPACE

These tasks were set by the AAT in December 2005.

This Exam based Assessment is in two sections.

You have to show competence in both sections, so attempt and aim to complete EVERY task in BOTH sections.

> Section 1   Processing exercise
> **Complete all six tasks**
>
> Section 2   10 tasks and questions
> **Complete all tasks and questions**

You should spend about 90 minutes on each section.

Include all essential workings within your answers, where appropriate.

Sections 1 and 2 both relate to the business described below.

INTRODUCTION

John McVee is the owner of an advertising business,which trades as Premier Space.

You are employed by the business as a bookkeeper.

The business uses a manual accounting system.

Double entry takes place in the main (general) ledger. Individual accounts of debtors and creditors are kept in subsidiary ledgers as memorandum accounts.

Bank payments and receipts are recorded in the cash book, which is part of the double entry system.

Assume today's date is 30 November 2006 unless you are told otherwise.

SECTION 1 – PROCESSING EXERCISE

You should spend about 90 minutes on this section.

DATA

Balances at the start of the day on 30 November 2006

The following balances are relevant to you at the start of the day on 30 November 2006:

	£
Credit suppliers	
Brown Ltd	2,000
Clarke and Crown	9,000
PPP Ltd	9,652
Lees Ltd	1,632
Purchases	286,000
Purchases returns	2,915
Purchases ledger control	39,874
Motor vehicles	4,610
Stationery	180
Rent and rates	1,758
Motor tax	180
VAT (credit balance)	15,490

Task 1.1

Enter these opening balances into the following accounts given on pages 372 to 375.

Subsidiary (purchases) ledger
Brown Ltd
Clarke and Crown
PPP Ltd
Lees Ltd

Main (general) ledger
Purchases
Purchases returns
Purchases ledger control
Motor vehicles
Stationery
Rent and rates
Motor tax
VAT

DATA

Transactions

The following transactions all took place on 30 November 2006 and have been entered into the relevant books of prime entry as shown below. No entries have yet been made into the ledger system. The VAT rate is 17½%.

Purchases day book

Date 2006	Details	Invoice number	Total £	VAT £	Net £
30 Nov	Brown Ltd	P129	7,050	1,050	6,000
30 Nov	Clarke and Crown	1983	3,525	525	3,000
30 Nov	PPP Ltd	Z120	10,575	1,575	9,000
30 Nov	Lees Ltd	398	5,875	875	5,000
	Totals		27,025	4,025	23,000

Purchases returns day book

Date 2006	Details	Credit note no	Total £	VAT £	Net £
30 Nov	Brown Ltd	CN19	47	7	40
30 Nov	PPP Ltd	CZ28	188	28	160
	Totals		235	35	200

Cash book

Date 2006	Details	Bank £	Date 2006	Details	VAT £	Bank £
30 Nov	Balance b/f	15,021	30 Nov	Motor vehicle		6,000
			30 Nov	Stationery	14	94
			30 Nov	Rent and rates		200
			30 Nov	Motor tax		90
			30 Nov	Clarke & Crown (creditor)		1,500
			30 Nov	Balance c/d		7,137
	Total	15,021			14	15,021
1 Dec	Balance b/d	7,137				

Task 1.2

From the day books and cash book shown above, make the relevant entries into the accounts in the subsidiary (purchases) ledger and main (general) ledger.

Task 1.3

Balance the accounts showing clearly the balances carried down at 30 November (closing balance).

Task 1.4

Enter the balances brought down at 1 December (opening balance), showing clearly the date, details and amount.

SUBSIDIARY (PURCHASES) LEDGER

Brown Ltd

Date 2006	Details	Amount £	Date 2006	Details	Amount £
30 NOV	PRDB	47	30 NOV	O/Bal	2000
30 NOV	Bal c/d	9003	30 NOV	PDB	7050
		9050			9050
			1 Dec	O/Bal	9003

Clarke and Crown

Date 2006	Details	Amount £	Date 2006	Details	Amount £
30 NOV	cashbook	1500	30 NOV	O/Bal	9000
30 NOV	Bal c/d	11025	30 NOV	PDB	3525
		12525			12525
			1 Dec	O/Bal	11025

PPP Ltd

Date 2006	Details	Amount £	Date 2006	Details	Amount £
30 Nov	PRDB	188	30 Nov	O/Bal	9652
30 Nov	Bal c/d	20039	30 Nov	PDB	10575
		20227			20227
			1 Dec	O/Bal	20039

Lees Ltd

Date 2006	Details	Amount £	Date 2006	Details	Amount £
30 Nov	Bal c/d	7507	30 Nov	O/Bal	1632
			30 Nov	PDB	5875
		7507			7507
			1 Dec	O/Bal	7507

MAIN (GENERAL) LEDGER

Purchases

Date 2006	Details	Amount £	Date 2006	Details	Amount £
30 Nov	O/Bal	286000	30 Nov	Bal c/d	309000
30 Nov	PDB	23000			
		309000			309000
1 Dec	B/Bal	309000			

Purchases returns

Date 2006	Details	Amount £	Date 2006	Details	Amount £
30 Nov	Bal c/d	3115	30 Nov	O/Bal	2915
			30 Nov	PRDB	200
		3115			3115
			1 Dec	O/Bal	3115

Purchases ledger control

Date 2006	Details	Amount £	Date 2006	Details	Amount £
30 Nov	PRDB	235	30 Nov	O/Bal	39874
30 Nov	Cashbook	1500	30 Nov	PDB	27025
30 Nov	Bal c/d	65164			
		66899			66899
			1 Dec	O/Bal	65164

Motor vehicles

Date 2006	Details	Amount £	Date 2006	Details	Amount £
30 Nov	O/Bal	4610	30 Nov	Bal c/d	10610
30 Nov	Cash book	6000			
		10610			10610
1 Dec	O/Bal	10610			

Stationery

Date 2006	Details	Amount £	Date 2006	Details	Amount £
30 Nov	O/Bal	180	30 Nov	Bal c/d	260
30 Nov	Cashbook	80			
		260			260
1 Dec	O/Bal	260			

Rent and rates

Date 2006	Details	Amount £	Date 2006	Details	Amount £
30 Nov	O/Bal	1758	30 Nov	Bal c/d	1958
30 Nov	Cash book	200			
		1958			1958
1 Dec	O/Bal	1958			

Motor tax

Date 2006	Details	Amount £	Date 2006	Details	Amount £
30 Nov	O/Bal	180	30 Nov	Bal c/d	270
30 Nov	Cash book	90			
		270			270
1 Dec	O/Bal	270			

VAT

Date 2006	Details	Amount £	Date 2006	Details	Amount £
30 Nov	PDB	4025	30 Nov	O/Bal	15490
30 Nov	Cashbook	14	30 Nov	PRDB	35
30 Nov	Bal c/d	11486			
		15525			15525
			1 Dec	O/Bal	11486

Task 1.5

Transfer the balances that you calculated in Tasks 1.3 and 1.4, and the bank balance, to the trial balance on page 377.

DATA

Other balances to be transferred to the trial balance.

	£
Fixtures and fittings	12,000
Stock	20,000
Petty cash control	120
Sales ledgers control	106,842
Capital	40,367
Sales	400,500
Sales returns	300
Discounts allowed	220
Wages	45,400
Insurance	1,800
Travel	1,928
Printing	750
Telephone	312
Professional fees	1,105
Miscellaneous expenses	620

Task 1.6

Transfer the balances that you calculated in Task 1.3, and the bank balance, to the trial balance on page 377.

Task 1.6

Transfer the balances shown above to the trial balance, and total each column.

Trial balance as at 30 November 2006

	Debit £	Credit £
Motor vehicles	10610	
Fixtures and fittings	12000	
Stock	20000	
Bank	7137	
Petty cash control	120	
Sales ledger control	106842	
Purchases ledger control		65164
VAT		11486
Capital		40367
Sales		400500
Sales returns	300	
Purchases	309600	
Purchases returns		3115
Discounts allowed	220	
Stationery	260	
Wages	45400	
Insurance	1800	
Rent and rates	1958	
Motor tax	270	
Travel	1928	
Printing	750	
Telephone	312	
Professional fees	1105	
Miscellaneous expenses	620	
Total	520632	520632

SECTION 2 – TASKS AND QUESTIONS

You should spend about 90 minutes on this section.

Answer all of the following questions on pages 378 to 385.

Write your answers in the spaces provided.

Note. You do not need to adjust the accounts in Section 1 as part of any of the following tasks.

Task 2.1

You have been asked to calculate the amount of VAT owing to HM Revenue and Customs for the last VAT quarter. All sales and purchases are subject to VAT at 17.5%.

a)   Complete the VAT calcuation summary below, clearly showing your workings.

VAT calculation summary

Sales £180,000 **excluding** VAT	VAT on sales =	£ 31500
Purchases £111,625 **including** VAT	VAT on purchases =	£ 16625
	VAT payable =	£ 14875
Workings:	180000 × 1.17 = 211500 VAF = 31500 111625 × 40/47 = 95000 VAT = 16625.	

b)   What will be the accounting entries required to record payment of this amount by cheque?

Account name	Debit	Credit
VAT account	14875	
Bank.		14875

Task 2.2

John McVee is considering buying some new office equipment and has asked the bank for an overdarft facility.

a) What is an overdraft facility?

Where the bank account can be overdrawn upto a pre-agreed amount ✓

b) Would the overdraft show in the trial balance of Premier Space as a debit or a credit balance? Circle the correct answer.

Debit / (Credit) ✓

Task 2.3

Premier Space operates a petty cash system with a monthly imprest level of £120. In November £98 was spent from petty cash.

a) What is the amount required to restore the imprest level?

£98 ✓

b) Will the restored amount be recorded on the debit or credit side of the petty cash book? Circle the correct answer.

(Debit) / Credit ✓

Task 2.4

Insert the missing word in each of the following sentences.

a) A cheque from a debtor has been *rejected* *-dishonoured* by the debtor's bank as there were insufficient funds in the account.

b) A *debit* card is used to make a payment electronically from a current account.

c) A cheque is said to be out of date when it is more than *6* months old.

Task 2.5

The accounting records of Premier Space consist of three ledgers: the main (general) ledger, the subsidiary (purchase) ledger and the subsidiary (sales) ledger.

In which ledger would you find the following accounts?

a)   L Jones Ltd (a supplier) *subsidiary (purchase) ledger*

b)   Loan from bank *main ledger*

c)   Sales returns *main ledger + subsidiary (sales) ledger*

d)   Discounts received *main ledger + subsidiary (purchase) ledger*

Task 2.6

A customer, B & D Ltd, has recently ceased trading, owing Premier Space £10,000 plus VAT.

What will be the entries required in the main (general) ledger to write off the £10,000 plus VAT, in the books of Premier Space?

Account name	Debit £	Credit £
Bad debts	10000	
VAT ~~Sales ledger control~~	1750	
Sales ledger ~~control~~ control		11750

Task 2.7

John McVee is considering changing from a manual to a computerised accounting system. He has asked you what customer documents the computer could produce, other than sales invoices.

List THREE other accounting documents that could be produced by computer to be sent out to customers.

i)   Statements

ii)   receipts

iii)   credit notes

Task 2.8

Note. Remember that you do NOT need to adjust, or refer to, the accounts in Section 1 or the previous tasks in Section 2.

The following information has become available.

a)   An amount of £85 has been debited to the insurance account instead of the rent and rates account.

b)   Premier Space buy from and sell to Protem Ltd. A contra entry is to be made for £200.

c)   An amount of £60 has been credited to the suspense account.

The following two errors have now been discovered:

i)   a payment of £900 has been recorded as £1,000 in the heat and light account
ii)   an amount of £40 has been omitted from the dioscounts allowed account

Record the journal entries needed in the ain (general) ledger, to deal with the above. You do not need to give dates and narratives.

THE JOURNAL

Details	Dr £	Cr £
a) Rent + rates	85	
Insurance		85
Amount debited to insu-		
rance in error.		
b) Purchase ledger control	200	
Sales ledger control		200
contra-entry for Protem		
Ltd.		
c) Discounts allowed	40	
Suspense	60	
Heat + light		100

Task 2.9

This is a summary of transactions with customers during the month of November.

	£
Balance of debtors at 1 November 2006	98,600
Goods sold on credit	41,642
Money received from credit customers	33,100
Discounts allowed	200
Goods returned by credit customers	100

a) Prepare a sales ledger control account from the above details. Show clearly the balance carried down at 30 November (closing balance) and brought down at 1 December (opening balance).

Sales ledger control

Date 2006	Details	Amount £	Date 2006	Details	Amount £
30 NOV	O/Bal	98600	30 NOV	Money received	33100
30 NOV	Goods sold	41642	30 NOV	Discounts allowed	200
			30 NOV	Goods refund	100
			30 NOV	Bal c/d	106842
		140242			140242
1 Dec	O/Bal	106842			

The following closing debit balances were in the subsidiary (sales) ledger on 30 November.

	£	
Black and Company	29,383	Debit
Arrowsmith Ltd	14,005	Debit
Gayfield Solicitors	250	Credit
BLK Ltd	17,050	Debit
Rosso and Company	23,362	Debit
Broadbents Ltd	22,792	Debit

b) Reconcile the balances shown above with the sales ledger control account balance you have calculated in part a).

	£
Sales ledger control account balance as at 30 November 2006	106842
Total of subsidiary (sales) ledger accounts as at 30 November 2006	106342
Difference	500

c) What may have caused the difference you calculated in part b)?

The entries for Gayfield Solicitors have most likely been posted to the wrong side of the account

Task 2.10

On 23 November Premier Space received the following bank statement as at 18 November:

CENTRAL BANK plc
52 The Parade, Darton, DF10 9SW

To: Premier Space   **Account No** 38920483   18 November 2006

STATEMENT OF ACCOUNT

Date 2006	Details	Paid out £	Paid in £	Balance £
01 Nov	Balance b/f			20,199 C
01 Nov	Cheque 600020	199 OB		20,000 C
04 Nov	Cheque 600023	2,800		17,200 C
08 Nov	Cheque 600024	155		17,045 C
09 Nov	Cheque 600026	250		16,795 C
10 Nov	Bank Giro Credit B & B Ltd		4,800	21,595 C
16 Nov	Cheque 600028	89		21,506 C
16 Nov	Direct Debit MBC	370		21,136 C
17 Nov	Direct Debit Bray & Co	5,000		16,136 C
18 Nov	Bank charges	25		16,111 C
18 Nov	Bank Giro Credit Guest Ltd		1,825	17,936 C

D = Debit C = Credit

The cash book as at 23 November 2006 is shown below.

Cash book

Date 2006	Details	Amount £	Date 2006	Cheque number	Details	Amount £
01 Nov	Balanvce b/f	20,000	01 Nov	600023	Baker Ltd	2,800
10 Nov	Smith & Jones	1,100	04 Nov	600024	Brown & Co	155
14 Nov	ALO Associates	1,250	04 Nov	600025	Potters Ltd	75
10 NOV	B+B Ltd	4800	04 Nov	600026	Roberts & Co	250
18 NOV	Guest Ltd	825	10 Nov	600027	Baxter Ltd	118
			10 Nov	600028	Cox & Co	89
			16 Nov		MBC	370
			17 Nov	DD	Brayt Co	5000
			18 Nov	DD	Chuges	25
			23 Nov		Bal c/d	20093
		28975				28975

24 Nov Bal b/d   20093 ✓

a) Check the items on the bank statement against the items in the cash book.

b) Update the cash book as needed.

c) Total the cash book and clearly show the balance carried down at 23 November (closing balance) and brought down at 24 November (opening balance).

   Note. You do not need to adjust the accounts in Section 1.

d) Using the information on page 384, complete the bank reconciliation statement as at 23 November.

Bank reconciliation statement as at 23 November 2006

		£
Balance as per bank statement		17936
Add: Smith+Jones	1100	
ALO Associates	1250	
	2350	20286
Less: Potters Ltd	75	
Baxter Ltd	118	
	(193)	20093
Balance as per the updated cash book		20093

ANSWERS

answers to chapter 1:
INTRODUCTION TO BUSINESS

1   ■   ownership and management

–   a sole trader and the partners in a partnership are the owners of the business and usually the managers as well

–   the owners of a limited company are the shareholders whilst the directors manage the company, often the shareholders are not directors

■   liability for debts

–   a sole trader and the partners in a partnership are liable for all of the debts of the business

–   the shareholders in a company have limited liability and therefore cannot be asked for any more monies than the amount paid for their shares

■   methods of taking out profit

–   sole traders and partners in a partnership will take money out of the business when they wish, known as drawings

–   the shareholders in a limited company will be paid a dividend normally twice a year

2   **Cash or credit?**

i)	purchase of goods for £200 payable by cash in one weeks time	Credit
ii)	writing a cheque for the purchase of a new computer	Cash
iii)	sale of goods to a customer where the invoice accompanies the goods	Credit
iv)	receipt of a cheque from a customer for goods purchased today	Cash
v)	purchase of goods where payment is due in three week's time	Credit

3

		Capital or revenue?
i)	purchase of a new computer paid for by cheque	Capital
ii)	purchase of computer discs by cheque	Revenue
iii)	purchase of a new business car on credit	Capital
iv)	payment of road tax on a new business car	Revenue
v)	payment of rent for the business premises	Revenue

4   A profit and loss account shows the historic picture of how the business has performed during the last accounting period. It shows the income and the expenses for the business for the period.

A balance sheet is a list of the assets and liabilities of the business on the last day of the accounting period.

answers to chapter 2:
BUSINESS DOCUMENTS – SALES

1

	List price total	Trade discount	Net total
i)	£416.70	£62.51	£354.19
ii)	£105.82	£15.87	£89.95
iii)	£ 96.45	£14.47	£81.98
iv)	£263.46	£39.52	£223.94
v)	£350.90	£52.64	£298.26

2

	Net total	VAT	Invoice total
i)	£258.94	£45.31	£304.25
ii)	£316.78	£55.43	£372.21
iii)	£82.60	£14.45	£97.05
iv)	£152.99	£26.77	£179.76
v)	£451.28	£78.97	£530.25

3

	Net total	VAT	Invoice total
i)	£258.94	£43.95	£302.89
ii)	£316.78	£53.77	£370.55
iii)	£82.60	£14.02	£96.62
iv)	£152.99	£25.97	£178.96
v)	£451.28	£76.60	£527.88

4

INVOICE

Southfield Electrical
Industrial Estate
Benham DR6 2FF
Tel 0303379 Fax 0303152
VAT Reg 0264 2274 49

To: Whitehill Superstores
28, Whitehill Park
Benham

Invoice number: 57104

Date/tax point: 8 January 2006

Order number: 32431

Account number: SL 44

Quantity	Description	Stock code	Unit amount £	Total £
8	Hosch Tumble Dryer	6060	300.00	2,400.00
2	Zanpoint Dishwasher	4425	200.00	400.00
				2,800.00
	Trade Discount			280.00

Net total	2,520.00
VAT	423.36
Invoice total	2,943.36

Terms
4% Settlement discount for payment within 10 days, otherwise 30 days net

INVOICE

Southfield Electrical
Industrial Estate
Benham DR6 2FF
Tel 0303379 Fax 0303152
VAT Reg 0264 2274 49

To:
Quinn Ltd
High Rocks Estate
Drenchley DR22 6PQ

Invoice number: 57105

Date/tax point: 8 January 2006

Order number: 24316

Account number: SL 04

Quantity	Description	Stock code	Unit amount £	Total £
14	Temax Mixer	3170	35.00	490.00
6	Temax Mixer	3174	46.00	276.00
				766.00
	Trade Discount			114.90

Net total		651.10
VAT		113.94
Invoice total		765.04

Terms
Net 30 days
E & OE

INVOICE

Southfield Electrical
Industrial Estate
Benham DR6 2FF
Tel 0303379 Fax 0303152
VAT Reg 0264 2274 49

To: Harper and Sons
30/34 High Street
Benham DR6 4ST

Invoice number: 57106

Date/tax point: 8 January 2006

Order number: 04367

Account number: SL 26

Quantity	Description	Stock code	Unit amount £	Total £
3	Hosch Washing machine	6150	260.00	780.00
	Trade Discount			78.00
			Net total	702.00
			VAT	119.16
			Invoice total	821.16

Terms
3% settlement discount for payment within 14 days, otherwise 30 days net
E & OE

5 **Weller Enterprises** – the invoice number, tax point, order number and account number have not been entered

– the terms do not mention the settlement discount that should be offered

– the VAT calculation has not taken account of the settlement discount offered - the VAT should be £453.60

QQ Stores – either the wrong stock code or wrong unit price has been used for the food processor as the list price of the 3162 processor is £120.00

– the calculation of the total of the food processor is incorrect it should be £980 not £890

– the trade discount has been incorrectly calculated - a figure of 15% has been used rather than 12%

answers to chapter 3:
DOUBLE ENTRY BOOKKEEPING

1   i)   James paid £20,000 into a business bank account in order to start the business;

Effect 1	Effect 2
Increase in cash	Capital of business set up

ii)   He paid an initial rental of £2,500 by cheque for the shop that he is to trade from;

Effect 1	Effect 2
Decrease in cash	Rent expense incurred

iii)   He purchased a van by cheque for £7,400;

Effect 1	Effect 2
Decrease in cash	Increase in asset - the van

iv)   He purchases £6,000 of goods for resale on credit;

Effect 1	Effect 2
Increase in purchases	Increase in creditors

v)   He sold goods for £1,000 - the customer paid by cheque;

Effect 1	Effect 2
Increase in cash	Increase in sales

vi)   He sold goods on credit for £4,800;

Effect 1	Effect 2
Increase in debtors	Increase in sales

vii)   He paid shop assistant's wages by cheque totalling £2,100;

Effect 1	Effect 2
Decrease in cash	Wages expense incurred

viii) He made further sales on credit for £3,900;

    Effect 1   **Effect 2**

    Increase in debtors   Increase in sales

ix) He purchases a further £1,400 of goods for resale by cheque;

    Effect 1   **Effect 2**

    Decrease in cash   Increase in purchases

x) £3,700 was received from credit customers;

    Effect 1   **Effect 2**

    Increase in cash   Decrease in debtors

xi) He paid £3,300 to credit suppliers;

    Effect 1   **Effect 2**

    Decrease in cash   Decrease in creditors

xii) He withdrew £800 from the business for living expenses.

    Effect 1   **Effect 2**

    Decrease in cash   Increase in drawings

2

Bank account				
	£			£
Capital (i)	20,000	Rent (ii)		2,500
Sales (v)	1,000	Van (iii)		7,400
Debtors (x)	3,700	Wages (vii)		2,100
		Purchases (ix)		1,400
		Creditors (xi)		3,300
		Drawings (xii)		800

Capital account			
	£		£
		Bank (i)	20,000

Rent account

	£		£
Bank (ii)	2,500		

Van account

	£		£
Bank (iii)	7,400		

Purchases account

	£		£
Creditors (iv)	6,000		
Bank (ix)	1,400		

Creditors account

	£		£
Bank (xi)	3,300	Purchases (iv)	6,000

Sales account

	£		£
		Bank (v)	1,000
		Debtors (vi)	4,800
		Debtors (viii)	3,900

Debtors account

	£		£
Sales (vi)	4,800	Bank (x)	3,700
Sales (viii)	3,900		

Wages account

	£		£
Bank (vii)	2,100		

Drawings account

	£		£
Bank (xii)	800		

3

Bank account

	£		£
Capital (i)	20,000	Rent (ii)	2,500
Sales (v)	1,000	Van (iii)	7,400
Debtors (x)	3,700	Wages (vii)	2,100
		Purchases (ix)	1,400
		Creditors (xi)	3,300
		Drawings (xii)	800
		Balance c/d	7,200
	24,700		24,700
Balance b/d	7,200		

Capital account

	£		£
		Bank (i)	20,000

Rent account

	£		£
Bank (ii)	2,500		

Van account

	£		£
Bank (iii)	7,400		

Purchases account

	£		£
Creditors (iv)	6,000		
Bank (ix)	1,400	Balance c/d	7,400
	7,400		7,400
Balance b/d	7,400		

Creditors account

	£		£
Bank (xi)	3,300	Purchases (iv)	6,000
Balance c/d	2,700		
	6,000		6,000
		Balance b/d	2,700

Sales account

	£		£
		Bank (v)	1,000
		Debtors (vi)	4,800
Balance c/d	9,700	Debtors (viii)	3,900
	9,700		9,700
		Balance b/d	9,700

Debtors account

	£		£
Sales (vi)	4,800	Bank (x)	3,700
Sales (viii)	3,900	Balance c/d	5,000
	8,700		8,700
Balance b/d	5,000		

Wages account

	£		£
Bank (vii)	2,100		

Drawings account

	£		£
Bank (xii)	800		

Trial balance

	Debits £	Credits £
Bank	7,200	
Capital		20,000
Rent	2,500	
Van	7,400	
Purchases	7,400	
Creditors		2,700
Sales		9,700
Debtors	5,000	
Wages	2,100	
Drawings	800	
	32,400	32,400

4 In the main ledger accounts the total sales on credit and receipts from credit customers have been entered into the debtors account, sales account and bank account. However this gives no information about how much is owed by each individual debtor. Therefore in many accounting systems a separate ledger is kept known as a subsidiary ledger in which the details of each debtor are kept in the form of a separate ledger account for each debtor. This subsidiary ledger is known as the sales ledger and is kept as well as the total figures in the main ledger. The debtors account in the main ledger, in such a system, tends to be known as the debtors control account.

Similarly with purchases on credit as well as recording the total credit purchases and payments to suppliers in the main ledger a subsidiary ledger is set up for creditors. This will have a ledger account for each individual credit supplier showing each invoice received and each payment made. The subsidiary ledger is known as the purchases ledger and the creditors account in the main ledger is known as the creditors control account.

5 Main ledger

Sales ledger control account

	£		£
Sales – H Simms	1,800	Bank – H Simms	900
Sales – P Good	3,000	Bank – P Good	1,400
Sales – K Mitchell	910	Bank – K Mitchell	910
Sales – C Brown	2,990	Bank – C Brown	490

Sales account

	£		£
		Sales ledger control	1,800
		Sales ledger control	3,000
		Sales ledger control	910
		Sales ledger control	2,990

Subsidiary ledger

H Simms account

	£		£
Sales	1,800	Bank	900

P Good account

	£		£
Sales	3,000	Bank	1,400

K Mitchell account

	£		£
Sales	910	Bank	910

C Brown account

	£		£
Sales	2,990	Bank	490

answers to chapter 4:
ACCOUNTING FOR CREDIT SALES

1 a) and b)

Sales day book

Date	Customer	Invoice number	Gross £	VAT £	Net £
2 Jan	Hoppers Ltd	6237	642.72	95.72	547.00
5 Jan	Body Perfect	6238	728.50	108.50	620.00
6 Jan	Esporta Leisure	6239	406.55	60.55	346.00
9 Jan	Langans Beauty	6240	267.90	39.90	228.00
12 Jan	Body Perfect	6241	643.90	95.90	548.00
16 Jan	Superior Products	6242	259.67	38.67	221.00
18 Jan	Esporta Leisure	6243	488.80	72.80	416.00
23 Jan	Hoppers Ltd	6244	279.65	41.65	238.00
26 Jan	Langans Beauty	6245	321.95	47.95	274.00
			4,039.64	601.64	3,438.00

Cross-cast check:

	£
Net	3,438.00
VAT	601.64
Gross	4,039.64

c) **Main ledger**

Sales ledger control account

	£		£
31 Jan SDB	4,039.64		

VAT account

	£		£
		31 Jan SDB	601.64

Sales account

	£		£
		31 Jan SDB	3,438.00

d) **Subsidiary ledger**

Hoppers Ltd account

	£		£
2 Jan SDB – 6237	642.72		
23 Jan SDB – 6244	279.65		

Body Perfect account

	£		£
5 Jan SDB – 6238	728.50		
12 Jan SDB – 6241	643.90		

Esporta Leisure account

	£		£
6 Jan SDB – 6239	406.55		
18 Jan SDB – 6243	488.80		

Langans Beauty account

	£		£
9 Jan SDB – 6240	267.90		
26 Jan SDB – 6245	321.95		

Superior Products account

	£		£
16 Jan SDB – 6242	259.67		

2 a) and b)

Sales day book

Date	Customer	Invoice number	SL Ref	Gross £	VAT £	Net £
5 Jan	Rocks Garden Supp	08663	22	687.14	102.34	584.80
7 Jan	Eridge Nurseries	08664	07	420.35	62.60	357.75
7 Jan	Abergaven G C	08665	16	904.16	134.66	769.50
9 Jan	Rother Nurseries	08666	13	740.25	110.25	630.00
				2,751.90	409.85	2,342.05

Cross-cast check:

	£
Net	2,342.05
VAT	409.85
Gross	2,751.90

c) **Main ledger**

Sales ledger control account

	£		£
9 Jan SDB	2,751.90		

VAT account

	£		£
		9 Jan SDB	409.85

Sales account

	£		£
		9 Jan SDB	2,342.05

Subsidiary ledger

Eridge Nurseries			SL 07
	£		£
7 Jan SDB – 08664	420.35		

Rother Nurseries			SL 13
	£		£
9 Jan SDB – 08666	740.25		

Abergaven Garden Centre			SL 16
	£		£
7 Jan SDB – 08665	904.16		

Rocks Garden Supplies			SL 22
	£		£
5 Jan SDB – 08663	687.14		

3   a) and b)

Sales returns day book

Date	Customer	Credit note number	Gross £	VAT £	Net £
17 Jan	Hoppers Ltd	1476	80.72	12.02	68.70
23 Jan	Esporta Ltd	1477	104.84	15.61	89.23
30 Jan	Superior Products	1478	13.80	2.05	11.75
			199.36	29.68	169.68

Cross-cast check:

	£
Net	169.68
VAT	29.68
Gross	199.36

c) **Main ledger**

Sales ledger control account

	£		£
31 Jan SDB	4,039.64	31 Jan SRDB	199.36

VAT account

	£		£
31 Jan SRDB	29.68	31 Jan SDB	601.64

Sales returns account

	£		£
31 Jan SRDB	169.68		

Subsidiary ledger

Hoppers Ltd account

	£		£
2 Jan SDB – 6237	642.72	17 Jan SRDB – 1476	80.72
23 Jan SDB – 6244	279.65		

Body Perfect account

	£		£
5 Jan SDB – 6238	728.50		
12 Jan SDB – 6241	643.90		

Esporta Leisure account

	£		£
6 Jan SDB – 6239	406.55	23 Jan SRDB – 1477	104.84
18 Jan SDB – 6243	488.80		

Langans Beauty account

	£		£
9 Jan SDB – 6240	267.90		
26 Jan SDB – 6245	321.95		

Superior Products account

	£		£
16 Jan SDB – 6242	259.67	30 Jan SRDB – 1478	13.80

4 a) and b)

Sales day book

Date	Customer	Invoice number	SL Ref	Gross £	VAT £	Net £
5 Jan	Rocks Garden Supp	08663	22	687.14	102.34	584.80
7 Jan	Eridge Nurseries	08664	07	420.35	62.60	357.75
7 Jan	Abergaven G C	08665	16	904.16	134.66	769.50
9 Jan	Rother Nurseries	08666	13	740.25	110.25	630.00
9 Jan	Rocks Garden Supp	1468	22	(343.57)	(51.17)	(292.40)
				2,408.33	358.68	2,049.65

Cross-cast check:

	£
Net	2,049.65
VAT	358.68
Gross	2,408.33

c) Main ledger

Sales ledger control account

	£		£
9 Jan SDB	2,408.33		

VAT account

	£		£
		9 Jan SDB	358.68

Sales account

	£		£
		9 Jan SDB	2,049.65

Subsidiary ledger

Eridge Nurseries   SL 07

	£		£
7 Jan SDB – 08664	420.35		

Rother Nurseries   SL 13

	£		£
9 Jan SDB - 08666	740.25		

Abergaven Garden Centre   SL 16

	£		£
7 Jan SDB – 08665	904.16		

Rocks Garden Supplies   SL 22

	£		£
5 Jan SDB – 08663	687.14	9 Jan SDB – 1468	343.57

answers to chapter 5:
RECEIVING MONEY

1   Who is the drawee? –   First National Bank

      Who is the payee?   –   J Peterson

      Who is the drawer? –   F Ronald

2

	Comments
Cheque from B B Berry Ltd	Words and figures differ
Cheque from Q Q Stores	Unsigned
Cheque from Dagwell Enterprises	Payee name is incorrect – Electronics instead of Electrical
Cheque from Weller Enterprises	Dated 6 January 2005 instead of 2006 – this cheque is therefore out of date

3   The cheque is valid but it has a special crossing which means that it can only be paid into the Drenchley branch of the Northern Bank.

4

	Comment and action
Cheque from T M Spence	The cheque guarantee card expired on 31 December 2005. Therefore this cheque cannot be accepted
Cheque from B Withers	The cheque guarantee card is for a different account from the account that the cheque is being written on. The customer is asked for the guarantee card for this account and if it is not available the cheque cannot be accepted
Cheques from C J Long	A cheque guarantee card can only be used to guarantee one cheque for each transaction. As the transaction exceeds the guarantee card limit the cheques cannot be accepted

5

	Comments
Payment from Rocks Garden Supplies	The remittance advice has been wrongly added up - the total should be £864.75
Payment from Eridge Nurseries	The cheque is invalid as the words and figures differ
Payment from Abergaven Garden Centre	This is perfectly acceptable and valid
Payment from Rother Nurseries	On the remittance advice Rother Nurseries has recorded invoice 08674 as £114.78 rather than £214.78 - therefore the amount of the payment is wrong

answers to chapter 6:
RECORDING RECEIPTS

1

		VAT	Net amount
i)	£145.28	£21.63	£123.65
ii)	£68.90	£10.26	£58.64
iii)	£258.73	£38.53	£220.20
iv)	£35.82	£5.33	£30.49
v)	£125.60	£18.70	£106.90

2 Cash receipts book

Date	Details	Total	VAT	Cash sales	Sales ledger	Sundry	Discounts allowed
		£	£	£	£	£	£
23 Jan	Hoppers Ltd	545.14			545.14		16.86
23 Jan	Superior Products	116.70			116.70		
24 Jan	Cash sales	128.46	19.13	109.33			
24 Jan	Esporta Leisure	367.20			367.20		11.36
25 Jan	Cash sales	86.75	12.92	73.83			
27 Jan	Body Perfect	706.64			706.64		21.86
27 Jan	Cash sales	58.90	8.77	50.13			
27 Jan	Langans Beauty	267.90			267.90		
		2,277.69	40.82	233.29	2,003.58	–	50.08

Cross-cast check:

	£
Sales ledger	2,003.58
Cash sales	233.29
VAT	40.82
Total	2,277.69

3 Double entry for discounts allowed:

DR Discounts allowed account
CR Sales ledger control account

4 Main ledger

Sales ledger control account

	£		£
20 Jan SDB	3,438.04	20 Jan SRDB	80.72
		27 Jan CRB	2,003.58
		27 Jan CRB – discount	50.08

VAT account

	£		£
20 Jan SRDB	12.02	20 Jan SDB	512.04
		27 Jan CRB	40.82

Sales account

	£		£
		20 Jan SDB	2,926.00
		27 Jan CRB	233.29

Discount allowed account

	£		£
27 Jan CRB	50.08		

Subsidiary ledger

Hoppers Ltd account

	£		£
27 Jan SDB – 623/	642.72	17 Jan SRDB – 1476	80.72
		23 Jan CRB	545.14
		23 Jan CRB – discount	16.86

Body Perfect account

	£		£
5 Jan SDB – 6238	728.50	27 Jan CRB	706.64
12 Jan SDB – 6241	643.90	27 Jan CRB – discount	21.86

Esporta Leisure account

	£		£
6 Jan SDB – 6239	406.55	24 Jan CRB	367.20
18 Jan SDB - 6243	488.80	24 Jan CRB – discount	11.36

Langans Beauty account

	£		£
9 Jan SDB – 6240	267.90	27 Jan CRB	267.90

Superior Products account

	£		£
16 Jan SDB – 6242	259.67	23 Jan CRB	116.70

answers to chapter 7:
THE BANKING SYSTEM

1   **Day 1**

The Benham branch of First National sends the cheque to the First National clearing department in London.

Day 2

The First National clearing department sorts all of the cheques received by bank.

The cheque from Hoppers Ltd is sent to the Central Clearing House together with the other cheques received by First National which have been written on Central bank.

The cheque is then sent to the clearing department of Central bank which sends the cheque to the Drenchley branch of Central bank.

Day 3

Provided the cheque is valid and correct it is then paid out of Hoppers Ltd's account and credited to Natural Production's account.

2

Notes/coins	Number	Total
		£
£50	3	150.00
£20	17	340.00
£10	26	260.00
£5	35	175.00
£2	7	14.00
£1	18	18.00
50p	15	7.50
20p	36	7.20
10p	47	4.70
5p	23	1.15
2p	41	0.82
1p	63	0.63
		979.00

3 Calculation of cash to be paid into the bank:

Cash in till Notes/coins	Number	Float required	Paid into bank	Total £
£20	5	–	5	100.00
£10	12	2	10	100.00
£5	13	2	11	55.00
£2	1	–	1	2.00
£1	17	5	12	12.00
50p	9	2	7	3.50
20p	4	–	4	0.80
10p	15	10	5	0.50
5p	12	10	2	0.10
2p	16	10	6	0.12
1p	19	10	9	0.09
				274.11

Date 27 Jan 2006

	£	p
Cash	274	11
Cheques	2003	58
Total	2277	69

DE LA RUE 0514

Date 27 Jan 2006

Cashier's stamp and initials

Bank Giro Credit

first national

No. of cheques **5**

First National High Street, Benham

Account *Natural Productions*

Paid in by

Cash	£ 274	p 11

Cheques + **2003.58**

£ **2277.69**

Sorting code number	Account number	Transcode
20-26-33	40268134	66

Please do not write or mark below this line or fold this voucher

Please detail cash and cheques overleaf

000123   20−26−33   40268134   66

Cash	£	p	Cheques	£	p	
£50 notes	–	–		545	14	*Hoppers Ltd CD-16-86*
£20 notes	100	00		116	70	*Superior Products*
£10 notes	100	00		367	20	*Esporta Leisure CD-11-36*
£5 notes	55	00		706	64	*Body Perfect CD-21-26*
£2 coins	2	00		267	90	*Langans Beauty*
£1 coins	12	00				
Other coins	5	11				
Total	274	11	Total	2003	58	

answers to chapter 8:
COMMUNICATION WITH CUSTOMERS

1

Harold & partners

	£		£
1 May Opening balance	1,367.83	7 May CRB	635.78
5 May SDB – 27465	998.20	7 May CRB – discount	33.46
12 May SDB – 27499	478.92	15 May SRDB – CN0364	106.34
20 May SDB – 27524	258.29	30 May CRB	663.66
		30 May CRB – discount	34.93
		31 May Closing balance	1,629.07
	3,103.24		3,103.24

T N Designs

	£		£
1 May Opening balance	2,643.56	8 May CRB	1,473.28
11 May SDB – 27491	828.40	24 May SRDB CN0381	253.89
18 May SDB – 27513	1,083.65	31 May Closing balance	2,828.44
	4,555.61		4,555.61

2

Debtor	Comment
Sunshine Sales	Only just within the credit limit. The major part of the debt is outside the credit terms of 30 days - Sunshine might be encouraged to pay up within the 30 day credit limit. However if this has always been the pattern then there is probably no problem here.
Groom Nurseries	No problems.
Bridge DIY	Although all of the debt is current it is over the credit limit for the customer so no more credit should be given without either payment received or management approval.
Erfield Gardens	The debt is over 30 days old and there has been no current activity on the account. This is a worrying situation and should be followed up.
Lye Nursery	The majority of the debt is current with only a small amount over 30 days. The concern however is the £89.32 due over 90 days. This must be investigated as it may be a disputed amount that will never be paid.

3

SHORT FURNITURE
ERIDGE ESTATE
BENHAM DR6 4QQ
Tel 0303312 Fax 0303300
VAT Reg 0361 3282 60

5 February 2006

Our ref: EG11/01/01

Purchase ledger manager
Erfield Gardens
Erfield House
Erfield Park
Benham DR6 6GL

Dear Sir

Overdue account

It would appear from our records that an amount of £435.77 has been owing from you for more than 60 days. We have enclosed a current statement showing all amounts outstanding and would be grateful if this amount can be settled by return of post.

We look forward to receiving your cheque.

Yours faithfully

Jane Trump

Sales ledger manager

1

GOODS RECEIVED NOTE

Whitehill Superstores

Supplier:	Southfield Electrical

GRN number: 04884

Date: 14 Jan 2006

Order number: 32581

Quantity	Description	Stock code
3	Zanpoint Fridge Freezer	4075
1	Zanpoint Tumble Dryer	4120
1	Hosch Washing Machine	6140

Received by: Charlie Rubble

Checked by: Jim Davids

Comments: 1 Zanpoint tumble dryer returned due to scratching

2

DEBIT NOTE

WHITEHILL SUPERSTORES
28 Whitehill Park
Benham DR6 5LM
Tel 0303446 Fax 0303447

To: Southfield Electrical
Industrial Estate
Benham
DR6 2FF

Debit note number: 0613
Date/tax point: 15 Jan 2006
Order number 32581
Delivery note number: 34976

Quantity	Description	Stock code	Unit amount	Total
			£	£
1	Zanpoint Tumble Dryer	4120	190.00	190.00

Reason: ....

Authorised by: ....   **Date:** ....

3

Supplier	Comment
A1 Wood Supplies	The invoice is for 50m of Oak but the delivery note and GRN show that only 45m was delivered. A credit note should be requested by sending out a debit note for the remaining 5m.
Polish People	The invoice is for the cherry polish at a price of £3.16 per litre whereas the purchase order shows a price of £2.99 per litre. A debit note should be issued requesting a credit note for the difference.
Woodwards Woods	The invoice is for 110m of teak but the delivery note has been amended to show that only 95m were actually received and this is confirmed by the GRN. A debit note should be issued requesting a credit note for the difference.

answers to chapter 10:
ACCOUNTING FOR CREDIT PURCHASES

1 Purchases day book

Date	Supplier	Invoice number	Gross £	VAT £	Purchases £	Stationery £	Packaging £
4 Jan	P J Phillips	03576	419.47	62.47	357.00		
6 Jan	Trenter Ltd	18435	502.90	74.90	428.00		
9 Jan	W J Jones	43654	246.75	36.75		210.00	
12 Jan	P J Phillips	03598	485.27	72.27	413.00		
16 Jan	Packing	28423	314.90	46.90			268.00
19 Jan	Supp	18478	612.17	91.17	521.00		
20 Jan	Trenter Ltd	84335	733.20	109.20	624.00		
24 Jan	O & P Ltd	28444	192.70	28.70			164.00
28 Jan	Packing	18491	432.40	64.40	368.00		
31 Jan	Supp	43681	122.20	18.20		104.00	
			4,061.96	604.96	2,711.00	314.00	432.00

Cross-cast check:

	£
Packaging	432.00
Stationery	314.00
Materials	2,711.00
VAT	604.96
Gross	4,061.96

Main ledger

Purchases ledger control account

	£		£
		31 Jan PDB	4,061.96

VAT account

	£		£
31 Jan PDB	604.96		

Purchases account

	£		£
31 Jan PDB	2,711.00		

Stationery account

	£		£
31 Jan PDB	314.00		

Packaging account

	£		£
31 Jan PDB	432.00		

Subsidiary ledger

P J Phillips account

	£		£
		4 Jan PDB 03576	419.47
		12 Jan PDB 03598	485.27

Trenter Ltd account

	£		£
		6 Jan PDB 18435	502.90
		19 Jan PDB 18478	612.17
		28 Jan PDB 18491	432.40

W J Jones account

	£		£
		9 Jan PDB 43654	246.75
		31 Jan PDB 43681	122.20

Packing Supplies account

	£		£
		16 Jan PDB 28423	314.90
		24 Jan PDB 28444	192.70

O & P Ltd account

£		£
	20 Jan PDB 84335	733.20

2   Purchases day book

Date	Supplier	Invoice number	Ref	Gross £	VAT £	Wood Purchases £	Polish/varnish purchases £	Other purchases £	Sundry £
27 Jan	Ephraim Supp	09642	PL39	340.39	49.39	291.00			
27 Jan	Cavendish Woods	06932	PL14	828.45	123.38	705.07			
27 Jan	Calverley Bros	67671	PL03	171.08	25.48		145.60		
27 Jan	Culverden & Co	36004	PL23	67.24	9.84			57.40	
				1,407.16	208.09	996.07	145.60	57.40	

Cross-cast check:

	£
Other purchases	57.40
Polish purchases	145.60
Wood purchases	996.07
VAT	208.09
Gross	1,407.16

Main ledger

Purchases ledger control account

£		£
	27 Jan PDB	1,407.16

VAT account

	£		£
27 Jan PDB	208.09		

Wood purchases account

	£		£
27 Jan PDB	996.07		

Polish/varnish purchases account

	£		£
27 Jan PDB	145.60		

Other purchases account

	£		£
27 Jan PDB	57.40		

Subsidiary ledger

Calverley Bros account PL 03

	£		£
		27 Jan PDB 67671	171.08

Cavendish Woods account PL 14

	£		£
		27 Jan PDB 06932	828.45

Culverden & Co account PL 23

	£		£
		27 Jan PDB 36004	67.24

Ephraim Supplies account PL 39

	£		£
		27 Jan PDB 09642	340.39

3 **Purchases returns day book**

Date	Supplier	Credit note No	Gross £	VAT £	Purchases £	Stationery £	Packaging £
10 Jan	P J Phillips	04216	115.15	17.15	98.00		
16 Jan	W J Jones	CN0643	65.80	9.80		56.00	
30 Jan	O & P Ltd	CN1102	145.70	21.70	124.00		
			326.65	48.65	222.00	56.00	–

Cross-cast check:

	£
Stationery	56.00
Purchases	222.00
VAT	48.65
Gross	326.65

Main ledger

Purchases ledger control account

	£		£
31 Jan PRDB	326.65	31 Jan PDB	4,061.96

VAT account

	£		£
31 Jan PDB	604.96	31 Jan PRDB	48.65

Purchases account

	£		£
31 Jan PDB	2,711.00	31 Jan PRDB	222.00

Stationery account

	£		£
31 Jan PDB	314.00	31 Jan PRDB	56.00

Packaging account

	£		£
31 Jan PDB	432.00		

Subsidiary ledger

P J Phillips account

	£		£
10 Jan PRDB 04216	115.15	4 Jan PDB 03576	419.47
		12 Jan PDB 03598	485.27

W J Jones account

	£		£
16 Jan PRDB CN0643	65.80	9 Jan PDB 43654	246.75
		31 Jan PDB 43681	122.20

O & P Ltd account

	£		£
30 Jan PRDB CN1102	145.70	20 Jan PDB 84335	733.20

answers to chapter 11:
MAKING PAYMENTS TO CREDIT SUPPLIERS

1

Invoice No	Payment date	Amount £
i)	6 February	437.66
ii)	17 January	315.82 (Working 1)
iii)	7 February	733.89
iv)	7 February	198.45
v)	19 January	600.64 (Working 2)
vi)	23 January	540.01 (Working 3)

Working 1

	£
Net	275.68
Less: discount	6.89
	268.79
Add: VAT £268.79 x 17.5%	47.03
	315.82

Working 2

	£
Net	527.00
Less: discount	15.81
	511.19
Add: VAT £511.19 x 17.5%	89.45
	600.64

Working 3

	£
Net	473.80
Less: discount	14.21
	459.59
Add: VAT £459.59 x 17.5%	80.42
	540.01

2

Invoice		Payment date	Amount of cheque
5 Jan	Henson Press	27 Jan	£329.00
8 Jan	GH Publications	3 Feb	£133.95
12 Jan	Ely Instruments	27 Jan	£640.00 – (2% x 640) + 109.76 £736.96
15 Jan	Hams Instruments	10 Feb	£362.89
19 Jan	CD Supplies	10 Feb	£135.22
22 Jan	Jester Press	27 Jan	£127.60 – (3.5% x 127.60) + 21.54 £144.67
22 Jan	Henson Press	17 Feb	£299.62
23 Jan	CD Supplies	27 Jan	£65.40 – (3% x 65.40) + 11.10 £74.54
25 Jan	Jester Press	27 Jan	£39.50 – (3.5% x 39.50) + 6.67 £44.79
25 Jan	Buser Ltd	27 Jan	£245.00 – (5% x 245.00) + 40.73 £273.48

3

Cheque counterfoil:
Date 27 Jan 2006
Henson Press
£ 329.00
003014

Cheque:
first national
20 - 26 - 33
003014   40268134
26 Pinehurst Place, London EC1 2AA
Date 27 Jan 2006
Pay Henson Press
Three hundred and twenty nine pounds
only
£ 329.00
140600
Cheque No.   Sort Code   Account No.
003014   20 – 26 – 33   40268134
Account Payee
NEWMANS

Cheque 1

Date 27 Jan 2006

Ely Instruments

Discount - 12.80

£ 736.96

003015

---

first national

26 Pinehurst Place, London EC1 2AA

Pay Ely Instruments

Seven hundred and thirty six pounds and 96 pence

140600
Cheque No.   Sort Code   Account No.

003015   20 – 26 – 33   40268134

20 - 26 - 33
003015 40268134

Date 27 Jan 2006

£ 736.96

NEWMANS

Cheque 2

Date 27 Jan 2006

Jester Press

Discount - 4.47

£ 144.67

003016

---

first national

26 Pinehurst Place, London EC1 2AA

Pay Jester Press

One hundred and forty four pounds and 67 pence

140600
Cheque No.   Sort Code   Account No.

003016   20 – 26 – 33   40268134

20 - 26 - 33
003016 40268134

Date 27 Jan 2006

£ 144.67

NEWMANS

Cheque 3

Date 27 Jan 2006

CD Supplies

Discount - 1.96

£ 74.54

003017

---

first national

26 Pinehurst Place, London EC1 2AA

Pay CD Supplies

Seventy four pounds and 54 pence

140600
Cheque No.   Sort Code   Account No.

003017   20 – 26 – 33   40268134

20 - 26 - 33
003017 40268134

Date 27 Jan 2006

£ 74.54

NEWMANS

Cheque 003018

Date 27 Jan 2006

Jester Press

Discount - 1.38

£ 44.79

003018

first national

26 Pinehurst Place, London EC1 2AA

Date 27 Jan 2006

Pay Jester Press

Forty four pounds and

79 pence

Account Payee

£ 44.79

20 - 26 - 33
003018 40268134

140600
Cheque No.   Sort Code   Account No.

003018   20−26−33   40268134

NEWMANS

Cheque 003019

Date 27 Jan 2006

Buser Ltd

Discount - 12.25

£ 273.48

003019

first national

26 Pinehurst Place, London EC1 2AA

Date 27 Jan 2006

Pay Buser Ltd

Two hundred and seventy three pounds

and 48 pence

Account Payee

£ 273.48

20 - 26 - 33
003019 40268134

140600
Cheque No.   Sort Code   Account No.

003019   20−26−33   40268134

NEWMANS

4

REMITTANCE ADVICE

To: P.T. Supplies
28 Farm Court Road
Drenchley DR22 4XT

From: Edgehill Designs

Date: 7 February 2006

Reference	Amount £	Paid (✓)
20671	107.22	✓
20692	157.63	✓
CN 04722	(28.41)	✓
20718	120.48	
20734	106.18	
CN 04786	(16.15)	

CHEQUE ENCLOSED	£236.44

Central Bank

18 - 26 - 44
004167 23341892

Date 7 Feb 2006

P.7. Supplies

£ 236.44

44, Main Road, Walkinghan.

Date 7 Feb 2006

Pay P.7. Supplies

Two hundred and thirty six pounds

44 pence

£ 236.44

140600
Cheque No.   Sort Code   Account No.

Account Payee

004167   004167   18−26−44   23341892   **Edgehill Designs**

answers to chapter 12:
RECORDING PAYMENTS

1

		VAT	Net total
i)	£254.68	£37.93	£216.75
ii)	£159.28	£23.72	£135.56
iii)	£ 49.69	£7.40	£42.29
iv)	£104.28	£15.53	£ 88.75
v)	£ 62.48	£9.30	£53.18
vi)	£823.55	£122.65	£700.90

2

	DR	Purchases ledger control account	£367.48
	CR	Cash	£367.48
	DR	Purchases ledger control account	£12.50
	CR	Discount received	£12.50

3

Date	Details	Cheque No	Total £	VAT £	Cash purchases £	Purchases ledger £	Sundry £	Discounts received £
23 Jan	Trenter Ltd	002144	1,110.09			1,110.09		28.47
23 Jan	Cash purchase	002145	105.79	15.75	90.04			
24 Jan	W J Jones	002146	246.75			246.75		
24 Jan	P J Phillips	002147	789.60			789.60		
24 Jan	Cash purchase	002148	125.68	18.71	106.97			
25 Jan	Packing Supp	002149	305.45			305.45		8.04
26 Jan	O & P Ltd	002150	703.87			703.87		18.72
27 Jan	Cash purchase	002151	95.00	14.14	80.86			
			3,482.23	48.60	277.87	3,155.76	–	55.23

Cross-cast check:

	£
Purchases ledger	3,155.76
Cash purchases	277.87
VAT	48.60
Total	3,482.23

Main ledger

Purchases ledger control account

	£		£
31 Jan PRDB	326.65	31 Jan PDB	4,061.96
27 Jan CPB	3,155.76		
27 Jan CPB – discounts	55.23		

VAT account

	£		£
31 Jan PDB	604.96	31 Jan PRDB	48.65
27 Jan CPB	48.60		

Purchases account

	£		£
31 Jan PDB	2,711.00	31 Jan PRDB	222.00
27 Jan CPB	277.87		

Discounts received account

	£		£
		27 Jan CPB	55.23

Subsidiary ledger

P J Phillips account

	£		£
10 Jan PRDB 04216	115.15	4 Jan PDB 03576	419.47
24 Jan CPB 002147	789.60	12 Jan PDB 03598	485.27

W J Jones account

	£		£
16 Jan PRDB CN0643	65.80	9 Jan PDB 43654	246.75
24 Jan CPB 002146	246.75	31 Jan PDB 43681	122.20

O & P Ltd account

	£		£
30 Jan PRDB CN1102	145.70	20 Jan PDB 84335	733.20
27 Jan CPB 002150	703.87		
27 Jan CPB discount	18.72		

Trenter Ltd account

	£		£
23 Jan CPB 002144	1,110.09	6 Jan PDB 18435	502.90
23 Jan CPB discount	28.47	28 Jan PDB 18491	432.40

Packing Supplies account

	£		£
25 Jan CPB 002149	305.45	16 Jan PDB 28423	314.90
25 Jan CPB discount	8.04	24 Jan PDB 28444	192.70

4   Cash payments book

Date	Details	Cheque No	Total £	VAT £	Purchases ledger £	Rent & rates £	Sundry £	Discounts received £
27 Jan	Henson Press	003014	329.00		329.00			
27 Jan	Ely Instr	003015	736.96		736.96			12.80
27 Jan	Jester Press	003016	144.67		144.67			4.47
27 Jan	CD Supplies	003017	74.54		74.54			1.96
27 Jan	Jester Press	003018	44.79		44.79			1.38
27 Jan	Buser Ltd	003019	273.48		273.48			12.25
27 Jan	Rates	SO	255.00			255.00		
27 Jan	Rent	DD	500.00			500.00		
			2,358.44	–	1,603.44	755.00	–	32.86

Cross-cast check:

	£
Rent & rates	755.00
Purchases ledger	1,603.44
Total	2,358.44

Main ledger

Purchases ledger control account

	£		£
27 Jan CPB	1,603.44		
27 Jan CPB - discounts	32.86		

Rent and rates account

	£		£
27 Jan CPB	755.00		

Discounts received

	£		£
		27 Jan CPB	32.86

Subsidiary ledger

Buser Ltd

	£		£
27 Jan CPB 003019	273.48		
27 Jan CPB discount	12.25		

CD Supplies

	£		£
27 Jan CPB 003017	74.54		
27 Jan CPB discount	1.96		

Ely Instruments

	£		£
27 Jan CPB 003015	736.96		
27 Jan CPB discount	12.80		

Henson Press

	£		£
27 Jan CPB 003014	329.00		

Jester Press

	£		£
27 Jan CPB 003016	144.67		
27 Jan CPB – discount	4.47		
27 Jan CPB 003018	44.79		
27 Jan CPB – discount	1.38		

5   Dear Sir

We have just received an invoice from yourselves for goods with a list price of £1,000 plus VAT giving an invoice total of £1,175. However we note that your normal practice is to grant our company a 20% trade discount as we have been regular customers of your business for a number of years. If the discount is given then the invoice total will be £940 (£1,000 x 20%) x 1.175). Therefore, if our company is still to receive a trade discount from you, please send a credit note for £235 and we will then pay the revised total.

Yours faithfully

A N Accountant

1   £68.34

2

RECEIPTS			PAYMENTS								
Date	Details	Amount £	Date	Details	Voucher number	Total £	VAT £	Travel £	Post £	Stationery £	Office supplies £
16 Jan	Bal b/f	120.00	23 Jan	Coffee	0721	3.99					3.99
			23 Jan	Stamps	0722	24.00			24.00		
			24 Jan	Taxi fare	0723	10.50	1.56	8.94			
			24 Jan	Paper	0724	6.97	1.03			5.94	
			26 Jan	Train fare	0725	13.60		13.60			
			27 Jan	Disks	0726	10.98	1.63				9.35
						70.04	4.22	22.54	24.00	5.94	13.34

Cross-cast check:

	£
Office supplies	13.34
Stationery	5.94
Postage	24.00
Travel	22.54
VAT	4.22
	70.04

Main ledger

VAT account

		£			£
27 Jan PCB		4.22			

Travel expenses account

		£			£
27 Jan PCB		22.54			

Postage account

		£			£
27 Jan PCB		24.00			

Stationery account

		£			£
27 Jan PCB		5.94			

Office supplies account

		£			£
27 Jan PCB		13.34			

answers to chapter 14:
PAYROLL ACCOUNTING PROCEDURES

1 a)

	£
Gross wage	440.00
PAYE	(77.76)
Employee's NIC	(43.18)
Pension contribution (440.00 x 5%)	(22.00)
Net pay	297.06

b)   £297.06 will be paid to Peter
£22.00 will be paid into the pension fund on his behalf
£170.29 (£77.76 + £43.18 + £49.35) will be paid to HM Revenue and Customs

c)

Wages expense account

	£		£
Gross wages control	440.00		
Gross wages control - employer's NIC	49.35		

Gross wages control account

	£		£
CPB – net pay	297.06	Wages expense	440.00
PAYE/NIC – PAYE	77.76	Wages expense – employer's NIC	49.35
PAYE/NIC – employee's NIC	43.18		
Pension contribution	22.00		
PAYE/NIC – employer's NIC	49.35		

PAYE/NIC creditor account

	£		£
		Gross wages control	77.76
		Gross wages control	43.18
		Gross wages control	49.35

Pension contribution account

	£		£
		Gross wages control	22.00

2

Employee	Gross annual salary £	Taxable annual salary £	Income tax @ 10% £	Income tax @ 22% £	NIC £	Net annual salary £
J Short	30,000	25,700	150	5,324	2,640	21,886
P Nielson	24,000	19,700	150	4,004	2,040	17,806
J Taylor	17,400	13,100	150	2,552	1,380	13,318
M Harris	15,500	11,200	150	2,134	1,190	12,026
J Philpott	14,600	10,300	150	1,936	1,100	11,414

answers to chapter 15:
BANK RECONCILIATION STATEMENT

1   **Transaction**   **Debit or credit?**

i)   £470.47 paid into the bank   Credit

ii)   Standing order of £26.79   Debit

iii)   Cheque payment of £157.48   Debit

iv)   Interest earned on the bank balance   Credit

v)   BACS payment for wages   Debit

2   **Cash receipts book**

Date	Details	Total £	VAT £	Sales ledger £	Music sales £	Instrument sales £	CD sales £	Discounts allowed £	Sundry £
27 Jan	Tunfield DC	594.69 ✓		594.69					
27 Jan	Tunshire CO	468.29 ✓		468.29				14.48	
27 Jan	Cash sales	478.90 ✓			478.90				
27 Jan	Tunfield BB	1,059.72 ✓		1,059.72				33.03	
27 Jan	Cash sales	736.58 ✓	109.70			626.88			
27 Jan	Cash sales	251.67	37.48				214.19		
27 Jan	Bank interest*	3.68							3.68
27 Jan	Tunfield AOS*	108.51		108.51					
		3,702.04	147.18	2,231.21	478.90	626.88	214.19	47.51	3.68

* Note: these items and the ticks relate to later activities in this chapter.

3   **Unmatched item**   **Action to be taken**

     Bank Giro Credit Tunfield AOS   This must be checked to any supporting documentation such as any remittance advice from Tunfield AOS or the original invoice - when it has been checked the amount should be entered into the cash receipts book

     Standing order to British Elec   The standing order schedule should be checked to ensure that this is correct and it should then be entered into the cash payments book

     Bank interest received   This should be entered into the cash receipts book

     Cash sales from CDs   The £251.67 cash sales from CDs do not appear on the bank statement. This is a reconciling item

     Cheques   Cheque numbers 003016, 003018 and 003019 are all unpresented cheques and will appear in the bank reconciliation statement

4   **Cash payments book**

Date	Cheque no	Details	Total £	VAT £	Purchases ledger £	Rent & rates £	Sundry £	Discount received £
27 Jan	003014	Henson Press	329.00 ✓		329.00			
27 Jan	003015	Ely Instr	736.96 ✓		736.96			12.80
27 Jan	003016	Jester Press	144.67		144.67			4.47
27 Jan	003017	CD Supplies	74.54 ✓		74.54			1.96
27 Jan	003018	Jester Press	44.79		44.79			1.38
27 Jan	003019	Buser Ltd	273.48		273.48			12.25
27 Jan	SO	Rates	255.00 ✓			255.00		
27 Jan	DD	Rent	500.00 ✓			500.00		
27 Jan	SO	British Elec	212.00 ✓				212.00	
			2,570.44		1,603.44	755.00	212.00	32.86

	£
Opening balance	379.22
Receipts	3,702.04
Payments	(2,570.44)
Amended cash book balance	1,510.82

5   Bank reconciliation statement as at 27 January 2006

	£	£
Balance per bank statement		1,722.09
Outstanding lodgement		251.67
		1,973.76
Unpresented cheques		
003016	144.67	
003018	44.79	
003019	273.48	
		(462.94)
Amended cash book balance		1,510.82

answers to chapter 16:
CONTROL ACCOUNT RECONCILIATIONS

1

Sales ledger control account

	£		£
Opening balance	12,589	Opening balance	900
Credit sales	12,758	Sales returns	1,582
Returned cheque	722	Cash received	11,563
		Discounts allowed	738
		Bad debt written off	389
		Closing balance	10,897
	26,069		26,069

2

Purchases ledger control account

	£		£
Purchases returns	728	Opening balance	8,347
Cash paid	8,837	Credit purchases	9,203
Discounts received	382		
Closing balance	7,603		
	17,550		17,550

3

		Control account	List of balances	Both
i)	Invoice entered into the sales day book as £980 instead of £890			✓
ii)	Purchase day book overcast by £1,000	✓		
iii)	Discounts allowed of £20 not entered into the cash receipts book			✓
iv)	An invoice taken as £340 instead of £440 when being posted to the subsidiary ledger		✓	
v)	Incorrect balancing of a subsidiary ledger account		✓	
vi)	A purchase return not entered into the purchases returns day book			✓

4   Main ledger

Sales ledger control account

	£		£
Opening balance	5,000	Cash receipts (2,400 + 3,600	
Sales (2,000 + 2,700 +		+ 1,100 + 4,800)	11,900
1,100 + 3,800)	9,600	Balance c/d	2,700
	14,600		14,600
Balance b/d	2,700		

Subsidiary ledger

H Simms account

	£		£
Opening balance	900	Cash receipt	2,400
Sales	2,000	Balance c/d	500
	2,900		2,900
Balance b/d	500		

P Good account

	£		£
Opening balance	1,600	Cash receipt	3,600
Sales	2,700	Balance c/d	700
	4,300		4,300
Balance b/d	700		

K Mitchell account

	£		£
Sales	1,100	Cash receipt	1,100

C Brown account

	£		£
Opening balance	2,500	Cash receipt	4,800
Sales	3,800	Balance c/d	1,500
	6,300		6,300
Balance b/d	1,500		

Reconciliation of subsidiary ledger balances with control account balance

	£
H Simms	500
P Good	700
K Mitchell	–
C Brown	1,500
Sales ledger control account	2,700

5   Main ledger

Purchases ledger control account

	£		£
Cash payment		Opening balance	2,700
(1,700 + 3,200 + 3,000)	7,900	Purchases	
Balance c/d	2,100	(1,600 + 2,500 + 3,200)	7,300
	10,000		10,000
		Balance b/d	2,100

Subsidiary ledger

J Peters account

	£		£
Cash payment	1,700	Opening balance	300
Balance c/d	200	Purchases	1,600
	1,900		1,900
		Balance b/d	200

T Sands account

	£		£
Cash payment	3,200	Opening balance	1,700
Balance c/d	1,000	Purchases	2,500
	4,200		4,200
		Balance b/d	1,000

L Farmer account

	£		£
Cash payment	3,000	Opening balance	700
Balance c/d	900	Purchases	3,200
	3,900		3,900
		Balance b/d	900

Reconciliation of subsidiary ledger balances with control account balance

	£
J Peters	200
T Sands	1,000
L Farmer	900
Purchases ledger control account	2,100

6

Sales ledger control account

	£		£
Balance b/d	13,452	Sales returns	100
		Bad debt	200
		Balance c/d	13,152
	13,452		13,452
Balance b/d	13,152		

	£
Subsidiary ledger list of balances	12,614
Over statement of receipt	180
Balance omitted	358
Amended total	13,152

7

Purchases ledger control account

	£		£
Discounts received (2 × 256)	512	Balance b/d	26,677
Balance c/d	27,165	Purchases day book	1,000
	27,677		27,677
		Balance b/d	27,165

	£
Subsidiary list of balances	27,469
Discount omitted	(64)
Debit balance (2 x 120)	(240)
Amended total	27,165

8   a)

		Voucher Total
		£
0473		12.60
0474		15.00
0475		19.75
0476		9.65
0477		10.00
0478		13.84
0479		4.26
0480		16.40
		101.50

Petty cash value

		£
£10 note	1	10.00
£5 note	4	20.00
£2 coin	3	6.00
£1 coin	7	7.00
50p coin	5	2.50
20p coin	8	1.60
10p coin	9	0.90
5p coin	4	0.20
2p coin	11	0.22
1p coin	8	0.08
		48.50

	£
Voucher total	101.50
Petty cash	48.50
Imprest amount	150.00

b) The petty cash control account in the main ledger is given below:

Petty cash control

		£			£
1 Jan	Balance b/d	150.00	31 Jan	Petty cash book	101.50
			31 Jan	Balance c/d	48.50
		150.00			150.00
1 Feb	Balance b/d	48.50			

Cash in the petty cash box   £48.50

answers to chapter 17:
PREPARING AN INITIAL TRIAL BALANCE

1

Sales ledger control account

	£		£
Opening balance	16,387	Cash receipts	15,388
Sales	17,385	Discounts allowed	734
		Sales returns	1,297
		Bad debt written off	479
		Balance c/d	15,874
	33,772		33,772
Balance b/d	15,874		

Purchases ledger control account

	£		£
Cash payments	10,756	Opening balance	11,529
Discounts received	529	Purchases	10,487
Purchases returns	926		
Balance c/d	9,805		
	22,016		22,016
		Balance b/d	9,805

2

Ledger account	Balance £	Debit or credit?
Sales	625,679	Credit
Telephone	1,295	Debit
Debtors	52,375	Debit
Wages	104,288	Debit
Purchases returns	8,229	Credit
Bank overdraft	17,339	Credit
Purchases	372,589	Debit
Drawings	38,438	Debit
Sales returns	32,800	Debit
Motor car	14,700	Debit
Creditors	31,570	Credit

3

	£	£
Motor vehicles	76,800	
Office equipment	36,440	
Sales		285,600
Purchases	196,800	
Bank overdraft		2,016
Petty cash	36	
Capital		90,000
Sales returns	5,640	
Purchases returns		4,320
Sales ledger control	42,960	
Purchases ledger control		36,120
VAT (credit balance)		15,540
Stock	12,040	
Telephone	1,920	
Electricity	3,360	
Wages	74,520	
Loan		36,000
Discounts allowed	7,680	
Discounts received		4,680
Rent	14,400	
Bad debts written off	1,680	
	474,276	474,276

1

Sales ledger control account

	£		£
Balance b/d	1,683	Cash received	14,228
Sales	15,899	Discounts allowed	900
		Bad debts written off	245
		Sales returns	1,467
		Balance c/d	742
	17,582		17,582

VAT account

	£		£
VAT on purchases	1,985	Balance b/d	2,576
		VAT on sales	2,368
Balance c/d	3,074	VAT on purchases returns	115
	5,059		5,059

2

	£	£
Motor vehicle	18,720	
Stock	2,520	
Bank (debit balance)	10,956	
Sales ledger control	5,280	
Purchases ledger control		3,840
Capital		48,000
Sales		78,000
Sales returns	6,000	
Purchases	50,400	
Purchases returns		3,240
Bank charges	120	
Discounts allowed	1,080	
Discounts received		720
Wages and salaries	26,160	
Rent and rates	7,440	
Telephone	1,224	
Electricity	3,060	
Bad debts written off	840	
	133,800	133,800

3 a) Journal entries

			£	£
i)	Debit	Sales ledger control	1,000	
	Credit	Sales		1,000
ii)	Debit	Electricity (in the TB)	1,642	
	Credit	Suspense		1,642
iii)	Debit	Discounts allowed (2 x £865)	1,730	
	Credit	Suspense		1,730
iv)	Debit	Sales ledger control	360	
	Credit	Cash book		360
v)	Debit	Purchases ledger control	120	
	Credit	Discounts received		120

b)

Suspense account

	£		£
Opening balance	3,372	Electricity	1,642
		Discounts allowed	1,730
	3,372		3,372

answers to chapter 19:
BUSINESS TRANSACTIONS AND THE LAW

1   i)   Offeror - Short Furniture
Offeree - Rother Nurseries

   ii)   Yes, there has been both offer and acceptance

   iii)   No, the stipulation about delivery from Rother Nurseries is a counter-offer that invalidates the original offer. It is now up to Short Furniture to decide whether or not to accept this counter-offer from Rother Nurseries.

2   No. The advertisement is an invitation to treat not an offer. When the customers call Short Furniture, that is the offer which Short Furniture can either accept or reject.

3   No. Acceptance cannot be in the form of silence. Therefore the fact that the customer has not responded means that there is no acceptance.

4   Yes. Acceptance is valid from the date on which it was posted ie, Friday of this week.

5   a)   The Data Protection Act 1998 affords protection to individuals over personal data that is held about them. The Act applies to records held on computer as well as records held in a manual system. The Act covers personal data which is data relating to an individual and that individual is known as the data subject.

b)   The eight principles of good information handling from the Data Protection Act are that information should be:

- fairly and lawfully processed

- processed for limited purposes

- adequate, relevant and not excessive

- accurate

- not held for longer than is necessary

- processed in line with the data subject's rights

- kept securely

- not transferred to countries outside the European Union unless there is adequate protection in those countries

answers to chapter 20:
INTRODUCTION TO MANAGEMENT INFORMATION

1   **Management task**

                                                                     Management role

	Management task	Management role
i)	estimating advertising costs for the following year	Planning
ii)	comparing this month' sales income to that for last month	Control
iii)	considering the opening of an additional factory	Decision-making
iv)	determining how many production employees are required for the following quarter's production	Planning
v)	comparing the actual costs for the month to the budgeted costs	Control
vi)	considering taking out a loan to help fund expansion	Decision-making

2
- amount of production planned
- productivity of production employees
- normal weekly hours of production employees
- number of possible overtime hours
- basic pay rates and overtime rates
- levels of absenteeism amongst production employees

3
- production budget showing quantity of goods to be produced
- materials usage showing the quantity of material required for the production
- materials cost budget showing the cost of the materials that must be purchased

1		Cost	Classification
	i)	Advertising costs in local paper	Expense
	ii)	Cost of imported wood	Materials
	iii)	Store keeper's wages	Labour
	iv)	New blades for saws	Expense
	v)	Cost of wood polish	Materials
	vi)	Accountant's salary	Labour
	vii)	Repair cost of delivery van	Expense
	viii)	Insurance of the cutting machinery	Expense
	ix)	Telephone bill	Expense

2

STOCK RECORD CARD

Stock code 02611

Date	In	Out	Balance
2006			
1 Jan			35 metres
2 Jan		25 metres	10 metres
5 Jan	45 metres		55 metres

STOCK RECORD CARD

Stock code P4612

Date	In	Out	Balance
2006			
1 Jan			15 metres
4 Jan		10 metres	5 metres
5 Jan	20 metres		25 metres

3

Employee	Total hours	Basic hours	Basic pay £	Overtime hours	Overtime pay £	Total gross £	Employers' NIC £
P Knight	38	35	357.00	3	45.90	402.90	39.16
P Anil	35	35	252.00	-	-	252.00	19.84
K Chappatte	39	35	297.50	4	51.00	348.50	32.19
H Dennis	37	35	252.00	2	21.60	273.60	22.60
K Fisher	38	35	227.50	3	29.25	256.75	20.45
J Hunt	40	35	297.50	5	63.75	361.25	33.82
D Jones	38	35	227.50	3	29.25	256.75	20.45
L Minns	41	35	252.00	6	64.80	316.80	28.13
S Percy	35	35	252.00	-	-	252.00	19.84
I Roberts	39	35	297.50	4	51.00	348.50	32.19
G Tracy	35	35	227.50	-	-	227.50	16.70
F Albert	37	35	248.50	2	21.30	269.80	22.12
L Gill	35	35	248.50	-	-	248.50	19.39
J Norman	41	35	248.50	6	63.90	312.40	27.57
T Stevens	38	35	248.50	3	31.95	280.45	23.48

4

	Cutting cost centre £	Assembly cost centre £	Finishing cost centre £	Marketing cost centre £	Admin cost centre £	Total £
Gross wages	2,873.12	5,301.57	4,781.56	3,350.50	1,079.20	17,385.95
Employer's NIC	261.14	480.70	415.70	292.81	92.90	1,543.25
	3,134.26	5,782.27	5,197.26	3,643.31	1,172.10	18,929.20

Workings:

Cutting
- gross wages 1,327.55 + 1,008.00 + (1/3 x 1,612.70) = £2,873.12
- employer's NIC 123.94 + 84.00 + (1/3 x 159.59) = £261.14

Assembly
- gross wages 1,008.00 + 1,026.40 + 1,445.00 + 1,284.60 + (1/3 x 1,612.70)
  = £5,301.57
- employer's NIC 84.00 + 86.30 + 138.63 + 118.58 + (1/3 x 159.59)
  = £480.70

Finishing
- gross wages 1,026.85 + 1,004.35 + 1,267.20 + 945.60 + (1/3 x 1,612.70)
  = £4,781.56
- employer's NIC 86.36 + 83.54 + 116.40 + 76.20 + (1/3 x 159.59)
  = £415.70

Marketing
- gross wages 994.00 + 1,234.70 + 1,121.80 = £3,350.50
- employer's NIC 82.25 + 112.34 + 98.22 = £292.81

1

INVOICE

Short Furniture
Eridge Estate
Benham DR6 4QQ
Tel 0303312 Fax 0303300
VAT Reg 0361 3282 60

To: Rother Nurseries
Rother Road
Benham

Invoice number: 08721

Date/tax point: 27 Jan 2006

Order number: 06148

Account number: SL 13

Quantity	Description	Stock code	Unit amount £	Total £
2	Coffee Table	CT002	96.00	192.00 (114)
6	Dining Chair	DC416	73.00	438.00 (111)

Net total	630.00
VAT	110.25
Invoice total	740.25

Terms
Net 30 days
E & OE

INVOICE

Short Furniture
Eridge Estate
Benham DR6 4QQ
Tel 0303312 Fax 0303300
VAT Reg 0361 3282 60

To: Fenband Stores
Victory Shopping Centre
Benham

Invoice number: 08722

Date/tax point: 27 Jan 2006
Order number: 43217

Account number: SL 61

Quantity	Description	Stock code	Unit amount £	Total £
7	Sunlounger	SL642	210.00	1,470.00
1	Bench	B443	110.00	110.00
				1,580.00
	Trade Discount			158.00

£1,323 (123)

£99 (122)

Net total	1,422.00
VAT	248.85
Invoice total	1,670.85

Terms
Net 30 days
E & OE

INVOICE

A1 Wood Supplies
Heath Park
Drenchley DR22 6KL
VAT Reg 4621 3117 04

To: Short Furniture
Eridge Estate
Benham DR6 4QQ

Invoice number: 764989

Date/tax point: 27 Jan 2006

Order number: 46794

Account number: S04

Quantity	Description	Stock code	Unit amount £	Total £
30m	Stripped Pine	P4612	12.38	371.40
40m	Oak	02611	15.87	638.80
				1,010.20
	Trade Discount			151.53

Net total	858.67 (211)
VAT	145.75
Invoice total	1,004.42

Terms
3% settlement discount for payment within 14 days, otherwise net 30 days
E & OE

INVOICE

Polish People
23/25 Main Street
Wakeham DR17 4ZF
Tel 0421666 Fax 0421667
VAT Reg 3692 9417 63

To: Short Furniture
Eridge Estate
Benham DR6 4QQ

Invoice number: 06715

Date/tax point: 27 Jan 2006

Order number: 04701

Account number: SL 13

Quantity	Description	Stock code	Unit amount £	Total £
40 litres	Exterior Wood Polish – cherry	88631	3.16	126.40
20 litres	Exterior Wood Polish – teak	88413	2.83	56.60

Net total		183.00
VAT		32.02
Invoice total		215.02

(234)

Terms
Net 30 days
E & OE

INVOICE

J. T. Turner
Black Horse House
Budlett DR4 6TM
VAT Reg 3667 1294 61

To:
Short Furniture
Eridge Estate
Benham DR6 4QQ

Invoice number: 06302

Date/tax point: 27 Jan 2006

Order number: 04699

Account number: SL 43

Quantity	Description	Stock code	Unit amount £	Total £
12 dozen	4″ cross head 2/8 screws	S428	3.83	45.96
30 dozen	3″ cross head 1/8 screws	S318	1.94	58.20
				104.16
	Trade Discount			15.62

Net total	88.54	(222)
VAT	14.87	
Invoice total	103.14	

Terms
4% settlement discount for payment within 10 days, otherwise 30 days net
E & OE

Code	Balance £	Amendment £	Updated balance £
111	16,387.50	438.00	
112	13,265.95		
113	9,326.20		
114	3,587.90	192.00	
115	1,037.00		
121	10,385.30		
122	7,256.30	99.00	
123	3,646.70	1,323.00	
124	3,027.60		
125	926.40		
211	35,287.74	858.67	
215	-		
216	-		
222	1,285.47	88.54	
223	1,036.80		
225	-		
226	-		
234	8,385.40	183.00	
235	-		
236	-		
245	-		
246	-		
255	-		
256	-		

2

	Cutting cost centre £	Assembly cost centre £	Finishing cost centre £	Marketing cost centre £	Admin cost centre £	Total £
Gross wages	2,873.12	5,301.57	4,781.56	3,350.50	1,079.20	17,385.95
Employer's NIC	261.14	480.70	415.70	292.81	92.90	1,543.25
	3,134.26	5,782.27	5,197.26	3,643.31	1,172.10	18,929.20
	(215)	(225)	(235)	(245)	(255)	

Coding listing – Income and expenditure – January 2006

Code	Balance £	Amendment £	Updated balance £
111	16,387.50	438.00	
112	13,265.95		
113	9,326.20		
114	3,587.90	192.00	
115	1,037.00		
121	10,385.30		
122	7,256.30	99.00	
123	3,646.70	1,323.00	
124	3,027.60		
125	926.40		
211	35,287.74	858.67	
215	-	3,134.26	
216	-		
222	1,285.47	88.54	
223	1,036.80		
225	-	5,782.27	
226	-		
234	8,385.40	183.00	
235	-	5,197.26	
236	-		
245	-	3,643.31	
246	-		
255	-	1,172.10	
256	-		

3

Expense	Totals £	Cutting £	Assembly £	Finishing £	Marketing £	Admin £
Blades	340	340				
Electricity 60% x 1,560	1,560	936	156	156	156	156
Advertising	550				550	
Rent 2,100 x 1,000/7,000 2,100 x 3,000/7,000 2,100 x 2,000/7,000 2,100 x 500/7,000	2,100	300	900	600	150	150
Telephone 70% x 420 30% x 420	420				294	126
	4,970	1,576	1,056	756	1,150	432
		(216)	(226)	(236)	(246)	(256)

Coding listing – Income and expenditure – January 2006

Code	Balance £	Amendment £	Updated balance £
111	16,387.50	438.00	
112	13,265.95		
113	9,326.20		
114	3,587.90	192.00	
115	1,037.00		
121	10,385.30		
122	7,256.30	99.00	
123	3,646.70	1,323.00	
124	3,027.60		
125	926.40		
211	35,287.74	858.67	
215	-	3,134.26	
216	-	1,576.00	
222	1,285.47	88.54	
223	1,036.80		
225	-	5,782.27	
226	-	1,056.00	
234	8,385.40	183.00	
235	-	5,197.26	
236	-	756.00	
245	-	3,643.31	
246	-	1,150.00	
255	-	1,172.10	
256	-	432.00	

4 **Coding listing – Income and expenditure – January 2006**

Code	Balance £	Amendment £	Updated balance £
111	16,387.50	438.00	16,825.50
112	13,265.95		13,265.95
113	9,326.20		9,326.20
114	3,587.90	192.00	3,779.90
115	1,037.00		1,037.00
121	10,385.30		10,385.30
122	7,256.30	99.00	7,355.30
123	3,646.70	1,323.00	4,969.70
124	3,027.60		3,027.60
125	926.40		926.40
211	35,287.74	858.67	36,146.41
215	-	3,134.26	3,134.26
216	-	1,576.00	1,576.00
222	1,285.47	88.54	1,374.01
223	1,036.80		1,036.80
225	-	5,782.27	5,782.27
226	-	1,056.00	1,056.00
234	8,385.40	183.00	8,568.40
235	-	5,197.26	5,197.26
236	-	756.00	756.00
245	-	3,643.31	3,643.31
246	-	1,150.00	1,150.00
255	-	1,172.10	1,172.10
256	-	432.00	432.00

5

	A	B	C	D
1	Cost code	£	£	£
2	10101	28,375	6,234	=B2+C2
3	10102	13,773	3,154	=B3+C3
4	10103	12,356	1,783	=B4+C4
5	10201	17,365	4,254	=B5+C5
6	10202	21,925	4,793	=B6+C6
7	10203	11,482	2,015	=B7+C7

answers to chapter 23:
COMPARISON OF COSTS AND INCOME

1

MEMO

To: Phil McKenna

From: Jane Mitchell

Date: 5 January 2007

Subject: Comparison of December 2006 production costs

Comparison of December 2006 costs to November 2006 costs

	December 2006 £	November 2006 £
Raw materials	2,968	5,216
Labour	1,635	2,667
Expenses	372	552
Total	4,975	8,435

It should be noted that production in November is normally greater than that of December in order meet demand for the Christmas market. Therefore the December 2006 costs are also compared to the costs for the same month in the previous year.

Comparison of December 2006 costs to December 2005 costs

	December 2006 £	December 2005 £
Raw materials	2,968	2,537
Labour	1,635	1,367
Expenses	372	350
	4,975	4,254

2

```
NOTE

To:          Phil McKenna

From:        Jane Mitchell

Date:        5 January 2007


Comparison of December 2006 costs to budget
```

	December 2006 costs		
	Actual	Forecast	Variance
	£	£	£
Raw materials	2,968	2,700	268 adverse
Labour	1,635	1,650	15 favourable
Expenses	372	420	48 favourable

3

	Month		Year to date	
	Forecast	Actual	Forecast	Actual
	£	£	£	£
July	8,700	8,500	8,700	8,500
August	8,100	8,500	16,800	17,000
September	9,800	9,900	26,600	26,900
October	8,600	9,000	35,200	35,900
November	8,500	8,500	43,700	44,400
December	9,900	9,600	53,600	54,000
January	7,400	7,100	61,000	61,100
February	7,800		68,800	
March	8,400		77,200	
April	8,500		85,700	
May	8,700		94,400	
June	8,800		103,200	

4

	A	B	C	D	E
1	Cost	Actual	Budget	Variance	Percentage
2	Materials	41,705	45,000	C2–B2	=(D2/C2)*100
3	Labour	68,376	60,000	C3–B3	=(D3/C3)*100
4	Expenses	25,357	22,500	C4–B4	=(D4/C4)*100

PRACTICE SIMULATION – UNIT 1

TUBNEY TECHNOLOGY LTD

ANSWERS

Task 1

Note on sale not invoiced

The delivery to Kendrick & Co could not be invoiced because the order asks for 100 PA220 parts, but the delivery note states that 1,000 RL188 parts have been delivered.

Action to be taken

The matter should be passed to Mark Alberts for checking.

Task 1 (continued)

INVOICE

Tubney Technology Ltd
Oxford Business Park
Oxford OX2 8VN
Phone: 01865 444555
Fax 01865 444666

To: Ardington plc

Invoice number: 8950

VAT Registration: 305 034 97 63

Date/tax point: 18 September 2006

Subsidiary (sales) ledger code: 100

Description	Quantity	Price £	Total £
MM936	1,000	0.50	500.00
AD897	2,000	0.35	700.00

Goods total		1,200.00
Trade discount @ 0%		0.00
Sub-total		1,200.00
VAT @ 17.5%		202.65
Invoice total		1,402.65

Settlement discount: 3.5% for payment in 14 days
(to be deducted when computing VAT) — £42.00

Task 1 (continued)

INVOICE

Tubney Technology Ltd
Oxford Business Park
Oxford OX2 8VN
Phone: 01865 444555
Fax 01865 444666

To: Dreadnought PC Ltd

Invoice number: 8951

VAT Registration: 305 034 97 63

Date/tax point: 18 September 2006

Subsidiary (sales) ledger code: 200

Description	Quantity	Price £	Total £
HighDensity 10 cm SIM cards as per quotation	500	–	1,950.00

Goods total		1,950.00
Trade discount @ 5%		97.50
Sub-total		1,852.50
VAT @ 17.5%		312.84
Invoice total		2,165.34

Settlement discount: 3.5% for payment in 14 days
(to be deducted when computing VAT)

£64.83

Task 1 (continued)

INVOICE

Tubney Technology Ltd
Oxford Business Park
Oxford OX2 8VN
Phone: 01865 444555
Fax 01865 444666

To: Lineman plc

Invoice number: 8952

VAT Registration: 305 034 97 63

Date/tax point: 18 September 2006

Subsidiary (sales) ledger code: 400

Description	Quantity	Price £	Total £
AD897	3,000	0.35	1,050.00
DF014	200	3.60	720.00
GW208	150	12.80	1,920.00

Goods total	3,690.00
Trade discount @ 0%	0.00
Sub-total	3,690.00
VAT @ 17.5%	623.14
Invoice total	4,313.14

Settlement discount: 3.5% for payment in 14 days
(to be deducted when computing VAT)

£129.15

Task 1 (continued)

INVOICE

Tubney Technology Ltd
Oxford Business Park
Oxford OX2 8VN
Phone: 01865 444555
Fax 01865 444666

To: PrimeTime Mobiles

Invoice number: 8953

VAT Registration: 305 034 97 63

Date/tax point: 18 September 2006

Subsidiary (sales) ledger code: 500

Description	Quantity	Price £	Total £
PA220	250	5.55	1,387.50
MM936	3,000	0.50	1,500.00

Goods total	2,887.50
Trade discount @ 5%	144.37
Sub-total	2,743.13
VAT @ 17.5%	463.24
Invoice total	3,206.37

Settlement discount: 3.5% for payment in 14 days
(to be deducted when computing VAT) £96.00

Task 2

CREDIT NOTE

Tubney Technology Ltd
Oxford Business Park
Oxford OX2 8VN
Phone: 01865 444555
Fax 01865 444666

To: Kendrick & Co

Credit note number: 650

VAT Registration: 305 034 97 63

Date/tax point: 18 September 2006

Subsidiary (sales) ledger code: 300

Item	Quantity	Price £	Total £
GW208 (Original invoice 8900 dated 8 Sept)	20	12.80	256.00

Goods total	256.00
Trade discount @ 0%	0.00
Sub-total	256.00
VAT @ 17.5%	43.23
Credit note total	299.23

Task 2 (continued)

CREDIT NOTE

Tubney Technology Ltd
Oxford Business Park
Oxford OX2 8VN
Phone: 01865 444555
Fax 01865 444666

To: Rondar plc

Credit note number: 651

VAT Registration: 305 034 97 63

Date/tax point: 18 September 2006

Subsidiary (sales) ledger code: 600

Item	Quantity	Price £	Total £
PA220 (Original invoice 8905 dated 10 Sept)	15	5.55	83.25

Goods total	83.25
Trade discount @ 0%	0.00
Sub-total	83.25
VAT @ 17.5%	14.05
Credit note total	97.30

Tasks 3 and 4

Invoices and credit notes should be authorised before despatch by: the Accounts Manager, Samir Aleffi.

Day's total settlement discount on invoices (to be agreed to discount analysis): £331.98 (42.00 + 64.83 + 129.15 + 96.00)

SALES DAY BOOK   Folio: SDB 38

Date 2006	Customer	Subsidiary (sales) ledger code: DR	Invoice number	Total £	VAT £	Net £
18-Sept	Ardington plc	100	8950	1,402.65	202.65	1,200.00
18-Sept	Dreadnought PC Ltd	200	8951	2,165.34	312.84	1,852.50
18-Sept	Lineman plc	400	8952	4,313.14	623.14	3,690.00
18-Sept	PrimeTime Mobiles	500	8953	3,206.37	463.24	2,743.13
						830.00
	Totals			11,087.50	1,601.87	9,485.63
	Main ledger codes			DR 2000	CR 6000	CR 4000

Tasks 3 and 4 (continued)

SALES RETURNS DAY BOOK

Folio: SRDB 9

Date 2006	Customer	Subsidiary (sales) ledger code: DR	Credit note number	Total £	VAT £	Net £
18-Sept	Kendrick & Co	300	650	299.23	43.23	256.00
18-Sept	Rondar plc	600	651	97.30	14.05	83.25
	Totals			396.53	57.28	339.25
	Main ledger codes			CR 2000	DR 6000	DR 5000

Tasks 4 and 7

MAIN LEDGER

2000 SALES LEDGER CONTROL ACCOUNT

Date 2006	Details	Folio	Amount £	Date 2006	Details	Folio	Amount £
18-Sept	Invoices	SDB 38	11,087.50	18-Sept	Credit notes	SRDB 9	396.53
				18-Sept	Receipts	CB 38	11,413.67
				18-Sept	Discounts allowed	CB 38	29.66

3000 DISCOUNT ALLOWED

Date 2006	Details	Folio	Amount £	Date 2006	Details	Folio	Amount £
18-Sept	Receipts	CB 38	29.66				

4000 SALES

Date 2006	Details	Folio	Amount £	Date 2006	Details	Folio	Amount £
				18-Sept	Invoices	SDB 38	9,485.63

5000 SALES RETURNS

Date 2006	Details	Folio	Amount £	Date 2006	Details	Folio	Amount £
18-Sept	Credit notes	SRDB 9	339.25				

6000 VAT

Date 2006	Details	Folio	Amount £	Date 2006	Details	Folio	Amount £
18-Sept	Credit notes	SRDB 9	57.28	18-Sept	Invoices	SDB 38	1,601.87

SUBSIDIARY (SALES) LEDGER

100 ARDINGTON PLC

Date 2006	Details	Folio	Amount £	Date 2006	Details	Folio	Amount £
22-Aug	Inv 8790	SDB 34	512.84	18-Sept	Cheque	CB 38	512.84
18-Sept	Inv 8950	SDB 38	1,402.65				

200 DREADNOUGHT PC LTD

Date 2006	Details	Folio	Amount £	Date 2006	Details	Folio	Amount £
19-Aug	Inv 8750	SDB 34	9,993.88	18-Sept	Cheque	CB 38	9,939.88
18-Sept	Inv 8951	SDB 38	2,165.34	18-Sept	Balance c/d		2,219.34
			12,159.22				12,159.22

300 KENDRICK & CO

Date 2006	Details	Folio	Amount £	Date 2006	Details	Folio	Amount £
5-Sept	Inv 8890	SDB 36	420.79	18-Sept	CN 650	SRDB 9	299.23
8-Sept	Inv 8900	SDB 37	1,496.16	18-Sept	Cash	CB 38	408.19
				18-Sept	Disc allowed	CB 38	12.60
				18-Sept	Balance c/d		1,196.93
			1,916.95				1,916.95

400 LINEMAN PLC

Date 2006	Details	Folio	Amount £	Date 2006	Details	Folio	Amount £
8-Sept	Inv 8910	SDB 37	569.82	18-Sept	BACS	CB 38	552.76
18-Sept	Inv 8952	SDB 38	4,313.14	18-Sept	Disc allowed	CB 38	17.06

500 PRIMETIME MOBILES

Date 2006	Details	Folio	Amount £	Date 2006	Details	Folio	Amount £
20-Aug	Inv 8765	SDB 34	4,264.05				
18-Sept	Inv 8953	SDB 38	3,206.37				

600 RONDAR PLC

Date 2006	Details	Folio	Amount £	Date 2006	Details	Folio	Amount £
13-May	Inv 6535	SDB 7	169.86	18-Sept	Credit note 651	SRDB 9	97.30
2-Jun	Inv 6590	SDB 10	210.87				

700 SLOMAX & PARTNERS

Date 2006	Details	Folio	Amount £	Date 2006	Details	Folio	Amount £
18-Sept	Balance b/d		3,972.09				

Task 5

Notes

Wrongly completed cheque

The cheque from the PrimeTime Mobiles cannot be paid in as it has not been signed.

Action to be taken

Return the cheque to the customer, requesting a properly completed one.

Disagreement with supporting documentation

The Dreadnought PC Ltd cheque agrees with the customer's supporting documentation, its remittance advice, but both disagree with the subsidiary (sales) ledger account and the discount analysis. This is because there is a transposition error of £54 in the customer's records.

Action to be taken

Pay in the cheque, but write to the customer pointing out that it has made a recording error and so has underpaid by £54, so this amount is still outstanding.

Task 5 (continued)

Contents of envelope handed in by Mark Albert with Kendrick & Co receipt

Value	Number	Total value £
£50	4	200.00
£20	8	160.00
£10	4	40.00
£5	1	5.00
£2	0	0.00
£1	2	2.00
50p	1	0.50
20p	2	0.40
10p	1	0.10
5p	3	0.15
2p	1	0.02
1p	2	0.02
		408.19

Tasks 6 and 8

MAIN LEDGER

1000 CASH BOOK CB 38

RECEIPTS

Date 2006	Details	Ref	Receipt £	Discount allowed £	Customer account £	Subsidiary (sales) ledger code
18-Sept	Kendrick & Co	Cash	408.19	12.60	408.19	300
18-Sept	Ardington plc	Cheque	512.84	0.00	512.84	100
18-Sept	Dreadnought PC Ltd	Cheque	9,939.88	0.00	9,939.88	200
17-Sept	Paying in total		10,860.91			
	Lineman plc	BACS	552.76	17.06	552.76	400
			11,413.67	29.66	11,413.67	
Main ledger codes				DR 3000	CR 2000	
				CR 2000		

Task 7

			Please detail cheques and cash overleaf

Date 18-Sept-06   Paid in by_____

Cashier's stamp

Bank giro credit

Bank: Oxford Bank plc
        High Street, Oxford, Ox2 7DF

Account: Tubney Technology Ltd

Paid in by: Lynsey Jones

NOTES		£	p
NOTES	£50	200	00
	£20	160	00
	£10	40	00
	£5	5	00
	£2	0	00
	£1	2	00
	50p	0	50
	20p, 10p, 5p	0	65
	2p, 1p	0	04
TOTAL CASH		408	19
Cheques		10,452	72
£		10,860	91

NUMBER
OF
CHEQUES

2

Sort code	Account number
25 - 45 - 78	98746510

Details of cheques	Amount	
	£	p
Ardington plc	512	84
Dreadnought PC Ltd	9,939	88
Total cheques carried over	10,452	72

Task 9

STATEMENT

Tubney Technology Ltd
Oxford Business Park
Oxford OX2 8VN

To: Dreadnought PC Ltd

Date: 18 September 2006

Subsidiary (sales) ledger code: 200

Date 2006	Transaction reference	Debit £	Credit £	Amount
19-Aug	Invoice 8750	9,993.88		9,993.88
18-Sept	Invoice 8951	2,165.34		12,159.22
18-Sept	Cheque received		9,939.88	2,219.34

Balance outstanding   2,219.34

Our terms are strictly 30 days, with 3.5% cash settlement discount available for payment within 14 days.

Task 9 (continued)

STATEMENT

Tubney Technology Ltd
Oxford Business Park
Oxford OX2 8VN

To: Kendrick & Co

Date: 18 September 2006

Subsidiary (sales) ledger code: 200

Date 2006	Transaction reference	Debit £	Credit £	Amount
5-Sept	Invoice 8890	420.79		420.79
8-Sept	Invoice 8900	1,496.16		1,916.95
18-Sept	Credit note 650		299.23	1,617.72
18-Sept	Cash received – thank you		408.19	1,209.53
18-Sept	Settlement discount given		12.60	1,196.93

Balance outstanding   1,196.93

Our terms are strictly 30 days, with 3.5% cash settlement discount available for payment within 14 days.

Task 10

Tubney Technology Ltd

Oxford Business Park, Oxford OX2 8VN

Phone: 01865 444555 Fax: 01865 444666

Ms U Ogangwe
Slomax & Partners
Success House
200 Old Kent Road
London SE2 9CV

18 September 2006

Dear Ms Ogangwe

Account 700: Current balance £3,972.09

We recently received your cheque for £2,078.65. Unfortunately the date on this cheque is 16 September 2005, so we were unable to bank it as the bank would reject it as out of date. I enclose the cheque. Please either amend the date or reissue it with correct details.

I would remind you that this substantial portion of your total debt (£2,078.65) is now more than 60 days old, and the remainder (£1,893.44) is also overdue.

Our credit terms are strictly 30 days. Our policy is for any account that becomes more than 60 days old to be automatically put 'on stop' until it is settled in full. I regret to tell you, therefore, that we will not be able to make any further supplies to you until we receive a cheque in settlement of your entire debt.

Once we have received a cheque for £3,972.09 (please ensure that it is dated 2006) we can return to normal trading with you, and will be able to fulfil the order that we received from you yesterday.

If you wish to discuss this matter further, please give me a call.

Yours sincerely

Samir Aleffi

Accounts Manager

Task 10 (continued)

MEMO

To: Mark Alberts, Sales Manager

From: Lynsey Jones, Accounts Assistant

CC: Samir Aleffi, Accounts Manager

Subject: Kendrick & Co payment method

Date;   18 September 2006

As your floor limit is only £100, you would have to call the credit card company to gain authorisation for Mr Kendrick to use his corporate credit card in payment of the firm's debts. In itself this should not be a problem, but it is subject to the credit limit on his card account.

Kendrick & Co's current account balance with us is £1,196.93, so it may not be possible for Mr Kendrick to settle the full balance with the credit card because he may not have sufficient credit on his card. However, he could pay us with cash or a cheque for any excess amount.

If he comes in tomorrow to do this then he will be able to take advantage of the settlement discount that is still available on Invoice 8900.

Lynsey

Task 11

EMAIL

From:	lynsey.jones@tubneytech.co.uk
To:	samir.aleffi@tubneytech.co.uk
CC:	
Subject:	Computerisation
Date:	18 September 2006

Message:

Hi Samir

Moving to a fully computerised accounts system does not mean that we have to move to a different sequence of invoice and credit note numbers, or different ledger codes. The computer can be programmed to make use of the same codes as we use manually, so disruption here should not occur.

We currently input invoice, credit note and cash receipts details to the computer.

This then produces the discount analysis and aged debtors analysis. If we computerise further these details could also be used by the system to draw up computerised day books (for sales, sales returns and cash), to post the day books to the main and subsidiary (sales) ledgers, and to prepare customer statements from the subsidiary (sales) ledger.

PRACTICE SIMULATION – UNIT 2

AMICA PRINTING CO.

ANSWERS

Tasks 1 and 3

INVOICE

Abingdon Paper Ltd
Milton Park
Abingdon
Oxon OX13 9AS
T: 01235 412233
F: 01235 412866

To: Amica Printing Company
McLaren Trading Estate
Wantage OX2 8SD

VAT Registration: 9175698745

Date/tax point: 22 September 2006

Quantity	Description	Unit amount £	Total £
5	100gsm Nordic White A1	200.00	1,000.00
4	260gsm Polar Ice A1	350.00	1,400.00

Good total	2,400.00
Trade discount @ 5%	120.00
Sub-total	2,280.00
VAT @ 17.5%	399.00
Invoice total	2,679.00

Terms
30 days net
E & OE

Errors or discrepancies: None.

Action to be taken: Record in purchase day book.

Invoice number: 6070

Tasks 1 and 3 (continued)

INVOICE

Feltham Bindery Ltd
Chertsey Road Trading Estate
Feltham
Middlesex TW12 5AB
T/F: 020 8371 5987

To: Amica Printing Company
McLaren Trading Estate
Wantage OX12 8SD

VAT Registration: 6873687344

Date/tax point: 22 September 2006

Description	Rate £	Total £
Consultancy report on installation of fully automated binding line, as per Sam Fisher's purchase order of 2 September 2006, and conversation with Alex Cook	4,250.00	4,250.00
Sub-total		4,250.00
VAT @ 17.5%		743.75
Invoice total		4,993.75

Terms: strictly 30 days net

Terms
30 days net
E & OE

Errors or discrepancies:
Amount charged does not agree with Sam Fisher's purchase order of 2 September.

Action to be taken:
Do not record in purchase day book. Talk to Alex Cook.

Invoice number: N/A
INVOICE

Tasks 1 and 3 (continued)

INVOICE

HAMBURG PRINT PLATES LTD
Highgrove Road
Newbury
Berks NY9 4BW
T: 01461 476431
F: 01461 547643

To: Amica Printing Company
McLaren Trading Estate
Wantage OX12 8SD

VAT Registration: 0547351034

Date/tax point: 22 September 2006

Description	Quantity	Rate £	Total £
Myobi 600 press plates	70	37.50	2,625.00
Hamburg 1000 print press plates	50	35.00	1,750.00
Hamburg 250 print press plates	100	25.00	2,500.00
Goods total			6,875.00
Trade discount @ 0%			0.00
Sub-total			6,875.00
VAT @ 17.5%			1,167.03
Invoice total			8,042.03

Cash (settlement) discount: 3% for payment in 7 days
(to be deducted when computing VAT), otherwise 30 days net

£206.25

Errors or discrepancies: None.

Action to be taken: Record in purchase day book.

Invoice number: 6071

Tasks 1 and 3 (continued)

INVOICE

Ilsley Inks Ltd
Ridgeway House
East Ilsley
Berks NY7 1LS
T: 01461 7576764
F: 01461 343463

To: Amica Printing Company
McLaren Trading Estate
Wantage OX12 8SD

VAT Registration: 0917757537

Date/tax point: 22 September 2006

Description	Quantity	Rate £	Total £
Cyan ink for Hamburg colour presses	15	20.00	300.00
Yellow ink for Myobi presses	20	12.50	250.00

Goods total	550.00
Trade discount @ 5%	27.50
Sub-total	522.50
VAT @ 17.5%	91.43
Invoice total	613.93

Terms: strictly 30 days net

Errors or discrepancies:
No evidence that goods have been delivered.

Action to be taken:
Do not record in purchase day book. Check whether Edward Hunt has purchase orders, delivery notes or goods received notes.

Invoice number: N/A

Tasks 1 and 3 (continued)

INVOICE

Sidney Stationers Ltd
40 Market Square
Wantage OX12 5KK
T: 01235 497611
F: 01235 576643

To: Amica Printing Company
McLaren Trading Estate
Wantage OX12 8SD

VAT Registration: 1473658734

Date/tax point: 22 September 2006

Description	Quantity	Price £	Total £
A4 lever arch files - red	200	1.49	298.00

Goods total		298.00
Trade discount	0%	0.00
Sub-total		298.00
VAT	17.5%	52.15
Invoice total		350.15

Terms: strictly 30 days net

Errors or discrepancies: None.

Action to be taken: Record in purchase day book.

Invoice number: 6072

Tasks 1 and 3 (continued)

INVOICE

Wantage Engineering Ltd
Grove Road
Wantage OX12 7SM
T: 01235 232155
F: 01235 235698

To: Amica Printing Company
McLaren Trading Estate
Wantage OX12 8SD

VAT Registration: 4654646446

Date/tax point: 22 September 2006

Description	Quantity	Price £	Total £
Print press cleaning fluid	50 litres	6.50	250.00
Machine oil	10 litres	5.00	60.00
Press tester units	25	15.00	475.00

Goods total			785.00
Trade discount	10%		78.00
Sub-total			707.00
VAT	17.5%		123.72
Invoice total			830.72

Cash (settlement) discount: 1% for payment in 21 days
(to be deducted when computing VAT), otherwise 30 days net   £7.07

Errors or discrepancies:

- Cross-casts wrong.
- Trade discount correctly stated at 10% but the full 10% has not been deducted.
- Cash (settlement) discount correctly calculated at 1%, but not deducted when computing VAT.

Action to be taken: Do not record. Send letter to supplier.

Invoice number: N/A

Tasks 1 and 2

Notes for conversation with Alex Cook
Re: Invoice from Feltham Bindery Ltd dated 22 September 2006

The amount of £4,250 plus VAT charged for the consultancy report on installing a binding line does not agree with the purchase order, which is for £3,250 plus VAT. The supplier's invoice states that the amount was agreed with Alex. Can she please clarify?

Notes for conversation with Edward Hunt

Re: Invoice from Ilsley Inks Ltd dated 22 September 2006

No documentation can be found to suggest that these inks were either ordered or delivered. Does Edward have the purchase order, delivery note and goods received note?

Task 1

AMICA PRINTING COMPANY

McLaren Trading Estate, Wantage OX12 8SD

Tel: 01235 687465 Fax: 01235 687412

Wantage Engineering
Grove Road
Wantage OX12 7SM

23 September 2006

Dear Sir/Madam

I am returning your invoice to us dated 22 September. I am afraid that we cannot record it as it contains a number of errors:

- while the unit prices stated on the invoice are correct, they have been crosscast incorrectly.

- trade discount of 10% has been correctly stated, but the actual calculation is wrong.

- the cash (settlement) discount of 1% has not been deducted when computing VAT. This means that the amount of VAT is incorrect.

Please send us a corrected invoice as soon as possible.

Yours faithfully

Hei Lam Cheng

Accounts Assistant

Tasks 2 and 3

CREDIT NOTE

HAMBURG PRINT PLATES LTD
Highgrove Road
Newbury
Berks NY9 4BW
T: 01461 476431
F: 01461 547643

To: Amica Printing Company
McLaren Trading Estate
Wantage OX12 8SD

VAT Registration: 0547351034

Date/tax point: 22 September 2006

Description	Quantity	Rate £	Total £
Hamburg 500 print press plates	5	30.00	150.00
Reason for credit Damaged (part of batch delivered and invoiced 15 September 2006)			

Goods total	150.00
Trade discount @ 0%	0.00
Sub-total	150.00
VAT @ 17.5%	25.46
Credit note total	175.46

Reduce cash (settlement) discount on original invoice by £4.50

Errors or discrepancies: None.

Action to be taken: Record in purchase returns day book.

Credit note number: 277

Tasks 2 and 3 (continued)

CREDIT NOTE

Ilsley Inks Ltd
Ridgeway House
East Ilsley
Berks NY7 1LS
T: 01461 7576764
F: 01461 343463

To: Amica Printing Company
McLaren Trading Estate
Wantage OX12 8SD

VAT Registration: 0917757537

Date/tax point: 22 September 2006

Description		Unit price £	Total £
Special order pigment 291 – 10 kilos		25.00	250.00
Reason for credit Incorrect pigment delivered and invoiced 15 September 2006			

Goods total		250.00
Trade discount @ 5%		12.50
Sub-total		237.50
VAT @ 17.5%		41.56
Credit note total		279.06

Errors or discrepancies: None.

Action to be taken: Record in purchase returns day book.

Credit note number: 278

Tasks 3 and 4

PURCHASE DAY BOOK

Folio: PDB 30

Invoice number	Supplier	Subsidiary (purchases) ledger code	Date 2006	Total £	VAT £	Purchases £	Stationery £
6070	Abingdon Paper	1101	22 Sept	2,679.00	399.00	2,280.00	
6071	Hamburg Print	1103	22 Sept	8,042.03	1,167.03	6,875.00	
6072	Sidney Stationers	1105	22 Sept	350.15	52.15		298.00
	Total			11,071.18	1,618.18	9,155.00	298.00
Main ledger codes				110 CR	220 DR	190 DR	210 DR

Tasks 3 and 4 (continued)

PURCHASE RETURNS DAY BOOK

Folio: PRDB 6

Credit note number	Supplier	Subsidiary (purchases) ledger code	Date 2006	Total £	VAT £	Purchases Returns £	Stationery £
277	Hamburg Print	1103	22 Sept	175.46	25.46	150.00	
278	Ilsley Inks	1104	22 Sept	279.06	41.56	237.50	
	Total			454.52	67.02	387.50	
Main ledger codes				110 DR	220 CR	200 CR	

519

Tasks 4 and 10

MAIN LEDGER

090 ADMINISTRATION

Date 2006	Details	Folio	Amount £	Date 2006	Details	Folio	Amount £
23 Sept	Cash book payments	CB 30	300.00				

110 PURCHASE LEDGER CONTROL ACCOUNT

Date 2006	Details	Folio	Amount £	Date 2006	Details	Folio	Amount £
23 Sept	Purchase returns	PRDB6	454.52	22 Sept	Balance b/d		7,186.79
23 Sept	CB payments	CB 30	12,008.65	23 Sept	Purchases	PDB 30	11,071.18
23 Sept	Discount rec'd	CB 30	201.75				
23 Sept	Balance c/d		5,593.05				
			18,257.97				18,257.97
				24 Sept	Balance b/d		5,593.05

120 DISCOUNT RECEIVED

Date 2006	Details	Folio	Amount £	Date 2006	Details	Folio	Amount £
				23 Sept	Discount rec'd	CB 30	201.75

Tasks 4 and 10 (continued)

MAIN LEDGER

130 FACTORY WAGES CONTROL

Date 2006	Details	Folio	Amount £	Date 2006	Details	Folio	Amount £
23 Sept	Net pay	CB 30	4,569.53	23 Sept	Total gross pay	Payroll Month 6	6,198.21
23 Sept	PAYE	Payroll Month 6	1,206.65				
23 Sept	Total ee's NIC	Payroll Month 6	422.03				

140 FACTORY WAGES EXPENSE

Date 2006	Details	Folio	Amount £	Date 2006	Details	Folio	Amount £
23 Sept	Total gross pay	Payroll Month 6	6,198.21				
23 Sept	Total er's NIC	Payroll Month 6	426.55				

150 PAYE/NIC CREDITOR

Date 2006	Details	Folio	Amount £	Date 2006	Details	Folio	Amount £
				23 Sept	PAYE	Payroll Month 6	1,206.65
				23 Sept	Ee's NIC	Payroll Month 6	422.03
				23 Sept	Total er's NIC	Payroll Month 6	426.55

170 POSTAGE

Date 2006	Details	Folio	Amount £	Date 2006	Details	Folio	Amount £

Tasks 4 and 10 (continued)

MAIN LEDGER

180 PRODUCTION EXPENSES

Date 2006	Details	Folio	Amount £	Date 2006	Details	Folio	Amount £
23 Sept	Petty cash	PCB 30	13.61				

190 PURCHASES

Date 2006	Details	Folio	Amount £	Date 2006	Details	Folio	Amount £
23 Sept	Purchases	PDB 30	9,155.00				

200 PURCHASES RETURNS

Date 2006	Details	Folio	Amount £	Date 2006	Details	Folio	Amount £
				23 Sept	Purchase returns	PRDB 6	387.50

210 STATIONERY

Date 2006	Details	Folio	Amount £	Date 2006	Details	Folio	Amount £
23 Sept	Purchases	PDB 30	298.00				
23 Sept	Petty cash	PCB 30	5.95				

Tasks 4 and 10 (continued)

MAIN LEDGER

220 VAT

Date 2006	Details	Folio	Amount £	Date 2006	Details	Folio	Amount £
23 Sept	Purchases	PDB 30	1,618.18	23 Sept	Purchase returns	PRDB 6	67.02
23 Sept	Petty cash	PCB 30	3.42				

SUBSIDIARY (PURCHASES) LEDGER

1101 ABINGDON PAPER LTD

Date 2006	Details	Folio	Amount £	Date 2006	Details	Folio	Amount £
23 Sept	Payment	CB 30	2,511.56	2 Sept	Invoice 5980	PDB27	✓2,511.56
23 Sept	Balance c/d		2,679.00	23 Sept	Invoice 6070	PDB 30	2,679.00
			5,190.56				5,190.56
				24 Sept	Balance b/d		2,679.00

1102 FELTHAM BINDERY LTD

Date 2006	Details	Folio	Amount £	Date 2006	Details	Folio	Amount £

Tasks 4 and 10 (continued)

SUBSIDIARY (PURCHASES) LEDGER

1103 HAMBURG PRINT PLATES LTD

Date 2006	Details	Folio	Amount £	Date 2006	Details	Folio	Amount £
23 Sept	Credit note 277	PRDB 6	✓ 175.46	5 Sept	Invoice 5982	PDB27	✓1,017.68
23 Sept	Payment	CB 30	8,682.50	15 Sept	Invoice 6040	PDB 29	1,754.62
23 Sept	Discount rec'd	CB 30	201.75	23 Sept	Invoice 6071	PDB 30	✓8,042.03
23 Sept	Balance c/d		1,754.62				
			10,814.33				10,814.33
				24 Sept	Balance b/d		1,754.62

1104 ILSLEY INKS LTD

Date 2006	Details	Folio	Amount £	Date 2006	Details	Folio	Amount £
23 Sept	Credit note 278	PRDB 6	279.06	2 Sept	Invoice 5985	PDB27	✓ 726.46
23 Sept	Payment	CB 30	726.46	15 Sept	Invoice 6042	PDB29	1,088.34
23 Sept	Balance c/d		809.28				
			1,814.80				1,814.80
				24 Sept	Balance b/d		809.28

1105 SIDNEY STATIONERS LTD

Date 2006	Details	Folio	Amount £	Date 2006	Details	Folio	Amount £
29 Aug	Credit note 250	PRDB5	✓17.62	28 Aug	Invoice 5965	PDB26	✓105.75
23 Sept	Payment	CB 30	88.13	23 Sept	Invoice 6072	PDB 30	350.15
23 Sept	Balance c/d		350.15				
			455.90				455.90
				24 Sept	Balance b/d		350.15

1106 WANTAGE ENGINEERING LTD

Date 2006	Details	Folio	Amount £	Date 2006	Details	Folio	Amount £

Task 5

STATEMENT

Lam,
Please pay ticked item.
Alex Cook

Abingdon Paper Ltd
Milton Park
Abingdon
Oxon OX13 9AS
T: 01235 412233
F: 01235 412866

To: Amica Printing Company
McLaren Trading Estate
Wantage OX12 8SD

VAT Registration: 9175698745

Date: 22 September 2006

Date	Transaction reference	Amount
1 Sept 2006	Invoice	2,511.56 ✓
22 Sept 2006	Invoice	2,679.00

Balance outstanding | 5,190.56

Our terms are strictly net 30 days

Discount to be taken: None

Discrepancies: None

Action to be taken about discrepancies: None

Tasks 5 and 9

STATEMENT

HAMBURG PRINT PLATES LTD
Highgrove Road
Newbury
Berks NY9 4BW
T: 01461 476431
F:01461 547643

Lam,
Please pay ticked items.
Cash discount of £201.75 to be
taken on invoice and credit note
dated 22 September 06.
Alex Cook

To: Amica Printing Company
McLaren Trading Estate
Wantage OX12 8SD

VAT Registration: 0547351034

Date: 22 September 2006

Date	Transaction reference	Amount	
4 Sept 2006	Invoice	1,017.68	✓
15 Sept 2006	Invoice	1,754.62	
22 Sept 2006	Credit note	−175.46	✓
22 Sept 2006	Invoice	8,042.03	✓

Balance outstanding   10,638.87

3% settlement (cash) discount is available for payment within 7 days. Otherwise, our terms are strictly net 30 days.

Discount to be taken:
£206.25 on invoice dated 22-Sept-06 less £4.50 on credit note dated 22-Sept-06 = £201.75

Discrepancies:
None

Action to be taken about discrepancies:
None

Task 5 (continued)

STATEMENT

Lam,
Please pay ticked item.
Alex Cook

Ilsley Inks Ltd
Ridgeway House
East Ilsley
Berks NY7 1LS
T: 01461 7576764 F: 01461 343463

To: Amica Printing Company
McLaren Trading Estate
Wantage OX12 8SD

VAT Registration: 0917757537

Date: 22 September 2006

Date	Transaction reference	Amount
1 Sept 2006	Invoice	726.46 ✓
22 Sept 2006	Invoice	1,088.34
22 Sept 2006	Credit note	-279.06

Balance outstanding | 1,535.74

Our terms are strictly net 30 days

Discount to be taken: None

Discrepancies: None

Action to be taken about discrepancies: None

Task 5 (continued)

STATEMENT

Lam,
Please pay ticked items.
Alex Cook

Sidney Stationers Ltd
40 Market Square
Wantage
OX12 5KK
T: 01235 497611
F: 01235 576643

To: Amica Printing Company
McLaren Trading Estate
Wantage OX12 8SD

VAT Registration: 1473658734

Date: 22 September 2006

Date	Transaction reference	Amount
27 Aug 2006	Invoice	105.75 ✓
28 Aug 2006	Credit note	−17.62 ✓
22 Sept 2006	Invoice	350.15

Balance outstanding — 438.28

Our terms are strictly net 30 days

Discount to be taken: None

Discrepancies: None

Action to be taken about discrepancies: None

Task 5 (continued)

REMITTANCE ADVICE

Amica Printing Company, McLaren Trading Estate, Wantage OX12 8SD
Tel: 01235 687465 Fax: 01235 687412

Supplier: Abingdon Paper Ltd

Subsidiary (purchase) ledger code: 1101

Date	Transaction reference	Amount (£)
2 September	Invoice	2,511.56
23 September	Cheque enclosed	-2,511.56

REMITTANCE ADVICE

Amica Printing Company, McLaren Trading Estate, Wantage OX12 8SD
Tel: 01235 687465 Fax: 01235 687412

Supplier: Hamburg Print Plates Ltd

Subsidiary (purchase) ledger code: 1103

Date	Transaction reference	Amount (£)
5 September	Invoice	1,017.68
23 September	Credit note	-175.46
23 September	Invoice	8,042.03
23 September	Cash discount taken	-201.75
23 September	Payment by BACS	- 8,682.50

Task 5 (continued)

REMITTANCE ADVICE

Amica Printing Company, McLaren Trading Estate, Wantage OX12 8SD
Tel: 01235 687465 Fax: 01235 687412

Supplier: Ilsley Inks Ltd

Subsidiary (purchase) ledger code: 1104

Date	Transaction reference	Amount (£)
2 September	Invoice	726.46
23 September	Cheque enclosed	-726.46

REMITTANCE ADVICE

Amica Printing Company, McLaren Trading Estate, Wantage OX12 8SD
Tel: 01235 687465 Fax: 01235 687412

Supplier: Sidney Stationers Ltd

Subsidiary (purchase) ledger code: 1105

Date	Transaction reference	Amount (£)
28 August	Invoice	105.75
29 August	Credit note	-17.62
23 September	Cheque enclosed	-88.13

Task 5 (continued)

Notes re: non-payment of cheque requisition

There is insufficient supporting evidence for the payment of the cheque requisition to Yarnton Estates Ltd. The cheque requisition does not state the nature of the expenditure, so it cannot be analysed. It should therefore be discussed with Alex Cook, who should decide whether payment can be made.

Tasks 5, 6, 9 and 10

MAIN LEDGER

100 CASH BOOK PAYMENTS · CB 30

Date 2006	Details	Cheque number/ BACS ref	Folio	Payment £	Admin £	Factory wages £	Petty cash £	Suppliers £	Discount received £	Subsidiary (purchases) ledger codes
23 Sept	Hamburg Print Plates Ltd	BACS	Remittance	8,682.50				8,682.50	201.75	1103
23 Sept	Abingdon Paper Ltd	Chq 546611	Remittance	2,511.56				2,511.56		1101
23 Sept	Ilsley Inks Ltd	Chq 546612	Remittance	726.46				726.46		1104
23 Sept	Sidney Stationers Ltd	Chq 546613	Remittance	88.13				88.13		1105
23 Sept	Children in Need	Chq 546614	Cheque req	300.00	300.00					
23 Sept	P Allen	Chq 546615	Payroll	732.73		732.73				
23 Sept	U Gupta	Chq 546616	Payroll	175.87		175.87				
23 Sept	Permanent payroll	BACS	Payroll	3,660.93		3,660.93				
23 Sept	Petty cash	Chq 546617	PCB 30	242.10			242.10			
				17,120.28	300.00	4,569.53	242.10	12,008.65	201.75	
			DR		090	130		110	110	
			CR						120	

Main ledger codes

Task 6

Amica Printing Company				
Employee: Pippa Allen	Employee no: FT683			
NI No: KS 82 01 92 M	Tax code: 475L	Date: 26 Sept 2006	Tax period: Mth 6	
Pay for FOUR weeks ending: 19 September 2006	Hours	Rate (£)	AMOUNT (£)	YEAR TO DATE (£)
Basic hours	150.00	5.50	825.00	
Time and a half	12.00	8.25	99.00	
Bonus		15.00	15.00	
PAY FOR PERIOD			939.00	4,695.00
PAYE			149.93	899.57
Employees' NI (Employer's NI £61.28)			56.34	
TOTAL DEDUCTIONS			206.27	
NET PAY			732.73	

Errors or discrepancies: None

Action to be taken: None

Task 6 (continued)

Amica Printing Company				
Employee: Usha Gupta	Employee no: FT685			
NI No: WL 29 30 48 P	Tax code: BR	Date: 26 Sept 2006	Tax period: Mth 6	
Pay for FOUR weeks ending: 19 September 2006	Hours	Rate (£)	AMOUNT (£)	YEAR TO DATE (£)
Basic hours	37.50	5.50	206.25	
Time and a half	4.00	8.25	33.00	
Bonus		5.00	5.00	
PAY FOR PERIOD			244.25	244.25
PAYE			53.73	53.73
Employees' NI (Employer's NI £17.50)			14.65	
TOTAL DEDUCTIONS			68.38	
NET PAY			175.87	

Errors or discrepancies: None

Action to be taken: None

FACTORY PAYROLL MONTH 6						
Employee:	Employee number	Pay for period £	PAYE £	Employee's NIC £	Net pay £	Employer's NIC £
Temporary factory payroll total						
Permanent factory payroll total		5,014.96	1,002.99	351.04	3,660.93	347.77
Total factory payroll						
Main ledger codes DR		140	130	130		140
CR		130	150	150		150
Payment by BACS - permanent						
Payment by cheque						

Task 7

EMAIL

To:	henrylynch@amica.co.uk
From:	heilamcheng@amica.co.uk
CC:	
Subject:	Larry Haynes
Date:	23 September 2006

Message:

Hi Henry

Thank you for your email regarding Larry Haynes. Sorry, but I could not leave the copy payslips and other details on your desk this morning as the documents are connected to the payroll and hence are highly confidential. I am also concerned about the security aspects of leaving such information on a desk.

To help Mr Haynes, I suggest that he comes to the office here, with you if he chooses, so I can hand the information to him in person.

Task 8

PETTY CASH VOUCHER

Number: *099*   Date: 23 Sept 2006

Expenditure		Amount
Stationery	Net	5.95
	VAT	1.04
	Gross	6.99

Supporting documentation:
Receipt dated 22 September 2006

Paid to:
Edward Hunt 23 September 2006

PETTY CASH VOUCHER

Number: *100*   Date: 23 Sept 2006

Expenditure		Amount
Production expenses	Net	13.61
	VAT	2.38
	Gross	15.99

Supporting documentation:
Receipt dated 22 September 2006

Paid to:
Larry Haynes 23 September 2006

Notes on why not all receipts have been paid out

The Post Office receipt, at £50.90, exceeds the authorised limit for claims to be paid out of petty cash. Martha Collins should be advised to submit an expenses claim form.

Task 8 (continued)

		To be paid out 23-Sept-05			
PETTY CASH LISTING					
Notes and coin in box	In petty cash box as at 22-Sept-06 £	Voucher number: 099 £	Voucher number: 100 £	Voucher number: £	In petty cash box as at 23-Sept-06 £
£50	0.00				
£20	40.00				40.00
£10	20.00		10.00		10.00
£5	15.00	5.00	5.00		5.00
£2	0.00				
£1	3.00	1.00			2.00
50p	1.50	0.50	0.50		0.50
20p	1.00	0.40	0.40		0.20
10p	0.20				0.20
5p	0.10	0.05	0.05		
2p	0.04	0.04			
1p	0.04		0.04		
Total	80.88	6.99	15.99		57.90

Tasks 8 and 10

160 PETTY CASH BOOK · **PCB 30**

Date 2006	Details	Receipts £	Date 2006	Voucher number	Payments £	Postage £	Production expenses £	Stationery £	VAT £
22 Sept	Balance b/d	80.88	23 Sept	099	6.99				1.04
			23 Sept	100	15.99		13.61	5.95	2.38
				Totals	22.98		13.61	5.95	3.42
				Interim Balance c/d	57.90				
					80.88				
23 Sept	Balance b/d	80.88	23 Sept	End of day balance c/d	300.00				
23 Sept	Cash	57.90			300.00				
		242.10							
23 Sept		300.00							
Main ledger codes					DR		180	210	220
					CR				

Task 9

OXBANK PLC   13 - 45 - 65

Cornmarket, Oxford OX1 4FG

Date

Date 23 September 2006

Pay Abingdon Paper Ltd

Two thousand five hundred

and eleven pounds and 56p only

Account Payee

£

£ 2,511.56

Cheque No.	Sort Code	Account No.
546611	546611	13-45-65	63500671

Amica Printing Company

OXBANK PLC   13 - 45 - 65

Cornmarket, Oxford OX1 4FG

Date

Date 23 September 2006

Pay Ilsley Inks Ltd

Seven hundred and twenty six pounds and

46p only

Account Payee

£ 726.46

£

Cheque No.	Sort Code	Account No.
546612	546612	13-45-65	63500671

Amica Printing Company

OXBANK PLC   13 - 45 - 65

Cornmarket, Oxford OX1 4FG

Date

Date 23 September 2006

Pay Sidney Stationers Ltd

Eighty eight pounds and 13p only

Account Payee

£ 88.13

£

Cheque No.	Sort Code	Account No.
546613	546613	13-45-65	63500671

Amica Printing Company

Task 9 (continued)

OXBANK PLC

13 - 45 - 65

Cornmarket, Oxford OX1 4FG

Date _23 September 2006_

Date

Pay _Children in Need_

Three hundred pounds only

Account Payee

£ _300.00_

£

Cheque No.	Sort Code	Account No.

546614

546614   13-45-65   63500671

Amica Printing Company

OXBANK PLC

13 - 45 - 65

Cornmarket, Oxford OX1 4FG

Date _23 September 2006_

Date

Pay _Pippa Allen_

Seven hundred and thirty two

pounds and 73p only

Account Payee

£ _732.73_

£

Cheque No.	Sort Code	Account No.

546615

546615   13-45-65   63500671

Amica Printing Company

OXBANK PLC

13 - 45 - 65

Cornmarket, Oxford OX1 4FG

Date _23 September 2006_

Date

Pay _Usha Gupta_

One hundred and seventy five

pounds and 87p only

Account Payee

£ _175.87_

£

Cheque No.	Sort Code	Account No.

546616

546616   13-45-65   63500671

Amica Printing Company

Task 9 (continued)

OXBANK PLC

13 - 45 - 65

Date

£

Cornmarket, Oxford OX1 4FG

Date 23 September 2006

Pay Cash

Two hundred and forty two pounds

and 10p only

Account Payee

£ 242.10

Cheque No.	Sort Code	Account No.

546617

546617

13-45-65

63500671

Amica Printing Company

PRACTICE SIMULATION – UNIT 3

WEASLEY SUPPLIES LTD

ANSWERS

Tasks 1 and 2

CB 241

RECEIPTS					PAYMENTS			
Sales ledger £	Other receipts £	Total £	Date 2006	Details	Cheque number	Total £	Purchases ledger £	Other payments £
4,486.85			1 June	Balance b/f				
4,776.15		4,776.15	5 June	Metrix plc				
			6 June	Horsfall Limited	331175	1,456.91	1,456.91	
7,715.96		7,715.96	12 June	Plympton Limited				
			16 June	Stainton and Co	331176	9,912.75	9,912.75	
			16 June	Inland Revenue	331177	3,901.25		3,901.25
15,901.22		15,901.22	19 June	Maidstone plc				
			23 June	Earley and Partners	331178	3,341.20	3,341.20	
2,816.55		2,816.55	23 June	Stenshaw Limited				
			25 June	Pickard Newton	331179	3,216.99	3,216.99	
2,451.88		2,451.88	29 June	Fitzroy Limited				
1926.34		1,926.34	30 June	Dove Ambleside				
				Medwith BC	SO	600.00		600.00
				Safeguard Insurance	SO	310.00		310.00
				Finance Leasing plc	SO	425.00		425.00
				Purchasecard plc	DD	2,341.89		2,341.89
				Salaries	CT	8,215.50		8,215.50
				Bank charges	CHGS	107.33		107.33
			30 June	Balance c/d		6,246.13		
35,588.10		40,074.95				40,074.95	17,927.85	15,900.97
		6,246.13	1 July	Balance b/d				

Task 3

Bank reconciliation statement at 30 June 2006

	£	£
Balance per bank statement at 30 June		7,750.99
Add: outstanding lodgement		1,926.34
		9,677.33
Deduct: unpresented cheque 331178	3,341.20	
discrepancy on cheque 331179	90.00	
		3,431.20
Balance per cash book at 30 June		6,246.13

Note for assessors: Some candidates may spot the discrepancy on cheque 331179 while performing Tasks 1 and 2, and may alter the cash book to reflect this. Such candidates will not have the £90.00 discrepancy as an item in their bank reconciliation for Task 3 and will not need the first journal in Task 4. This alternative approach is acceptable and should not be penalised.

Task 4

JOURNAL

Date 2006	Account names and narratives	Debit £	Credit £
30 June	Cash at bank	90.00	
	Purchases ledger control account		90.00
	Being correction of mistake in recording cheque 331179		
30 June	Bad debts	1,233.75	
	Sales ledger control account		1,233.75
	Being write-off of balanced owed by Driftway Limited		

Task 5

MAIN (GENERAL) LEDGER

Account Sales ledger control account

Debit				Credit	
Date 2006	Details	Amount £	Date 2006	Details	Amount £
1 June	Balance b/f	30,914.66	30 June	Bank	35,588.10
30 June	Invoices in month	32,617.80	30 June	Journal: bad debt	1,233.75
			30 June	Balance c/d	26,710.61
		63,532.46			63,532.46
1 July	Balance b/d	26,710.61			

Account Purchases ledger control account

Debit				Credit	
Date 2006	Details	Amount £	Date 2006	Details	Amount £
30 June	Bank	17,927.85	1 June	Balance b/f	19,334.02
30 June	Balance c/d	21,697.62	30 June	Invoices in month	20,201.45
			30 June	Journal: cheque misstated	90.00
		39,625.47			39,625.47
			1 July	Balance b/d	21,697.62

Task 6

Creditors reconciliation at 30 June 2006

	£
Total of balances in subsidiary (purchases) ledger	21,607.62
Balance on control account	21,697.62
Discrepancy	90.00

Explanation of discrepancy

It seems likely that the journal relating to cheque number 331179 has not yet been actioned in the subsidiary ledger. Once this is adjusted for the balance owing to Pickard Newton becomes zero, and the total balances amount to £21,697.62, agreeing with the balance on the control account.

Task 7

PETTY CASH BOOK   PCB 52

Receipts £	Date 2006	Details	Voucher number	Total £	VAT £	Postage £	Stationery £	Other expenses £
200.00	1 June	Balance b/f						
	5 June	Postage	358	4.26		4.26		
	9 June	Stationery	359	12.87	1.91		10.96	
	12 June	Tea, coffee etc	360	7.02				7.02
	16 June	Postage	361	3.12		3.12		
	18 June	Stationery	362	13.51	2.01		11.50	
	23 June	Stationery	363	6.58	0.98		5.60	
	26 June	Stationery	364	5.73	0.85		4.88	
	27 June	Postage	365	5.90		5.90		
	30 June	Tea, coffee etc	366	6.50				6.50
		Totals		65.49	5.75	13.28	32.94	13.52
	30 June	Balance c/d		134.51				
200.00				200.00				

549

Task 7 (continued)

Notes and coin in the petty cash tin, 30 June 2006

	Number	Total value £
£20	4	80.00
£10	3	30.00
£5	2	10.00
£1	8	8.00
50p	8	4.00
20p	8	1.60
10p	8	0.80
5p	1	0.05
2p	2	0.04
1p	2	0.02
		134.51

Petty cash reconciliation

Date: 14 July 2006

	£
Balance per petty cash book	134.51
Total of notes and coin	134.51
Discrepancy (if any)	NIL

Explanation of difference (if any)

N/A

Task 8

Trial balance at 30 June 2006

DESCRIPTION	Ledger balances	
	Dr £	Cr £
Administration expenses	3,276.88	
Bad debts	2,010.76	
Bank	6,336.13	
Business rates	1,800.00	
Capital		46,745.76
Fixed assets	25,219.05	
HMRC		4,003.51
Insurance	930.00	
Leasing costs	1,275.00	
Petty cash	134.51	
Purchases	64,016.83	
Purchases ledger control		21,697.62
Purchases returns		1,125.31
Salaries expense	35,211.81	
Sales		96,558.43
Sales and distribution expenses	2,006.81	
Sales ledger control	26,710.61	
Sales returns	1,327.44	
Stock	7,270.00	
VAT control		3,995.20
Suspense account		3,400.00
Totals	177,525.83	177,525.83

Tasks 9 and 10

Date 2006	Account names and narrative	Dr £	Cr £
30 June	Suspense account Purchases returns Being purchases returns of £200 wrongly debited to the returns account	400.00	400.00
	Suspense account Capital Being cash receipt previously not posted	3,000.00	3,000.00

Account Suspense

Debit			Credit		
Date 2006	Details	Amount £	Date 2006	Details	Amount £
30 June	Jnl: purchase returns Jnl: capital introduced	400.00 3,000.00	30 June	To balance TB	3,400.00
		3,400.00			3,400.00

Task 11

EMAIL

From: Kim Wendell

To: Ari Pottle

CC:

Subject: Re: Correcting the trial balance

Date: 7 July 2006

Message:

Hi Ari

I've made the changes you mentioned in your email. The effects are as follows.

First, the purchases returns figure (a credit balance on the trial balance) will increase by £400.

Second, the capital figure (also a credit balance on the trial balance) will increase by £3,000.

Finally, the £3,400 credit balance on suspense account will vanish, having been replaced by the above.

The net effect is that the trial balance will balance without any suspense account.

Regards, Kim

PRACTICE SIMULATION – UNIT 4

AVONTREE LTD

ANSWERS

Task 1

DATA INPUT SHEET				
Sales invoices		Date: 9 June 2006		
			Coding	
Invoice number	Customer	Amount £	Revenue centre	Type of revenue
52711	Megabooks Limited	124.15	100	400
52712	Books Plus	103.80	100	500
52713	Empstone Books Ltd	145.80	100	400
52714	Win Hong Books	161.20	200	300
52715	Tradesales Limited	120.00	100	400
52716	Palmer and Company	299.52	100	400
52717	Business Books	148.40	100	500
52718	Megabooks Limited	228.80	100	400

Task 2

EMAIL

From: | Parfraz Mehdi

To: | Emily Padden

CC: |

Subject: | Checks on purchase invoices

Date: | 9 June 2006

Message:

I have just checked a batch of purchase invoices. I have noticed the following discrepancies.

1. We have an invoice for £400 plus VAT from Editype Limited. I can find no purchase order corresponding to this. Please could you let me know if an order was raised.

2. We have an invoice from Litho Printing Ltd in respect of 5,000 copies of The Wars of the Roses. Only 500 copies appear to have been ordered (our order number 2271).

3. We have an invoice from Decofix Ltd for repainting the accounts office. This has been coded 660-710. I think it should be 660-720.

Task 3

DATA INPUT SHEET

Payroll

Date: 9 June 2006

Detail	Amount £	Coding Cost centre	Type of expenditure
Gross pay	10,900.00	660	730
Employer NIC	967.95	660	730

Task 4

AVONTREE LIMITED					
PROFIT AND LOSS ACCOUNT					
Date: 31 May 2006					
		YTD			
Account code	Account name	This year	Last year	Variance £	Variance %
100-300	UK sales: primary	75,600	74,100	+1,500	+2.0
100-400	UK sales: secondary	100,900	108,700	-7,800	-7.2
100-500	UK sales: higher	98,700	95,000	+3,700	+3.9
610-720	Typesetting: expenses	15,300	16,000	-700	-4.4
620-720	Editing: expenses	16,400	15,700	+700	+4.5
630-710	Printing & binding: materials	40,100	36,500	+3,600	+9.9
640-710	Distribution: materials	4,600	6,100	-1,500	-24.6
650-720	Marketing: expenses	16,400	15,900	+500	+3.1
660-720	Establishment: expenses	5,600	5,200	+400	+7.7
660-730	Establishment: salaries	34,200	33,000	+1,200	+3.6

Task 5

REPORT

To: Emily Padden

From: Parfraz Mehdi

Subject: Variances YTD, May 2006

Date: 9 June 2006

I attach the schedule of variances, showing YTD figures to end of May for both this year and last.

In the following cases the variances exceed 5% of last year's figure.

- Account 100–400: down 7.2% on last year

- Account 630–710: up 9.9% on last year

- Account 640–710: down 24.6% on last year

- Account 660–720: up 7.7% on last year

PRACTICE EXAM 1 – UNIT 3

WM PRINTING

ANSWERS

Tasks 1.1– 1.4

SUBSIDIARY (PURCHASES) LEDGER

TGB Ltd

Date 2006	Details	Amount £	Date 2006	Details	Amount £
30 June	PRDB	47	30 June	Balance b/f	3,000
30 June	Balance c./d	8,828	30 June	PDB	5,875
		8,875			8,875
			1 July	Balance b/d	8,828

Compton & Co

Date 2006	Details	Amount £	Date 2006	Details	Amount £
30 June	Cash book	3,000	30 June	Balance b/f	8,600
30 June	Balance c./d	6,775	30 June	PDB	1,175
		9,775			9,775
			1 July	Balance b/d	6,775

Rowley Associates

Date 2006	Details	Amount £	Date 2006	Details	Amount £
30 June	PRDB	94	30 June	Balance b/f	10,432
30 June	Balance c./d	20,913	30 June	PDB	10,575
		21,007			21,007
			1 July	Balance b/d	20,913

Elton & Lowe Ltd

Date 2006	Details	Amount £	Date 2006	Details	Amount £
			30 June	Balance b/f	1,750
30 June	Balance c./d	4,100	30 June	PDB	2,350
		4,100			4,100
			1 July	Balance b/d	4,100

MAIN (GENERAL) LEDGER

Purchases

Date 2006	Details	Amount £	Date 2006	Details	Amount £
30 June	Balance b/f	285,200			
30 June	PDB	17,000	30 June	Balance c/d	302,200
		302,200			302,200
1 July	Balance b/d	302,200			

Purchases returns

Date 2006	Details	Amount £	Date 2006	Details	Amount £
			30 June	Balance b/f	3,000
30 June	Balance c./d	3,120	30 June	PRDB	120
		3,120			3,120
			1 July	Balance b/d	3,120

Purchases ledger control

Date 2006	Details	Amount £	Date 2006	Details	Amount £
30 June	PRDB	141	30 June	Balance b/f	40,698
30 June	Cash book	3,000	30 June	PDB	19,975
30 June	Balance c./d	57,532			
		60,673			60,673
			1 July	Balance b/d	57,532

Motor vehicles

Date 2006	Details	Amount £	Date 2006	Details	Amount £
30 June	Balance b/f	5,000			
30 June	Cash book	6,000	30 June	Balance c/d	11,000
		11,000			11,000
1 July	Balance b/d	11,000			

General repairs

Date 2006	Details	Amount £	Date 2006	Details	Amount £
30 June	Balance b/f	200			
30 June	Cash book	160	30 June	Balance c/d	360
		360			360
1 July	Balance b/d	360			

Insurance

Date 2006	Details	Amount £	Date 2006	Details	Amount £
30 June	Balance b/f	2,900			
30 June	Cash book	150	30 June	Balance c/d	3,050
		3,050			3,050
1 July	Balance b/d	3,050			

Motor tax

Date 2006	Details	Amount £	Date 2006	Details	Amount £
30 June	Balance b/f	180			
30 June	Cash book	90	30 June	Balance c/d	270
		270			270
1 July	Balance b/d	270			

VAT

Date 2006	Details	Amount £	Date 2006	Details	Amount £
30 June	PDB	2,975	30 June	Balance b/f	15,560
30 June	Cash book	28	30 June	PRDB	21
30 June	Balance c./d	12,578			
		15,581			15,581
			1 July	Balance b/d	12,578

565

Tasks 1.5 and 1.6

Trial balance as at 30 June 2006

	Debit £	Credit £
Motor vehicles	11,000	
Office equipment	15,000	
Stock	17,500	
Bank	12,214	
Cash	186	
Sales ledger control	106,842	
Purchases ledger control		57,532
VAT		12,578
Capital		30,710
Sales		418,200
Sales returns	2,605	
Purchases	302,200	
Purchases returns		3,120
Discounts allowed	350	
Motor tax	270	
General repairs	360	
Wages	42,181	
Insurance	3,050	
Rent	3,000	
Rates	2,100	
Stationery	620	
Telephone	800	
Heat and light	1,300	
Miscellaneous expenses	562	
Total	522,140	522,140

SECTION 2

Task 2.1

a) The words and figures do not match
    The cheque is not signed

b) The customer must be contacted, the problem explained and a new cheque requested.

Task 2.2

Debit	£	Credit	£
Purchases ledger control	50	Sales ledger control	50

Task 2.3

	£
Output VAT (£122,000 × 17.5%)	21,350
Input VAT (£9,870 × 17.5/117.5)	(1,470)
Amount payable	19,880

Task 2.4

A trade discount is offered:

■ to reward a valued customer
■ due to the customer being in the trade rather than a member of the general public
■ to recognise bulk buying from the customer.

A settlement discount is offered to encourage the customer to pay the amount due earlier, thus helping cash flow.

Task 2.5

When a cheque is paid into a bank it must pass through the clearing system in order for the funds to be passed from the payer's bank account to the payee's bank account.

Task 2.6

a)   Revenue
b)   Revenue
c)   Capital
d)   Revenue

Task 2.7

Integrated accounting software is a software system that ensures that all relevant accounts within the system are linked together. Therefore when one entry is made to the system all relevant accounts are simultaneously updated.

Task 2.8

JOURNAL

Account name	Dr £	Cr £
a) Heat and light	78	
Miscellaneous expenses		78
b) Rent	450	
Cash Book/Bank		450
c) Stationery	25	
Suspense	75	
Insurance		100

Task 2.9

a)

Sales ledger control

Date 2006	Details	Amount £	Date 2006	Details	Amount £
1 June	Balance b/d	100,102	30 June	Bank	32,250
30 June	Sales	40,140	30 June	Discounts allowed	150
			30 June	Returns	1,000
			30 June	Balance c/d	106,842
		140,242			140,242
1 July	Balance b/d	106,842			

b)

	£
Sales ledger control account balance as at 30 June 2006	106,842
Total of Subsidiary (sales) ledger accounts as at 30 June 2006	106,992
Difference	150

c) In the sales ledger control account there is a credit entry of £150 for discounts allowed. If this had been omitted from the individual accounts in the Subsidiary (sales) ledger then this would account for the difference of £150.

Task 2.10

a) to c)

Cash book

Date 2006	Details	Amount £	Date 2006	Cheque Number	Details	Amount £
1 June	Balance b/f	21,421	3 June	300175	Mills Ltd	3,550
25 June	Paper Design	1,500	3 June	300176	Baker & Brown	368
27 June	Bate Ltd	2,000	4 June	300177	Legge Ltd	100
14 June	Low & Lodge	12,100	4 June	300178	Parker Papers	412
21 June	BGC Ltd	1,569	6 June	300179	Beta Ltd	300
			17 June	300180	Paper UnLtd	158
			20 June		Bedford MBC	210
			21 June		LTM Ltd	4,800
			21 June		Bank charges	97
			28 June		Balance c/d	28,595
		38,590				38,590
29 June	Balance b/d	28,595				

d) **Bank reconciliation statement as at 28 June 2006**

	£	£
Balance as per bank statement		25,495
Add: outstanding lodgements		
Paper Design	1,500	
Bate Ltd	2,000	
		3,500
Less: unpresented cheques		
300177 Legge Ltd	100	
300179 Beta Ltd	300	
		(400)
Balance as per updated cash book		28,595

PRACTICE EXAM 2 – UNIT 3

THE GARDEN WAREHOUSE

ANSWERS

Tasks 1.1– 1.4

SUBSIDIARY (SALES) LEDGER

Creations Limited

Date 2006	Details	Amount £	Date 2006	Details	Amount £
30 June	PRDB	8,756	30 June	SRDB	4,700
30 June	SDB	2,115	30 June	Closing balance	6,171
		10,871			10,871
1 July	Opening balance	6,171			

Jackson and Company

Date 2006	Details	Amount £	Date 2006	Details	Amount £
30 June	Opening balance	4,814	30 June	Cash book	3,650
30 June	SDB	9,870	30 June	CB - discounts	100
			30 June	Closing balance	10,934
		14,684			14,684
1 July	Closing balance	10,934			

Loxley Limited

Date 2006	Details	Amount £	Date 2006	Details	Amount £
30 June	Opening balance	6,320	30 June	SRDB	423
30 June	SDB	3,055	30 June	Closing balance	8,952
		9,375			9,375
1 July	Opening balance	8,952			

PTT Limited

Date 2006	Details	Amount £	Date 2006	Details	Amount £
30 June	Opening balance	4,500			
30 June	SDB	7,050	30 June	Closing balance	11,550
		11,550			11,550
1 July	Opening balance	11,550			

MAIN (GENERAL) LEDGER

Office equipment

Date 2006	Details	Amount £	Date 2006	Details	Amount £
30 June	Opening balance	3,500			
30 June	Cash book	5,250	30 June	Closing balance	8,750
		8,750			8,750
1 July	Opening balance	8,750			

Sales

Date 2006	Details	Amount £	Date 2006	Details	Amount £
			30 June	Opening balance	321,650
			30 June	SDB	18,800
30 June	Closing balance	340,450			340,450
		340,450			
			1 July	Opening balance	340,450

Sales returns

Date 2006	Details	Amount £	Date 2006	Details	Amount £
30 June	Opening balance	15,800			
30 June	SRDB	4,360	30 June	Closing balance	20,160
		20,160			20,160
1 July	Opening balance	20,160			

Sales ledger control

Date 2006	Details	Amount £	Date 2006	Details	Amount £
30 June	Opening balance	112,636	30 June	SRDB	5,123
30 June	SDB	22,090	30 June	Cash book	3,650
			30 June	CB – discounts	100
			30 June	Closing balance	125,853
		134,726			134,726
1 July	Opening balance	125,853			

Discounts allowed

Date 2006	Details	Amount £	Date 2006	Details	Amount £
30 June	Opening balance	750			
30 June	Cash book	100	30 June	Closing balance	850
		850			850
1 July	Opening balance	850			

Motor expenses

Date 2006	Details	Amount £	Date 2006	Details	Amount £
30 June	Opening balance	1,225			
30 June	Cash book	350	30 June	Closing balance	1,575
		1,575			1,575
1 July	Opening balance	1,575			

Rent and rates

Date 2006	Details	Amount £	Date 2006	Details	Amount £
30 June	Opening balance	3,600			
30 June	Cash book	1,200	30 June	Closing balance	4,800
		4,800			4,800
1 July	Opening balance	4,800			

VAT

Date 2006	Details	Amount £	Date 2006	Details	Amount £
30 June	SRDB	763	30 June	Opening balance	11,463
30 June	Closing balance	13,990	30 June	SDB	3,290
		14,753			14,753
			1 July	Opening balance	13,990

Tasks 1.5 and 1.6

Trial balance as at 30 June 2006

	Debit £	Credit £
Motor vehicles	5,200	
Office equipment	8,750	
Stock	17,000	
Cash at bank	5,040	
Petty cash control	60	
Sales ledger control	125,853	
Purchases ledger control		56,713
VAT owing to HM Revenue & Customs		13,990
Loan from bank		15,000
Capital		27,798
Sales		340,450
Sales returns	20,160	
Purchases	206,511	
Purchases returns		862
Discount received		248
Discount allowed	850	
Wages	50,425	
Heat and light	963	
Motor expenses	1,575	
Rent and rates	4,800	
Travel expenses	1,650	
Telephone	1,006	
Accountancy fees	2,530	
Miscellaneous expenses	2,688	
Total	455,061	455,061

SECTION 2

Task 2.1

a)
		£
Invoice total		210.87
Less: discount (180 x 2%)		(3.60)
		207.27

b) ii) To offer a lower price to an organisation within the same trade.

c) i) Those placing large orders

Task 2.2

The Garden Warehouse are entitled to a refund from HM Revenue and Customs.

Task 2.3

a) WR50 or WB50 or PL50
b) Subsidiary purchases ledger

Task 2.4

a) The trial balance will balance
b) The trial balance will balance
c) The trial balance will balance
d) The trial balance will not balance

Task 2.5

Open a suspense account in order to make the trial balance balance.

Task 2.6

a) Speed of processing - time saved
    Accuracy
    Presentation
    More efficient

b) Profit and loss account
    Balance sheet
    Aged debt analysis
    VAT return
    Stock report
    Trial balance
    Ledger accounts
    Customer statements
    Bank reconcilation statement

c) Password security
    Physical security for hardware
    Regular backup copies
    Minimise risks to computer environment

Note that for each part of this task only *two* answers were required.

Task 2.7

Rent receivable account
Non-trade debtors control account

Task 2.8

JOURNAL

Account name	Dr £	Cr £
a) Motor tax account	70	
Miscellaneous expenses account		70
b) Purchases account	1,000	
Purchases ledger control account		1,000
c) Bad debts expense account	200	
VAT account	35	
Sales ledger control account		235

Task 2.9

a)
Purchases ledger control

Date 2006	Details	Amount £	Date 2006	Details	Amount £
30 June	Cash book	16,193	1 June	Opening balance	53,386
30 June	Cash bk - discounts	380	30 June	PDB	20,500
30 June	PRDB	600			
30 June	Closing balance	56,713		Balance c/d	
		73,886			73,886
			1 July	Opening balance	56,713

b)

	£
Purchase ledger control account balance as at 30 June 2006	56,713
Total of Subsidiary (sales) ledger accounts as at 30 June 2006	57,093
Difference	380

c)   Discounts received have been omitted from the subsidiary (purchases) ledger.

The subsidiary ledger total is £380 higher than that of the control account. Therefore, as the discounts received total £380 it is likely that they have only been posted to the control account in the main ledger and not to the subisdiary (purchase) ledger.

Task 2.10

Cash book

Date 2006	Details	Amount £	Date 2006	Cheque Number	Details	Amount £
01 June	Balance b/f	15,619	01 June	008301	Portman Bros	2,650
10 June	A Parker	550	01 June	008302	Tether & Tie	1,986
10 June	L Westwood	6,140	06 June	008303	D Price	8,432
15 June	CCC Limited	1,260	06 June	008304	Mundon Limited	1,407
22 June	B Williams	142	22 June	008305	Hacket Limited	350
22 June	**Bank interest**	**26**	**15 June**		**Droitwich CC**	**100**
			20 June		**Cranston Ins**	**250**
			22 June		**Overdraft fee**	**50**
			22 June		**Bank charges**	**16**
			28 June		**Balance c/d**	**8,496**
		23,737				23,737
29 June	**Balance b/d**	**8,496**				

PRACTICE EXAM 3 – UNIT 3

PREMIER SPACE

Tasks 1.1– 1.4

SUBSIDIARY (PURCHASES) LEDGER

Brown Ltd

Date 2006	Details	Amount £	Date 2006	Details	Amount £
30 Nov	PRDB	47	30 Nov	Opening balance	2,000
30 Nov	Closing balance	9,003	30 Nov	PDB	7,050
		9,050			9,050
			1 Dec	Opening balance	9,003

Clarke and Crown

Date 2006	Details	Amount £	Date 2006	Details	Amount £
30 Nov	Cash book	1,500	30 Nov	Opening balance	9,000
30 Nov	Closing balance	11,025	30 Nov	PDB	3,525
		12,525			12,525
			1 Dec	Closing balance	11,025

PPP Ltd

Date 2006	Details	Amount £	Date 2006	Details	Amount £
30 Nov	PRDB	188	30 Nov	Opening balance	9,652
30 Nov	Closing balance	20,039	30 Nov	PDB	10,575
		20,227			20,227
			1 Dec	Opening balance	20,039

Lees Ltd

Date 2006	Details	Amount £	Date 2006	Details	Amount £
			30 Nov	Opening balance	1,632
30 Nov	Closing balance	7,507	30 Nov	PDB	5,875
		7,507			7,507
			1 Dec	Opening balance	7,507

MAIN (GENERAL) LEDGER

Purchases

Date 2006	Details	Amount £	Date 2006	Details	Amount £
30 Nov	Opening balance	286,000			
30 Nov	PDB	23,000	30 Nov	Closing balance	309,000
		309,000			309,000
1 Dec	Opening balance	309,000			

Purchases returns

Date 2006	Details	Amount £	Date 2006	Details	Amount £
			30 Nov	Opening balance	2,915
30 Nov	Closing balance	3,115	30 Nov	PRDB	200
		3,115			3,115
			1 Dec	Opening balance	3,115

Purchases ledger control

Date 2006	Details	Amount £	Date 2006	Details	Amount £
30 Nov	PRDB	235	30 Nov	Opening balance	39,874
30 Nov	Cash book	1,500	30 Nov	PDB	27,025
30 Nov	Closing balance	65,164			
		66,899			66,899
			1 Dec	Opening balance	65,164

Motor vehicles

Date 2006	Details	Amount £	Date 2006	Details	Amount £
30 Nov	Opening balance	4,610			
30 Nov	Cash book	6,000	30 Nov	Closing balance	10,610
		10,610			10,610
1 Dec	Opening balance	10,610			

Stationery

Date 2006	Details	Amount £	Date 2006	Details	Amount £
30 Nov	Opening balance	180			
30 Nov	Cash book	80	30 Nov	Closing balance	260
		260			260
1 Dec	Opening balance	260			

Rent and rates

Date 2006	Details	Amount £	Date 2006	Details	Amount £
30 Nov	Opening balance	1,758			
30 Nov	Cash book	200	30 Nov	Closing balance	1,958
		1,958			1,958
1 Dec	Opening balance	1,958			

Motor tax

Date 2006	Details	Amount £	Date 2006	Details	Amount £
30 Nov	Opening balance	180			
30 Nov	Cash book	90	30 Nov	Closing balance	270
		270			270
1 Dec	Opening balance	270			

VAT

Date 2006	Details	Amount £	Date 2006	Details	Amount £
30 Nov	PDB	4,025	30 Nov	Opening balance	15,490
30 Nov	Cash book	14	30 Nov	PRDB	35
30 Nov	Closing balance	11,486			
		15,525			15,525
			1 Dec	Balance b/d	11,486

Tasks 1.5 and 1.6

Trial balance as at 30 November 2006

	Debit £	Credit £
Motor vehicles	10,610	
Fixtures and fittings	12,000	
Stock	20,000	
Cash bank	7,137	
Petty cash control	120	
Sales ledger control	106,842	
Purchases ledger control		65,164
VAT owing to HM Revenue & Customs		11,486
Capital		40,367
Sales		400,500
Sales returns	300	
Purchases	309,000	
Purchases returns		3,115
Discount allowed	220	
Stationery	260	
Wages	45,400	
Insurance	1,800	
Rent and rates	1,958	
Motor tax	270	
Travel expenses	1,928	
Printing	750	
Telephone	312	
Professional fees	1,105	
Miscellaneous expenses	620	
Total	520,632	520,632

SECTION 2

Task 2.1

a)

VAT calculation summary

Sales		
£180,000 **excluding** VAT	VAT on sales =	£31,500
Purchases		
£111,625 **including** VAT	VAT on purchases =	£(16,625)
	VAT payable =	£14,875

b)

Account name	Debit	Credit
VAT account	14,875	
Bank account		14,875

Task 2.2

a) A form of borrowing where the current account can be overdrawn up to an agreed amount.
b) Credit

Task 2.3

£98
Debit

Task 2.4

a) A cheque from a debtor has been **dishonoured** by the debtor's bank as there were insufficient funds in the account.

b) A **debit** card is used to make payment electronically from a current account.

c) A cheque is said to be out of date when it is more than **six** months old.

Task 2.5

a) Subsidiary (purchases) ledger
b) Main ledger
c) Main ledger
d) Main ledger

Task 2.6

Account name	Debit £	Credit £
Bad debts expense	10,000	
VAT	1,750	
Sales ledger control		11,750

Task 2.7

Any three from:

- Statement of account
- Overdue account letter
- Delivery/advice note
- Credit note
- Order acknoweldgement

Task 2.8

JOURNAL

Account name	Dr £	Cr £
a) Rent and rates	85	
Insurance		85
b) Purchases ledger control	200	
Sales ledger control		200
c) Discounts allowed	40	
Suspense	60	
Heat and light		100

Task 2.9

a)

Sales ledger control

Date 2006	Details	Amount £	Date 2006	Details	Amount £
1 Nov	Opening balance	98,600	30 Nov	Cash book	33,100
30 Nov	Sales day book	41,642	30 Nov	Cash bk - discounts	200
			30 Nov	SRDB	100
			30 Nov	Closing balance	106,842
		140,242			140,242
1 Dec	Balance b/d	106,842			

b)

	£
Sales ledger control account balance as at 30 November 2006	106,842
Total of subsidiary (sales) ledger accounts as at 30 November 2006	106,342
Difference	500

The subsidiary (sales) ledger amount for Gayfield solicitors could have been listed as a debit balance rather than a credit balance.

Task 2.10

Cash book

Date 2006	Details	Amount £	Date 2006	Cheque Number	Details	Amount £
01 Nov	Balance b/f	20,000	01 Nov	600023	Baker Ltd	2,800
10 Nov	Smith & Jones	1,100	04 Nov	600024	Brown & Co	155
14 Nov	ALO Associates	1,250	04 Nov	600025	Potters Ltd	75
			04 Nov	600026	Roberts & Co	250
			10 Nov	600027	Baxter Ltd	118
			10 Nov	600028	Cox & Co	89
			16 Nov		MBC	370
10 Nov	**B&B Ltd**	**4,800**	**17 Nov**		**Bray & Co**	**5,000**
18 Nov	**Guest Ltd**	**1,825**	**18 Nov**		**Bank charges**	**25**
			28 Nov		**Balance c/d**	**20,093**
		28,975				**28,975**
29 Nov	**Balance b/d**	**20,093**				

d)   **Bank reconciliation statement as at 23 November 2006**

	£	£
Balance as per bank statement		17,936
Add: Smith and Jones	1,100	
ALO Associates	1,250	
		2,350
Less: Potters Ltd	75	
Baxter Ltd	118	
Total to subtract		(193)
Balance as per updated cash book		20,093